Drunkard

Drunkard

A Hard-Drinking Life

Neil Steinberg

Dutton

DUTTON
Published by Penguin Group (USA) Inc.
375 Hudson Street, New York, New York 10014, U.S.A.
Penguin Group (Canada), 90 Eglinton Avenue East, Suite 700, Toronto, Ontario M4P 2Y3, Canada (a
division of Pearson Penguin Canada Inc.); Penguin Books Ltd, 80 Strand, London WC2R 0RL,
England; Penguin Ireland, 25 St Stephen's Green, Dublin 2, Ireland (a division of Penguin Books Ltd);
Penguin Group (Australia), 250 Camberwell Road, Camberwell, Victoria 3124, Australia (a division of
Pearson Australia Group Pty Ltd); Penguin Books India Pvt Ltd, 11 Community Centre, Panchsheel
Park, New Delhi—110 017, India; Penguin Group (NZ), 67 Apollo Drive, Rosedale, North Shore
0632, New Zealand (a division of Pearson New Zealand Ltd); Penguin Books (South Africa) (Pty) Ltd,
24 Sturdee Avenue, Rosebank, Johannesburg 2196, South Africa

Penguin Books Ltd, Registered Offices: 80 Strand, London WC2R 0RL, England

Published by Dutton, a member of Penguin Group (USA) Inc.

First printing, June 2008
10 9 8 7 6 5 4 3 2 1

"Ol' Man River" by Jerome Kern and Oscar Hammerstein II
© 1927 by Universal Music
All Rights Administered by ASCAP
Used by Permission. All Rights Reserved

"Pain" by Jimmy Eat World
Used by permission.

 REGISTERED TRADEMARK— MARCA REGISTRADA

LIBRARY OF CONGRESS CATALOGING-IN-PUBLICATION DATA

Steinberg, Neil.
    Drunkard : a hard-drinking life / by Neil Steinberg.
        p. cm.
    ISBN 978-0-525-95065-3
    1. Steinberg, Neil. 2. Alcoholics—Illinois—Chicago—Biography. 3. Alcoholics—Illinois—Chicago—
Rehabilitation. I. Title.
    HV5293.S75A3 2008
    616.86'1092—dc22
[B]   2007051603

Printed in the United States of America
Set in Fairfield
Designed by Alissa Amell

While the author has made every effort to provide accurate telephone numbers and Internet addresses
at the time of publication, neither the publisher nor the author assumes any responsibility for errors, or
for changes that occur after publication. Further, the publisher does not have any control over and does
not assume any responsibility for author or third-party Web sites or their content.

For my brother,
Samuel Steinberg

A Note on Names

This is a book of fact. The events all happened the way they were described, in the order they occurred; the people involved are real individuals who said the things I quote them saying, based on notes taken at the time, on printed records and on memory. No one is a composite or imaginary character.

Some names, however, have been changed.

The Chapman Center at Highland Park Hospital is a real place, and I kept its name because I think the treatment there was, in the main, beneficial, and I want readers to be able to avail themselves of it without being forced to resort to sleuthing. I changed the names of the professionals who worked with me there, however, so that I might describe them freely without embarrassing them or subjecting them to unwanted public attention.

All the names of the fellow patients in rehab and the people I encounter in the program, as well as various concerned neighbors, have also been changed, even those who wanted their names used, because of the sensitive and private nature of recovery and what they had to say. I also changed some identifying details for the same reason. I understand that the "anonymous" in Alcoholics Anonymous is taken very seriously, and some members will be horrified at the idea of my repeating anything said "within these rooms," even if the identity of the speaker is disguised. But I did not feel I could adequately tell my story without referring to a little of what happens at meetings, and they should know that I considered the matter carefully before proceeding as I did. Of course AA in no way endorses or is responsible for this book.

My colleagues at the *Chicago Sun-Times* are identified by their real names, with the exception of Prissy, who was aghast at the thought of being in a book, as well as Peter Baker, who could use a fig leaf of privacy given his very public life, and Walt Decker, whose story seemed too personal and raw to attribute.

My family is all identified by their real names, with the exception of "Aunt Betty," which is a pseudonym.

Author's Note

If there are only two types of stories—a stranger arrives in town or a man goes on a journey—then this book is both. Well into middle age, when I thought everything in my life was settled, an unexpected visitor arrived and moved in, so slowly that I barely noticed until he was part of me, our souls merged, until his seemingly inseparable presence forced me to go on a journey that changed the type of person I am.

Perhaps this story—about a suburban guy, a functioning drunkard who fell down the rabbit hole of alcoholism and then had to struggle back—will relate to you. Perhaps you're facing the same problem yourself, or trying not to face it, or know someone who is facing or avoiding it. Perhaps you like to stand at a bar, or enjoy other delicious and perilous recreations, and wonder about what it's like for those who stray over the line and are lost.

Whoever you are, here is my story. While I do hope that it helps you if you need help—hope that it lets you see change is possible, that your life today does not have to be your life as it always will be—that isn't really why I tell it. I tell it because that is what people in my situation do. We tell our stories because we have to, because doing so somehow redeems us.

Drunkard

"Yet why not say what happened?"

—Robert Lowell

I

"Ha, Ha, You in Jail"

Introduction

The thing about jail is it has bars and guards and they won't let you out.

That might sound obvious, and the part about bars and guards certainly *is* obvious. But the key word in the first sentence, when in jail, is "you." They won't let *you* out. Because jail is something that's supposed to happen to other people. Lesser people. Desperate junkies who rob liquor stores, warped crazies who shoot their neighbors, heartless men who murder their wives for the insurance money. Criminals. People worthy of jail.

Suddenly into the mix pops "you" and it's a shock, a sharp twist in reality and a hint that your life is not unfolding as you planned.

Or, to put it succinctly, as a previous occupant of my cell did when he scratched this bit of taunting graffiti into the beige metal wall: "HA, HA, YOU IN JAIL."

––––––––––

Now and then I peer through the bars. Not expecting anything, just to pass the time. The hallway is empty and dead-of-night silent, glazed brick, except for a security camera I can barely see, hard to the right. Directly in front is a high, small window where, for a while, a crescent moon appears. I am thankful for that moon, as thankful as I can be for anything under the circumstances.

The bars do not rattle. That only happens in the movies. Instead, the bars are the most solid substance I have ever held—thick, cold, immobile. Trying to shake them is like kicking a fire hydrant.

Once an hour they check on me, to see that I haven't killed myself. Not during the few moments I am at the bars, but while I am lying in my bunk, gazing blankly at the ceiling, or turned to face the wall. I hear a distant, complex, echoing clank, then footsteps, and feel a brief sense of somebody's head flashing by, even though I keep my eyes on the ceiling or on the wall. One time the guard—a woman—says, "Still awake?" with a touch of maternal concern in her voice, and I am grateful for that too.

Suicide certainly crosses my mind. I could hang myself from the bars. But the intent never settles seriously upon me—it's more a tormenting possibility, one of the countless agonies that lurch into mind, along with head-slapping regret and the irrational dread that the police station could flood and I would drown here, reaching through the bars, calling for help that doesn't come as the rising icy waters foam and rush around me.

But I wouldn't do it, wouldn't hang myself on the bars. First, I'd probably goof it up and merely look ridiculous, caught up in my homemade rope, shoulder pressed hard against my cheek, suspended like a marionette. And second, I couldn't do that to the boys. It isn't a weight I want my sons to carry around. "No, my father's dead. He hung himself in jail when I was nine."

Suicide must be a common impulse, though. That's why my clothes were taken—shirts can be shredded into ropes. They also took my shoes. Laces are strong enough to do the job in a pinch. Even my eyeglasses, though how a person could kill himself with a delicate pair of wire-framed spectacles is beyond my imagination. They dress me in a white paper jumpsuit designed to thwart being turned into an effective rope, since it starts to rip apart after just one night of twisting and tossing and clawing at myself on the thin black foam mattress.

My only companions in the cell are a pair of blankets made out of some kind of disposable black felt. The police officer processing me—taking the fingerprints and photos—observes that typically prisoners are given *one* blanket. Implying that my getting two blankets constitutes soft treatment. And while I appreciate the gesture, and keep one blanket wrapped around me like a shawl, there is also something abject about being wrapped in a blanket in a cell. A lunatic who haunts the grand Wacker Drive colonnade of the Civic Opera Building in downtown Chicago sometimes wraps himself in a dark blanket, hand outstretched, crying loudly for pity. Suddenly he and I have too much in common.

I have no watch, so can only sense the hours trudge by because of the moon transiting the window. An endless, insomniac rondo of regret and anger, a desperate, futile desire to go back in time, only a few hours, to Before This Happened. At one point I pray to God—rare for me. I offer him a deal: Let me sleep until dawn and I'll believe in You forever.

A bargain, really.

But God remains aloof, as is his habit. Preoccupied elsewhere, molding distant galaxies perhaps.

Instead dawn comes on schedule, a gradual brightening at the little window, and shortly afterward a police officer brings a doughnut and a cardboard half-pint carton of milk in a brown paper bag. He pokes the bag through a wide slot in the bars designed for passing trays. My first inclination is not to eat—lack of hunger, coupled with a child's desire to refuse food, to evoke pity. Look, the poor guy isn't eating! But the day ahead is uncertain, and somewhere within me the sensible suburban man operating on autopilot figures he had better take advantage of the opportunity offered by the brown paper sack. I gulp the milk and eat most of the doughnut, without savor, like an animal, breaking it up and pushing the pieces into my mouth with my fingertips. But I can't finish it, and leave about a quarter of the doughnut behind. My deep subconscious notes that if I'm not eating part of a chocolate doughnut, I must really be in trouble.

Chapter One

Were everyone like Phyllis, I wouldn't be in this mess. Phyllis is the bartender at the Billy Goat Tavern. Not the famous one, the basement bar off lower Michigan Avenue, a subterranean haunt where Mike Royko drank his vodka tonics and terrorized the tourists. Not the one John Belushi parodied on *Saturday Night Live*: "Cheezborger, cheezborger, cheezborger! No fries, cheeps!" Not the one where generations of newspapermen drank themselves into the grave or Alcoholics Anonymous—and really, which is worse?—leaving behind their forgotten bylines yellowing on the wall over the bar.

No, Phyllis is the bartender at Goat II on Washington Street, about a mile away, a straggler in owner Sam Sianis' constantly expanding herd of Goats—he has one at the Merchandise Mart, Navy Pier, even O'Hare Airport. At this secondary Goat, there is only one byline yellowing on the wall—mine—segregated from the rest of Chicago journalism. I resist bringing it in. But Phyllis insists, bugging me for a solid year.

"This is your home bar," she says, and eventually I give in.

Phyllis' voice—I wish you could hear it. A blunt, South Side–tomboy's voice marinated for half a century in nicotine and booze. A bleating, so-what-buddy voice, the voice of a woman

who has stood behind a bar for decades and has seen everything, twice. A metal-spoon-banging-against-a-pan voice when
barking at misbehaving drunks—"You! Moron! Out! Now!"—
but soft and concerned when one of her favorites drags his sorry
ass into the Goat for a cup of comfort.

"Oh boy, look at you," Phyllis says, sliding the drink toward
me. "Tough day?"

I always mean to ask Phyllis to bring me a photo of herself as
a young lady. She must have been a stunner. She still has the
rack, the sparkle in her eyes, though they are lost in wrinkles—
sorry, Phyl, constrained by the realm of fact, as I like to say. She
has the cheekbones. Hearts must have broken. But I never
ask—it seems, I don't know, *forward*. And with all the smutty
things the other barflies say to her—the guffawing, blow-me-
Phyllis remarks they get away with because they too are regu-
lars—I am inclined not to be suggestive with Phyllis in any
manner. "Respect Phyllis!" I bark at them when they say something crude, smacking my palm on the bar.

My loyalty is rewarded. The glass is always waiting. The instant she sees me burst through the front door, her hand shoots
under the bar. While I unshoulder the leather strap and set my
briefcase down on the littered floor, plant a foot on the brass rail
and my belly against the bar, she grabs the stubby rocks glass,
fills it with a handful of ice, and then brims it off with Jack
Daniel's and sets it down on a square napkin—an unnecessary
nicety since the bar is brown linoleum. She is so quick about
fixing the drink that I sometimes suspect she senses me coming
and starts to pour before the door opens.

I love that. I will not lie to you. The magically arriving glass
is my Pulitzer, my round of applause from the world. Love it. I
sneak glances at the strangers at the bar and it is all I can do to
keep from throwing my shoulders back, waving a hand over the

glass, and exuding, "See that? I don't even have to order. I belong here. I'm the king of the bar."

Though I don't say it, I think it. Every time.

I don't drink right away. No, no, no. That would be wrong.
Overeager. As frantic as I sometimes am, staring intently at other,
lesser bartenders, who often lag, too slow to notice me, too slow
to get off the phone, too slow to find the Jack—*there, you idiot,
right there!*—so slow I want to slap the bar and snarl, "Hurry the
hell up!" As eager as I sometimes am, moving down the bar and
dipping my head to catch their attention. As carefully as I track
the composition of the drink—the glass, the ice, the booze—
once it has arrived, I always pause to gaze for a rapt moment at
the filled glass, the ice, the Jack, the square napkin, the dark linoleum bar. The twirling universe stops dead, the Jack its mo-
tionless epicenter. I pick up the glass and take a long draw.

You probably do not drink whiskey. You might not drink at
all—a third of the country doesn't, a statistic that astounds me,
the way I am astounded by the fact that one-third of all Americans believe in UFOs and two-thirds believe in angels.

But whiskey tastes wonderful—sweet and smoky, cold and
comforting. The first sip doesn't do much but reassure: the
overture, the fugue, the opening beat of the orchestra saying,
"Just wait; you're in the right place." Soon—two sips, three—
the glass is half empty and the grating clank of the day begins to
soften and fade. I've made it. I am rescued, plucked from the
icy chop and flopped gratefully into the lifeboat, covered with a
wool blanket and heading for home. Maybe I'll talk to the guys
at the bar. Hello, Franz. Hello, Gino; he pilots a boat of some
kind. "Ahoy, Captain," is what I actually say, and if he isn't
preoccupied sweet-talking some bottle-blond bar girl who has
strayed into his clutches—her face slack, mesmerized as he
tightens his coils around her—he'll greet me in return.

Maybe I'll pull the folded hard copy of tomorrow's column out of my suit jacket pocket and give it a quick read. Contentment, to spread the pages on the bar, pen poised in my left hand, drink waiting at my right. I smile, reading quietly to myself. Most reporters want to break big stories—to uncover news, reveal scoops. That never meant much to me. I assume politicians are corrupt, assume hidden crimes are committed. Nothing surprising there. What I really want to do is to write something funny—to give people such as myself, reading newspapers in bars, something fresh to laugh at. That is the limit of my ambition, to write it and, I suppose, to have somebody notice.

To that end, if the bar is not too crowded and sometimes even if it is, I'll share a funny bit with Phyllis. "Here, read this," I say, passing the copy across the bar. Phyllis, God bless her, drops whatever she's doing and stands there, the back of her index finger to her lips, reading the item with one eye while scanning her flock with the other. She chuckles, her eyes crinkling, a muted "heh-heh-heh." A long moment passes.

"That's good," she finally says, handing the column back, and I exhale, fold the pages and tuck them away, reassured. Somebody likes it. I touch the lip of my empty glass with my finger, look directly into Phyllis' eyes, and she pours. Usually I don't even have to do that. Phyllis is there without my having to go through the effort of touching my glass. In fact, usually I have to put my flat hand over the rim, because I have home to think about. Two, three drinks tops. I drink with an eye on my watch—at 5:15 p.m. I must leave, promptly, to catch the 5:25 out of Union Station. If I've just begun that third drink, I might dump it into my wax cup of water and take it with me, sipping the bourbon through a straw on the sidewalk, disguised as soda. Fooling the world.

Phyllis figures the tab, which at my special rate is never much. I tip well.

"See ya, Phyl," I call over my shoulder.

"Say 'hi' to Edie and the boys for me," Phyllis says, but I never do, because that would tell my wife I have been at the Goat. Can't do that. Not everyone is like Phyllis.

———————

The 5:25 Metra Milwaukee District North Line pulls into Northbrook Station at 6:02. Not a bad ride at all. Usually each passenger has a seat to himself. Etiquette demands that people walk the length of the train, looking for an empty seat, before they plop next to another person.

This troubles and fascinates me, because really, what's the harm of sitting next to somebody? A slight pressure on your shoulder? The presence of another human at your elbow? The need to put your briefcase on your lap? There must be something awful about other people, given how we cringe away from them. I must feel that way as well, because I too take the long walk. I want to spread out, slump, be comfortable, and shrink from the exasperated "oh, all right" glance that a person gives, gathering up his belongings so I can sit next to him.

The bar car stops my trek. Nothing fancy—a metal counter in the middle of the car, blocking the double doors to the platform. Since you have to enter the bar car from either end, it tends to fill up last and there are often empty seats there. They serve beer, wine, and simple mixed drinks, as well as chips, popcorn, and pretzels.

On the train I shift to wine. The airline bottles of Jack Daniel's they serve look paltry and lost amid the ice after Phyllis' bottomless pours. After bourbon, wine feels like a temperance beverage. Like moderation.

"I'll have a red wine," I say.

"Cabernet or merlot?" the bartender mechanically replies, and I answer, "Either. It doesn't matter—they both taste the same to me." Which they do. It's wine. It tastes like wine. I take my plastic cup and my little green bottle or two, go back to my seat and read a book, or read the column yet again, or watch the loading docks and the gritty trackside landscape roll by.

Before long the parked semitrailers and gravel lots give way to townhomes and golf courses. Northbrook Station is a pleasant, modern affair, sturdy brick. After scorning people walking the length of the train, looking for an empty seat, when I get off the train I tuck myself behind the lowered crossing gate, while the rest of the passengers stand in front, waiting for the train to pull away so they can stampede across the tracks. I'm pleased with this little bit of separation, counting down the ten seconds it takes for the gate to lift, wondering where they're all rushing to in such a goddamn hurry.

Even waiting, I still get home first. My house is less than two blocks away. That's why we bought it. A block from the train, in one direction and, in the other, a block from the elementary school. Convenient. A ramshackle 1905 farmhouse, with a sort of turret in front. To some it would seem a palace: five bedrooms, a half acre of yard, lots of trees, big back deck, tire swing hanging from an enormous, one-hundred-fifty-year-old sugar maple that fills the front yard and dwarfs the house.

To others it might seem a dump: gray aluminum siding, roof about to go, piebald yard with a scattering of balls there so long they've begun to fade in the sun and sink into the ground, a jumbled interior including, in one bedroom, a closet whose bottom is two feet off the floor.

To me it's fancy—I love the turret, love the little black spire on top that some farmer made out of curlicue sheet metal, and especially the big tree, branching into three enormous sub-trunks, its bark thick and deeply furrowed, like the armored skin of some prehistoric beast. I tell people that we didn't buy the house; we bought the tree and the house just happened to come with it.

When I cross the street from the train station, turn the corner, and see the house, framed between two enormous American elms, I feel happy to come home. Even after living there for five years, I walk toward it thinking, *That's my house.* I can hardly believe it. Who thought I'd be a guy who owns a house with a front porch and a bay window and a big sugar maple with a tire swing? A house all lit up like a cruise ship in the evening darkness.

Sometimes my boys see me and come running—I have two boys, Ross and Kent. They are nine and eight, but still sometimes shout, "Dad!" and race up to me full bore, and I spread my arms and brace myself for a hug that almost knocks me over. Big boys.

Inside, walking to the door to greet me, is Edie. My wife. The prudent man never writes anything about his wife that won't fit at the bottom of an anniversary card. But I've put Edie into my columns for almost twenty-five years, back to the days when we were in our early twenties and dating. I do it out of a blend of sincere sentiment, open braggartry, and the constant need to fill space. I consider her interesting, which might be the biggest compliment a man can pay his wife after being together for decades. Four weeks before I find myself in a jail cell, I write an item in my column headlined "Reader, she married me," a bit of prose that you may file under "tempting fate":

People who meet my wife invariably say the same thing. "How could somebody so pretty, so nice, end up marrying *you?*"

Their voices drip with amazement, and they really get their back into that "you," like Frank Thomas smacking a fastball into the stands, infusing that single syllable with a heavy dose of befuddlement and wonder. "How could she marry *you*?"

Sometimes they stop and begin to apologize, realizing what they've said—kind of an insult to me, really—but I wave it off. I've asked her that myself, because it is something of a mystery.

"You make me laugh," she always answers, and while that isn't my first choice—I would have preferred "Your smoldering good looks haunted my dreams and set my heart aflame"—it will have to do. It is enough. And I do make her laugh, sometimes intentionally, such as the elaborately planned joke that drew a great guffaw while she was in labor, undergoing a contraction, with our first son. I was immensely proud of that—few audiences are tougher than a woman about to give birth.

While she pops up now and again in the margins of this column, I rarely sing her praises directly. First, so as not to brag. A guy bragging about his wife is a guy about to get divorced.

And second, because there is an inherent risk in writing about somebody, and I don't want to foul the nest. It was in a column twenty-three years ago that I—unfamiliar with the term "strawberry blonde"—referred to her hair as "dishwater blonde," which I thought was the proper term. It wasn't. I would be reluctant to bring it up now, had she ever forgotten or forgiven me for it, but she hasn't, so I don't really lose anything by using the deathless error as an example of why I tend to draw the veil.

Long-standing gripes aside, the beauty of being with

somebody so long—our first date was in 1982—is that you can see them grow and change over the years. When I met her, she was a student at Northeastern—the one in Chicago—working at Mindscape Gallery, an art glass place in Evanston. The clerks were all pretty young women who worked on commission and I, naive, mistook their desire to sell stuff as an interest in myself as a person. She said she was studying philosophy, and I asked her if she had ever read Sartre's *Nausea*. She said no.

"Then you're not studying philosophy," I replied, with characteristic smugness she would devote her life to deflating. It wasn't much of an opening exchange—not exactly Nick and Nora—but it was a start.

She went to law school and joined a white-shoe law firm—it was always funny to run into people who knew her in high school as a quasi-hippie-chick artist, to register their jaw-dropping shock when confronted with this razor-cool attorney in a gray pinstriped outfit.

Maybe that's why I don't write about her—not enough room to do her justice. Anyway, for whatever reason, she married me, exactly fifteen years ago today, and I'm deeply grateful for that.

That might seem like something oddly personal to run in a big-city newspaper, but that's the kind of column it is. The readers seem to enjoy it; they feel they know me, know my kids, my wife, know the "leafy suburban paradise" of Northbrook, as I call it in a kind of mocking trope, a parody of Homer's "wine dark sea." It's a razzing affection, since Northbrook really is the scrub sink catchall for those striving suburbanites who can't assemble the necessary funds to live in its tonier neighbors— Highland Park, Glencoe, Wilmette, Winnetka. Put it this way:

downtown Highland Park boasts a Saks Fifth Avenue, a Williams-Sonoma, a Restoration Hardware, and a collection of similarly snooty stores. The most prominent features of downtown Northbrook are a hot dog stand, an old auto garage, a car parts store, and a softball field.

Edie loves it, and she stands out among the suburban matrons, at least in my eyes. At forty-five, Edie still carries herself with the air she had when I met her at twenty-two. She is no longer ready to go out for the evening by slipping into a purple unitard and a pair of jeans. But still trim, with her long strawberry blond hair cascading down her back. She's not going to cut it, she tells me, but instead become one of those old women with long hair. I say that's fine with me—as if she'd change for my sake if it weren't. Having watched plastic surgery performed, my advice to her has always been: Grow old.

All is not cooing doves and sweet sympathy, of course. This is, after all, a marriage. I don't like that she doesn't work—it made sense the first five or eight years when the kids were young, but nearly a decade on, with the boys approaching middle school, the benefits of her being at home seem counterbalanced by our deepening pit of debt.

She doesn't like that I drink—I can see her face fall when she greets me at the door, looks into my eyes, and detects it. The glow, the softening of my features, the flush in my cheeks. She describes it as a slight drooping in the corner of my mouth.

"Like my grandmother after she had her stroke," she says with disgust.

This fuzziness in me touches off an opposite reaction in her: a hardening, a sneer, a quick turn of the head, a swap of cheek for lips, and then a silent retreat into the kitchen.

I write off her concerns to wifely nagging, sparked by

oversensitivity; if I even think about taking a drink she can later smell it. Sometimes she lets it pass, sometimes she doesn't.

"You've been drinking," she says.

"I had a glass of wine on the train," I say, ruffling up a false indignation, ignoring the two or three bourbons at the Billy Goat.

My attitude is: I work, I earn a good paycheck, you get to stay home with the kids and do whatever you want. Drinking is something I've earned the right to do. It's mine, my pride and joy and solace, and you can't take it away.

"It isn't as if I come home and beat you," I say.

Thus we deadlock and the years click by. Occasionally the system will swing out of control—a festive lunch with a publicist stretches into dinner. Suddenly I'm not on the 5:25. Suddenly it's nine p.m. and loud and noisy and happy and I look around and register my surroundings and think, *Whoops, I better call Edie and tell her where I am,* and I'm yelling on a cell phone from the Old Town Ale House.

"Honey," I slur. "Shomething's come up!"

Two or three times a year it is one a.m. and I'm walking down a deserted stretch of suburban highway, looking for a cab, after sleeping through my stop and the five stops beyond it. Edie meets me at the door, her face frozen with contempt, then turns wordlessly and heads upstairs to sleep in the guest room. Once she sleeps there for three nights straight while I pour on the charm. She turns to me, eyes afire. "Not a drop! Never again!" And I have to keep from laughing, because that's just crazy. A week later it's forgotten—at heart she is an easygoing child of the sixties, and we'll be at a restaurant, and I'll order a glass of wine. She purses her lips but no more. The second glass always earns me an annoyed glare.

Then one night the pattern breaks.

Chapter Two

Disasters usually require a confluence of circumstance, a string of small accidents. The pilot, preoccupied with a faulty indicator light; the co-pilot, battling a head cold; the mountain peak, shrouded in fog.

In this case, I drove into work the day before. It's late September, the holidays are approaching, and I need a new tuxedo—my old one is tight from too much high living. I drive in so I can stop by the men's store I like to go to, a big discount suit place.

Since I have the car, I figure I'll take something home from the office. Efficiency. My eyes set on a big gift box containing a beautiful crystal bottle of cognac, a gift from the Taiwanese that has been sitting there since the previous December. I figure it will look good on the office bookshelf at home.

Usually we don't keep booze in the house. We used to. When we lived in the city, the bottles crowded a high shelf in the pantry. Bottles left over from parties, gifts from publicists, brands I bought myself and liked to drink from time to time. But the liquor developed a habit of disappearing. I knew something was up when I drank the rue-flavored grappa. We'd had that bottle for years—it was vile, a decorative bottle with mummified bitter branches of rue jammed into it. But the other bottles disappeared faster than they were replaced. And then the rue-flavored grappa was gone.

But I think that maybe we'll change that. I am riding high, in control of things. Over the summer, the New York *Daily News* tries to hire me. I don't go—we can't agree on a contract—but it boosts my status here. In August, the family and I head happily up to the Grand Hotel on Mackinac Island, to hike and ride in carriages. I sit on the long, long porch, drinking my Jack Daniel's, feeling that I have finally figured things out. We will spend a week every summer here, I tell myself, the boys capering in the pool, the successful daddy taking his drink on this magnificent porch. Life is sweet.

Back home, the Saturday before everything blows up, Edie makes cheese fondue, from scratch, and brings home a bottle of white wine and a bottle of kirsch—for the fondue—and a bottle of red, for us. I see those bottles on the counter, lick my lips, and think, *Restraint, restraint.* At dinner, I sip—it's like holding back a brace of surging hounds—and manage to leave behind half a bottle of red, wanting to encourage her. This is the kind of elegance we will have in life. We will have fondue and candlelight and wine. She doesn't notice me sneaking a slug out of the kirsch bottle when I put it away on the high shelf.

Bringing the cognac home is the next step toward what I consider "normalcy"—a house full of booze that I can drink whenever I like, because I do not have a problem. I was like that once. I will be that way again. The bottle of cognac—flat, round, lovely, with a centaur etched into it—looks elegant in my office upstairs, on a bookshelf next to the lamp with the brass bulldog chewing a cigar and wearing a bowler hat.

The night before it happens, I pop up at two a.m. and can't sleep. Nothing works. Not counting backward. Not thinking calming thoughts. My blood roars in my ears.

"I think I'm going to have a heart attack," I tell Edie, who is sleeping, or was, and battling a migraine. "I'm eating too much, drinking too much."

At three a.m. I get out of bed and go to the office. Why not read the newspapers online and, hey, drink a bit of this cognac? It's three a.m.—late last night, not early tomorrow morning. By five a.m. about a third of the bottle is gone and I reel off to bed.

At seven a.m. Edie wakes me and the world returns with a white flash and a roar. Time for work. After an exhausted, semi-drunk rush into the shower. I feel like a boxer about to pitch forward onto the mat, so lousy that, even as the train is pulling into Union Station, I know I'm going to stop at the Goat. No decision, no debate. Drinking in the morning is stupid and I've only done it six or eight or a dozen times in my life, but I feel lousy and know a vodka tonic will help set things right, and it does and the second one sets things righter. A third would be too stupid, so I have a beer.

If anyone at the ten a.m. editorial board meeting notices, they don't say anything. It's Wednesday, so my column is in the paper and not due again until tomorrow. I write an editorial and then go to lunch with an old friend from Berea, the little town— once sandstone capital of the world—where I grew up in Ohio.

Patti was a cheerleader. We went to high school together. Bright-eyed, apple-cheeked, then and now. She e-mailed me a few months back, asking for some vague professional help regarding a business she wants to start, and we had a long boozy lunch in July, one of those aforementioned lunches where I end up walking down the side of the road at one a.m. You'd think that would have been warning aplenty. But no.

We eat steak and drink wine at a little steakhouse by the

paper. I haven't lived in Berea for twenty-seven years, and it's so nice to talk to somebody from home, somebody who knows everybody I know, somebody who is pretty and friendly and will drink wine at Gene & Georgetti with me and laugh and clink glasses. So very pleasant. It takes a concentration of will to pull away at three p.m. and go back to work to see if anything has developed. It hasn't. I put my feet on my desk and close my eyes and fall asleep.

At a quarter to five, I take my briefcase and head for the train, stopping of course at the Goat for a couple drinks. And wine on the train.

I arrive home at six p.m. as always. Edie has ordered pizza from Tonelli's, which doesn't deliver. So I drive to get the pizza and stop, as I like to do, to have a drink at the bar at Tonelli's while I wait for the pizza to be ready, picking at the rice crackers and watching the TV.

Now it's eight p.m. The pizza has been eaten. I'm up in my office, playing chess with Ross. And there, on the bookshelf, is the cognac and wouldn't a cognac taste good about now? A capper to a good day. A perfect day. Elegant, in a snifter I happen to have right here—always a glass or two stashed in a discreet corner of my office. So I'm sitting there, at the Italian chess table with the walnut drop leaves, holding my glass of cognac, playing chess with my eldest son, and Edie comes into the office—she doesn't do that often. Normally I have time to set the glass behind a frame on the desk. She sees the glass in my hand, and while she knows that I have been drinking, the glass is the proof. She doesn't say anything then. We put the boys to bed. Now it's almost ten p.m. She is getting ready for bed. I write an e-mail to my agent in New York—a paragraph mentioning that I've been kicking around some ideas. Not a comma out of place.

I go to bed. Slip under the covers. Another day done.

"I did it again," I say to her in the darkness. "I went to Gene & Georgetti's and ate too much, drank too much, spent too much."

Edie is not sympathetic.

"Don't you wake me in the middle of the night when I have a migraine and then go drinking again the next day."

Within moments, we're at it.

"You bitch," I say.

"Get out," says Edie. "I'm not sleeping with you. You're a drunk. You smell. I'm not smelling you all night. You say yesterday you're worried about eating too much and drinking too much and then you go and do it again today. Get out."

In another frame of mind I might have meekly done it, but this time I dig in. I refuse. "This is my bed, my house," I say. "You get out; you go sleep in the guest room."

So she does, but I follow her, and the rest of the memory is a jangling flash of images. I'm screaming at her—"You cunt!"—she's crying, grabbing the phone. "Go away! You're scaring me," she says. "I'm calling 911," which just outrages me. Scaring her? Me? Her loving husband? What a lousy thing to say. We go around the house. Edie tells me not to go up toward the boys' rooms, but I do. Kent is up, a frightened little face peering from a darkened room. We are just outside his door. I'm yelling. She has the phone, she's dialing, she says, she's going to dial, she has the phone up against her head and I suddenly swing, an arcing open-handed slap, knocking the phone hard against the side of her head. She howls, her face contorted and hideous, Edvard Munch's *The Scream*, and runs away, wailing at Kentie, "Call 911! Call 911!" I retreat to the kitchen, roiling, look around like a cornered animal, pause, then rip the phone out of the wall and hurl it across the room.

Now it's quiet. I am sitting in the front entranceway, on the red chair. A knock at the door and I get up to answer it. The police, young, polite but insistent. Two, then four. Suddenly the house is filled with police, plus a social worker and others. Many people, some upstairs talking to Edie, others downstairs talking to me. I feel as sober as I've ever been, but very tired, answering questions. "We're going to have to arrest you," they say, almost apologetically, and handcuff me behind my back. That is a surprise. The handcuffs are cold metal and tight. A firm hand is on my shoulder, guiding me. I twist to look at the stairs up to the bedroom as I'm led out the front door.

Chapter Three

The next day I get out of jail. One night in the Northbrook lockup, a doughnut, then whisked to the Cook County Jail satellite at the Skokie Courthouse.

One night is plenty.

To make the transfer that morning, a police officer puts a wide leather belt, like a weightlifter's belt, around my waist. At navel level, a metal ring, and he handcuffs me through the ring, so I can't lift my arms to attack anybody.

"I read your column," says the officer cuffing me.

Nobody else knows I'm here except for my wife. They give you a phone call in jail, just like the movies. The night they book me, I call the City Desk at the *Sun-Times*.

"You're up late," says Phyllis Gilchrist, a night editor.

"Could you leave a note for Nancy?" I say. "Tell her I won't be filing tomorrow."

That surprises me, later, when I think about it. I didn't call my brother, Sam, or set somebody to work trying to get me out. My parents live in Colorado and there's nothing they could do except worry. Besides, they're going on vacation to Greece in a few days; better not to tell them at all. Let them go untroubled. Sam lives nearby. But why disturb him at eleven p.m.? Let him sleep. The cops say that nothing will happen until the morning, and I believe them.

Outside, a beautiful, bright autumn morning. The police officer driving me to the Skokie Courthouse says he is freshly divorced, but already working on a new family with his girlfriend. He understands troubles with the wife.

That's how men do it, I think. Shed one wife and family, pick up another. Keep moving forward. Not quite my way. I tend to stick with people. I dated my high school girlfriend for six years, all through college, long distance. I could present that as loyalty. But maybe it's just timidity and lack of imagination.

We arrive at the Skokie Courthouse and I'm taken in through a back bay, delivered like a carton of bananas. Someone signs for me and I'm deposited on a bench, by myself in a windowless room, waiting to be processed. The night's haul of miscreants from other suburbs arrives—a scruffy, rail-thin eighteen-year-old drug addict with a foreign name. A heavy bikerish woman with coarse skin and tiny eyes concealed somewhere within her puffy, hard face.

A county cop walks me to a cell. I've traded the tattered white jumpsuit back for the khaki green shorts and the olive-green T-shirt I went to bed in, a shirt that says, in Hebrew, "Golani" on the front—the Israeli Army—with a big yellow star on the back. I wonder how that will go over with the skinheads and tattooed white supremacists in jail.

No need to worry. I'm led to a cell by myself—no bars, but a thick Plexiglas door that slides. A long metal bench, not quite wide enough to lie on comfortably.

Hours pass. Young men in brown DOC jumpsuits are moved this way and that through the corridor outside my cell. They are lined up standing against the wall, told to spread their arms and legs, and patted down. They kick off their sneakers so guards with flashlights and latex gloves can peer inside their shoes. I pace the cell, singing to myself to pass the time. "Amazing Grace" seems apt.

They transfer me to a waiting area—a narrow room, locked door, the walls above waist-level thick Plexiglas. A pair of stools are bolted to the floor in front of a counter—obviously someone on the other side will meet with me, eventually. Twenty minutes crawl by. I feel caged and fervently wish I had something to read, to distract myself.

Finally a woman about my age—tall, thin, careworn—appears. She introduces herself as Jeanne Bishop, a Cook County public defender. She was randomly assigned to me, but says she knows me—we went to Northwestern together. *Oh lovely,* I think. "Hail to purple, hail to white, hail to thee, Northwestern. . . ." She acts as if we're old friends, though I don't recall her at all. Happens to me all the time; I tend to linger in people's minds while they slip out of mine. Still, I pretend to remember her. That seems both polite and, under the circumstances, prudent.

I will have to post bond, Jeanne says, or have someone post it for me. I could put it on a credit card, but my credit cards are in my wallet at home. Edie might show up in court and post my bond. Or she might not. Can she phone anyone for me? I think of my brother, Sam, but he's downtown at work—he works in the county treasurer's office and this is crunch time for property taxes. I ask her to phone—incredibly—my mother-in-law, Edie's mother. She's eighty, but spry and red-haired, and I can see her showing up to spring me out of jail. Otherwise, I give her my brother's office number. Maybe he'll come.

She asks me if I'm receiving any treatment for alcoholism. I tell her I've gone to Alcoholics Anonymous a couple of times under duress and hated it. More recently, during the summer, I've been seeing a therapist—also Edie's idea—a hippieish woman in her late fifties named Sarah who is helping me battle drink with tea, cinnamon cookies, and supportive hugs.

I am led back to the cell, slightly reassured. Somebody is making calls for me. Without a watch, I can't tell the time, but gauge that it's around noon when I see them serving lunch—a bologna sandwich and a cup of juice Saran-wrapped to a molded cardboard tray. The famous Cook County Jail bologna sandwich. I am not hungry, just wish for the distraction of eating. But they never bring me a tray and I don't want to draw attention to myself by asking for one.

An hour or so later, I am transferred to a holding cell with prisoners up from the main jail at 26th and California. Hardcore guys, lanky and muscled, scarred and tattooed, black and Hispanic. We're crowded in with no place to sit. When somebody uses the stainless-steel toilet at the back, we all know it through three senses.

The guards call names. Prisoners leave with a swagger and complainingly return. "Oh *man*! I gotta come back in a *month!*" The waiting builds, the feeling of being in the wings, of wanting to go on, get it over with, anything to get out of here.

Finally I am ushered into the courtroom, which seems enormous after the small rooms I have been in for the past fourteen hours. A guard tells me to keep my hands behind my back and my eyes forward. A courtroom full of people—men in suits, women in skirts. I feel undressed in my beltless green shorts and army T-shirt.

I expect to see Edie as she always is—warm, relaxed, looking at me with concern since, heck, I've been in jail all night. Some fanciful part of my brain must still be functioning as before, because I hold out for the possibility there'll be a twinkle in her eye—*I hope you learned your lesson, buddy. Now let's get you out of here and oh, by the way, try not to drink so much.*

"Eyes forward!" a guard barks when I sneak a glance to my left, and my eyes snap back to the judge, a fierce Hispanic woman. One glimpse of Edie is enough to throw me. She is pale, drawn, shaken.

Jeanne Bishop begins:

"On behalf of Mr. Steinberg, Judge, he is forty-five years old. He is the coowner, along with his wife, of their home in Northbrook. They have lived at that same address and owned that home for five years. He has two children, eight and nine. He is married. He has a brother, Sam Steinberg, who's present in court here."

That's a relief. Sam's here.

"If Mr. Steinberg is not permitted to return to his home, he could live with his brother. . . . This is his very first arrest in his entire life."

My wife is sworn in.

"Have there been other incidents prior to this?" the judge asks.

"You mean physical incidents? No," says Edie. "He has never hit me. Previously he's been drunk a lot; but no, no physical violence. This is the first time ever."

"Any emotional or verbal abuse?"

"No."

"How do you feel about your husband right now; are you afraid of him?"

"I am not afraid of him. I want him to get help for alcoholism. That's the problem. It's been an ongoing problem for the last few years. He tries to stop, but it continually builds up. I found after the police left yesterday he brought home a huge bottle of cognac on Tuesday. I found it in his office yesterday night after the police left. It was two-thirds empty. I found two empty containers of Jack Daniel's and an empty bottle of port. I believe that he needs help, but he has to be the one to instigate that."

"For how long has he been drinking like this?" the judge asks.

"He's been having a problem the last couple years," my wife says. "He always drank, but the problem has been bad for the last few years. . . . He would fall asleep on the train all the time because he had been drinking so much. He came home and he had been staggering home from Deerfield Station with the knee of his suit bloody because he was falling down drunk."

That first lunch with Patti last July. No cabs. Midnight, and I didn't want to bother Edie, so I walked the three miles. There was a slope at the side of the road and I slipped on the gravel. A sober man might have done the same thing at noon. I came home with my pants leg torn open and flapping at the knee, a big bloody gash, like the principal at the end of *Ferris Bueller's Day Off*. Not a pretty sight.

Edie isn't done. Her delivery is calm and lawyerly. I think of a tape she made years ago, practicing her litigation technique.

"This past year when my father died and we were sitting shivah a week later—that's the mourning period—we were having Shabbat dinner. He showed up so drunk he could not even stand and he took a cab home from Chicago to my mother's house. He was able to get there. He told me he was frightened because he could not remember anything the next day when he woke up.

"So he's been having a terrible battle with alcohol. He did try to go for help, but he would not admit he was an alcoholic. He stated he just wanted to be a regular person, to have wine and beer at social occasions and he tried doing that, but now he's been drinking again every day. And apparently he's been drinking hard liquor and just slipping, and I love him very much, but he needs to remedy that."

"There is a problem and he has been trying to get help," summarizes Jeanne Bishop. "He did tell me that he had been attending some counseling, some Alcoholics Anonymous."

"Mr. Steinberg," the judge asks me, "do you think that you have an alcohol problem?"

"Yes," I say.

"Would you say that you are an alcoholic?"

"Yes, your honor," I say.

The tone in the room shifts slightly. Admitting the truth seems to earn points—they must get a lot of fierce denial. A lot of angry drunks. The judge sharply orders me to attend a minimum of twenty-eight days of an alcohol rehab program—inpatient, at a facility where I'll stay full-time. Plus a domestic violence evaluation.

"I want him in the program within the next seven days," the judge says. My gut sinks. I'm going into rehab.

The judge gives me a warning. "Unless you want to help yourself, nothing is going to work. So that you know, it's a shame that you have gotten to this point; but, if you do not obey the special conditions of bond, one of them being inpatient treatment, then I will have to revoke your bail and I will put you in jail. Believe it or not, Cook County Jail has one of the best drug and alcohol treatment programs, but that's my last resort. I do want you in a good program."

Then I'm back in the lockup. I meet in a side room with Margaret Egan, my probation officer—*my probation officer*, I think grimly, trying out the words. She is clipped, efficient. She says that even though a judge has just ordered me to enter inpatient rehab upon pain of imprisonment, that it is really more of a suggestion than a command.

"Your treatment is up to those making your evaluation to decide," she says. "The judge can't mandate a certain course of medical treatment."

She takes out her business card, flips it over, and on the back writes "Highland Park Hospital" and "Chapman Center." I'm to call them and set up an appointment.

I'm taken to a cell large enough to hold one hundred people, but it's empty except for me. Being so close to getting out makes me nervous and I pace, then gaze out the door, my hands cupped around my eyes. A guard shows up, orders me to step back, unlocks the door, and leads me to an office, where I sign a couple of forms, am handed a square plastic bag holding my belt, watch, and driver's license, and am directed out a door on the other end of the room.

My brother, Sam—five years younger, three inches taller, with a mustache and a goatee—is standing in the hallway, looking sharp in a business suit and crisp necktie. Sam is the guy you want waiting for you when you get out of jail. He handles billions of dollars for the Cook County treasurer's office, massive financial transactions where he saves taxpayers money by shaving costs and keeping the capital working.

He smiles tentatively and I thank him for coming.

"No problem," Sam says. He is carrying a hanging bag—my hanging bag. "Edie pulled some clothes together for you."

We walk to the car service Lincoln Continental Sam has taken from downtown and settle into the backseat, the black leather cool against the back of my legs. Definitely the way to be sprung. He tells the driver to go to his house in Arlington Heights.

"How's Edie?" I ask.

"She didn't spend a lot of time talking to me," he says. "She didn't seem happy. I promised her I wouldn't let you drink."

"And you won't," I say. "It'll be my own doing."

"Have you eaten?"

"A doughnut this morning."

"We'll go get something after you get settled."

"I need a shower."

Sam lives in a split-level with his wife and two middle school kids, in comfort but not luxury, with a sleeper couch in the basement where I will live for at least the next three days. Too many men in my situation return home and kill their wives, so Illinois law requires no contact—no going home, not even a phone call—for seventy-two hours. That meshes with my mood. Frankly, I feel like never going home. I dig a beer out of the refrigerator.

"That's better," I say, after a long pull. "Thanks for coming to get me."

"That's what brothers are for."

"I wasn't sure you'd come—I know you're busy."

"No problem."

I shower—wonderful after a night in jail—and change my clothes. Edie has been thorough, but no wallet, which feels strange, and no wedding ring. It's still on the base of the lamp on the night table at home, where I parked it when I went to bed.

Last night.

We go out for sushi. A small, elegant place, pearl-gray walls, dim little glass oil lamps lit, in the lull between lunch and dinner. We sit at the sushi bar and drink hot sake. I have fallen through the looking glass and am now unmoored—not living at my house, but with my brother, Sam.

"Maybe I'll just divorce her and start again." I muse. I am

forty-five. The rondo of home to work, work to home became oppressive long ago. Drinking at the Goat is my only break—a little "me time," as they say. Edie certainly saw her chance, certainly leaped to enlist the law to do her dirty work. She saw her opportunity and she took it. Maybe this can be my opportunity too.

"She pushed me off a cliff," I tell Sam. "This isn't my fault."

We go back to his house. Evening comes. Sam goes up to sleep. You'd think, with the insomniac night before, I'd sleep now. But no, too much has happened. I'm living in Sam's basement. He has an IKEA wine rack along one wall—nice, expensive bottles. Opening one would be a betrayal of his hospitality. Besides, I'd have to go upstairs and hunt up a corkscrew. I examine them more closely. One bottle is cheap Japanese plum wine with a screw-on cap. I open that up and drink it dry while watching a black-and-white John Wayne movie on a small TV. The bottle empty, I climb upon the open sleeper couch and fall asleep.

The next morning, Sam and I drive to the Arlington Heights train station. It's sunny, cloudless, another great day in September. He buys the newspaper, buys my ticket. I feel dependent— no wallet, no ring—the troubled brother being taken on an outing.

"Here's money," Sam says, as if reading my mind, handing over sixty-five dollars. "Will that be enough?"

"That'll be enough; thanks." I put it in my pants pocket. No money clip.

We stand waiting for the train. One approaches in the distance.

If it's an express, I think in an offhand way, *if it doesn't slow down here, I should just jump in front and be done with it.* It isn't an express, but our train, and I didn't mean that anyway. At least I think I didn't mean it.

We arrive at Northwestern Station—not my usual station; another wrong note—and split up, agreeing to meet back at five p.m. I consider going directly to the Goat for a drink, but don't. That would be a bad idea. I have things to do.

The *Sun-Times* moved its offices a year ago, after our publisher, the reptilian crook David Radler, sold the building out from under us in a deal with Donald Trump. Now our offices are new and clean, but off-the-beaten-track—Wolf Point, where the Chicago River branches north and south. The newsroom is very quiet at nine a.m. My office is off the sports department, empty before lunch, desolate on a good day. I hang up my suit jacket, turn on the computer. Today is Friday. There is an editorial board meeting to attend and Sunday's column to write.

The meeting breaks up in half an hour. I go back to my office, fish the card out of my pocket, and phone the Chapman Center. A young man answers. Is it an emergency? No? Great, we'll see you Monday for your intake evaluation. I immediately call Margaret Egan to tell her I've done it—everything by the book, no slipping up, no going back to jail.

Now the tough part. I walk over to the office of the editor in chief, John Barron, a dapper, put-together fellow about my age, tall, always in an immaculate shirt and tie, vaguely resembling Hugh Grant but without the roguishness. His brother is a priest.

"Do you have room for one more problem this morning?" I ask, chatty and conversational. He waves me into his office, with its panoramic view south down the Chicago River, the Sears Tower, all the way to U.S. Cellular Field.

I close the door behind me.

"There's been some trouble . . ." I begin, outlining the situation, what happened and, more important, what's going to happen. I don't know if my schedule will be my own. There's an evaluation Monday and after that, who knows? I may be somewhere inpatient—that's what the court ordered, but there seems to be some wiggle room. I'll try to go somewhere outpatient, so I can continue to work.

John listens carefully. I'm amazed at how easily he adapts to this crisis, as if employees walk in every day and lay out lurid tales of personal collapse. Maybe they do. He says the right words of empathy and concern. I'm to concentrate on getting better and not worry about work. We shake hands and I walk out, thinking, *That went well.*

Then to my column for Sunday. Typically, I would write about the pair of very interesting days that have just transpired. But that seems like a bad idea. So instead I write about a reporter who went to jail rather than reveal her sources—she's being accused of doing it unnecessarily, as a stunt. Nobody, I write, putting my fresh experience to work, stays in jail if they don't have to.

At eleven thirty, with the column shaping up, I hurry over to the Shamrock Club, a small bar next door to the *Sun-Times,* just north of the Merchandise Mart. Not as welcoming as the Goat, but three blocks closer, and they make a great cheeseburger, which I order, along with one, two, three, four glasses of Jack Daniel's on ice. The booze transforms my mood from vague numb dread to entirely numb dread. The guy on the stool to my left is some sort of construction worker, a biker, sipping light beer on his lunch break. He is divorced, and his advice is: Stay married. Don't be the one to leave the house. Don't risk your kids, because you end up never seeing them and it ruins your life. After four Jacks it occurs to me that I have drunk a lot, so I have a Sam Adams for dessert and go back to the paper.

After dinner in Arlington Heights, the newspaper calls—Don Hayner, who keeps being given ever-grander titles yet always remains the same lanky South Side guy in charge of the newsroom. He says he's sorry, but they can't run my Sunday column—it'll seem too odd when the news comes out.

"They spiked my column," I tell Sam, covering the mouthpiece.

Which leads to the second point: The paper has to print something about my arrest.

"We'd run it if it were somebody at the *Trib*," Don says. So it doesn't seem that we ducked the story. Makes sense. Do I want to comment? I think of the response that Peter Baker, my old boss, gives to hostile reporters: "You're going to throw me in the shit; don't ask me to jump in and splash around for you." I don't say that. Instead I say: "No, I don't want to comment."

But half an hour later I call Don back. They were so solid and supportive of me—if a comment from me will help the story, then I'll make a comment. I've spent too many years prying quotes out of people at their moment of deepest personal crisis to duck out now, when it's my turn. He thanks me. In a few minutes a reporter, Shamus Toomey, calls. He is very apologetic. We go over the facts as supplied by the Northbrook Police Department. He wants a quote.

Exhaling, I look around the cluttered little kitchen. What does a person say? Take responsibility, I tell myself. No self-pity. No excuses. People hate that.

"I'm deeply humiliated to have brought this misfortune on my family and am eager to do what is necessary to set it right," I say, in one breath. He thanks me and hangs up. I stand up and take a beer from the refrigerator.

Saturday morning Sam and I go out to pick up bagels. It seems every person in the bagel place is reading the *Sun-Times*. Truly, like in a movie, each patron is holding the paper up high, open to the page. Since when is the *Sun-Times* so popular in the suburbs? My story is on page two, the headline run across four columns of type: "*Sun-Times* columnist Steinberg charged with domestic battery."

Back at his house, Sam has errands to run—stuff to buy, kids to chauffeur. I sit on the big leather sofa in the living room. He goes upstairs to do something, and I leap up and quickly charge my coffee from a new bottle of The Macallan in his pantry. I had bought it for him the month before, for his fortieth birthday. Good stuff. But I can't care about that now.

My day is spent there, on the sofa, watching TV, slowly drinking the bottle, first mixed with coffee, then not. Sam later tells me that he never thought I was an alcoholic before—that he always thought the problem was Edie being a scold—until he saw me sit on his couch and put away that bottle of The Macallan.

That afternoon, the phone rings. Sam takes the call. He looks up at me. "Edie," he says, handing over the phone.

"The boys miss you," she says, cold and straight to the point, no greeting, no how-are-you. She puts Ross on the phone. "Hi, Daddy!" he says brightly. "When are you coming home? Can you read *The Odyssey* to me over the phone?"

I tell him I would, but I don't have the book. I've read to him since he was a toddler. *Alice's Adventures in Wonderland*. The Harry Potter books. *Treasure Island*. Lately we've been reading first *The Iliad*—it's supposed to be read aloud—and now *The Odyssey*. You'd think that I would be the one forcing him. Actually, it's the other way around. While I'm generally glad to do it, some evenings I'm tired, reluctant. The book can be an endless

rondo of gift giving, banquet hosting, and monster fighting. But
he insists.

Edie tells me she wants me to come home tomorrow morning, eleven a.m., while the boys are in Sunday school. I meekly
tell her I will. So much for divorcing her and starting anew. Do-
mesticity has a gravity that pulls you back in. You need momentum to break away, and the notion of going to live in the Red
Roof Inn so I can continue being a drunkard just doesn't spark
my boosters.

The *Tribune* phoned, she says, but she didn't talk to them.
Do I want the reporter's number? No, I say, I don't want to talk
to the *Tribune*.

So tomorrow I'll have to see her. And the boys. I've wondered
what to say to them. What comes to mind is to get down on one
knee, look each carefully in the eye, first one and then the other,
and say, "Boys, I just want you to know something: that your
mother murdered me, murdered our family, and destroyed everything we built together."

I drain my last beer of the night and go to bed about eleven
p.m. I have to stop drinking because I'll be seeing Edie in the
morning. But I'm up at one a.m., sweating and rolling around
the sleeper sofa in the basement. My nervous system screams
that it's time to drink again. A racking need I think of as "the
claw." My body hurts, hungers. Pulling the sheets off, I kick and
thrash on the bare sleeper couch mattress. I sit up in alarm, as
if the room were on fire, then lie back down. This is the pit, I
tell myself, this is John Lennon's "Cold Turkey." Still, I'm not
desperate enough to open the fine wines that Sam has cellared
in his basement. I can't go home in a few hours with this stuff
pouring out of my system. I go upstairs in the dimness and rum-
mage through the refrigerator. The beer is gone. I try some
crème liqueur, but it's rank, curdled. No Macallan in the

cabinet—must have polished that off. I find a dusty bottle of Bombay Sapphire gin with a few tablespoons in it and drink that, warm, standing in the kitchen in my boxer shorts. It is enough to let me crawl back into my basement hole and fall asleep for a few hours.

Chapter Four

Sam announces we're going to his health club to exercise. Sweating out yesterday seems a good plan. His gym is a white, airy, modern affair—a health center with tall ceilings, new equipment, large windows—a dazzling suburban exercise Olympus.

While he fills out my guest registration at the front desk, I notice a stack of Sunday *Tribune*s in a wire rack next to the counter selling T-shirts and necessities.

"Why bother?" Sam says. "Ignore it."

"Easier if I get it out of the way," I say. I heft up a fat Sunday *Trib* and yank out the Metro section. I'm not on the front page at least. But it is on page three and it is a shock—five columns wide, splashed across the top of the page. "Columnist charged with abuse" in forty-eight point type, the headline size they would use for an elementary school fire, a fire where kids got hurt. I read the story. Unlike the *Sun-Times*, the *Trib* does not tread lightly. It points out that I could go to jail for a year.

Returning the paper to the stack, I feel nausea and a kind of tingling vertigo. Sam has vanished somewhere—to get a lock maybe. There is an open stairway leading up to the second level, ringing the atrium, and I imagine bolting up the stairs and plunging headfirst over the railing. That would do it. Not exactly the hero's exit, I tell myself, shaking the feeling off, as Sam returns and we head into the locker room.

Sam has an iPod. "Here, listen to this," he says. The song is "Pain" by something called Jimmy Eat World. A single second of pulsing guitar, then:

"I don't feel the way I've ever felt. . . ."

Pulling on boxing gloves, I fling myself at the heavy bag, planting my feet, hitting it for all I'm worth, which isn't much. Left left left, right right right, left right, left right.

"Anyone can see my every flaw," Jimmy sings. "It isn't hard. Anyone can say they're above this all. . . ." I pause only to slip off a glove and replay the song.

". . . it's a false sense of accomplishment, every time I quit. . . ."

Again and again. Half a dozen times.

". . . these are *hard* times," the singer drawls. "Oh oh oh. I can't let it bother me."

The designated hour approaches. We get into Sam's big Toyota Highlander and start driving over to my house, maybe twenty minutes east. But we've got too much of a jump. I don't want to get there early. So we pull over into a little park. It's another lovely day, more like spring than fall. We walk around a small retention pond disguised as a lake and ringed by a concrete sidewalk.

How can I do this? I wonder. What kind of life can I have?

Sam offers a metaphor.

"Let's say you're a ballplayer—forty-five years old, solid career," he begins. "Obviously the end is in sight, but you figure you've got another season or two. Then one day you tear up your knee. That's it. It doesn't matter what you want. It doesn't matter whether you're ready or not, you can't play anymore. You can go to Wrigley Field. You can sit in the stands and watch other people play. But if you try to climb onto the field, if you toss your leg over that fence, they'll put you in jail. Look at drinking that way. You've had a fine career drinking. Now it's time to hang up the spikes."

I like that, the image of the battered veteran ballplayer with the blown-out knee. Nothing as strengthening as an original metaphor. We get to my house—they've painted the new porch white while I was away. Life goes on whether I'm there or not.

Edie's older sister, Janice, answers the back door—the emissary. We embrace.

My wife is sitting at the island in the kitchen. She has a blank piece of yellow lined paper before her on the granite countertop and a freshly sharpened pencil. Her eyes are fire.

"I want the location of all the liquor you have hidden in the house—the champagne in the basement, that old scotch—we're selling them all on eBay," she announces. "And I want you to stop swearing in front of the boys."

Not the best beginning. There are a couple bottles of good champagne from Ross' birth year—1995—in the basement. I figured we'd open them when he gets older. And a bottle of single malt from the year I was born—1960 Scapa—I bought a decade earlier and had been saving for the right time. I don't want to sell them, but that doesn't seem important right now.

"Fine," I say. I know enough not to promise anything. My general attitude is: I'm in this situation, this mess, and I'm going to work to get out of it. This is one of those times when only actions count—words mean nothing.

"I'm going to try my best," I say. "Whether it's with your help or without it is up to you."

She isn't placated and says some angry things—I don't recall what exactly, only Janice hovering nearby, gingerly pointing out to her sister that I'm here, I'm going into the program and willing to do my best, and she should perhaps meet me in the middle. We stumble on in this regard until Ross and Kent mercifully return from Sunday school, dropped off by a friend. I hear the commotion at the back door and go to greet them, big hugs, their dear faces alight, as if I'm returning from a business trip. I almost expect them to ask for presents.

Get it out of the way, I figure, still bent over from the hugs.

"Boys, I just want you both to know something," I begin, looking each in the eye in turn. "I want you to know that your mother was absolutely right in what she did, and that none of this is your fault, and everything is going to be okay."

Ross and I rush upstairs to read *The Odyssey* in his bedroom, its walls still aqua from when he was a baby, with the masses of stuffed toys that he loves. He sprawls on his bed, beaming, expectant, body limp with pleasure. I turn to where we left off several days and an eternity ago.

The goddess Circe, whose brew turns men into pigs, is warning Odysseus of two perils he will face once he leaves her island. Charybdis, the gulping whirlpool, and Scylla, "the yelping horror," a six-headed monster. Scylla cannot be defeated, Circe warns, so just accept the loss of however many men she snatches from your ship as you speed past. Whatever you do, don't stop and fight.

Yes, yes, Odysseus says, impatiently. But how do I fight it?

"So stubborn," the goddess begins. "Hell-bent yet again on battle and feats of arms? Can't you bow to the deathless gods themselves? Scylla's no mortal, she's an immortal devastation, terrible, savage, wild, no fighting her, no defense—just flee the creature."

That's the ticket, I tell myself, smiling at the kind of ironic coincidence that some consider the hand of God. Booze is my Scylla. No engaging, no defeating it. This is a battle I can't win, only run away from it as fast as I can. "Row hard for home." Good advice, if I can take it. Odysseus can't.

That goddess is cramping my style, he tells himself, girding for battle. "I donned my heroic armor, seized long spears in both my hands and marched out the half-deck, forward, hoping from there to catch the first glimpse of Scylla. . . ."

Is that being a hero? To be unable to leave monsters alone?

I sleep in the guest room. Which is not the pristine and cozy refuge that the phrase "guest room" implies, with perhaps a lace-covered night table and a nautical theme. Rather it is a small extra room crammed with stacks of books, cardboard boxes, luggage, a dresser stuffed with towels, and those big bulk packages of toilet paper they sell at Costco. A guest could barely walk into it.

In the morning the boys, playing computer games in my office in the next room, hear me stirring and rush in and fling themselves on the bed, with joyful hugs. I hold them tight, register their presence, am glad to be home.

"I'll walk the boys to school," I tell Edie later, when they're about to leave.

"You don't have to," Edie snaps. "They can walk themselves."

But they want me to and I want to. In the middle of our block, Ross briefly takes my hand, as if out of habit, then lets it go. I kiss both boys on the tops of their heads. Kent, who normally can't be kissed in public without scanning the bushes to see if his entire class is lurking, isn't self-conscious now, but calmly accepts my lips against his hair.

I have to be at Chapman for my evaluation at 12:45 p.m.

Until it's time to leave, I flap around the house, nervous, distracted, searching for a form I need from court. Edie drives me to the hospital—I don't want to drive myself because I'm not sure where I'll go.

"You have to choose between your two loves—booze or me," she says. "I know you'll make the right choice."

She parks. It's 12:42. We need to hurry, I say, worrying that if I'm late they'll slap me back in jail. We go to the third floor. The Chapman Center is basically a corridor. Edie reads a magazine while I fill out forms.

The director, Sally, comes to get me. She leads me back to a tiny office—room only for a small metal desk and a single chair for a visitor.

How are you supposed to be helped, I wonder, clutching arrogance like a blanket, by someone whose office is smaller than your own?

We sit down. There is no ceremony, no welcome, no ritual marking of the moment. Sally keeps her eyes on her computer screen and asks a series of questions. How many drinks a day on average do you have? How old were you when you began drinking?

I try to answer. On average? Three? Five? I first got drunk at the Chardon Inn, drinking pitchers of beer with the other junior camp counselors, so I was fifteen or sixteen. There was also a time at Passover, but I don't remember how old I was.

Any alcoholism in your family?

"My aunt," I say. "Aunt Betty. I remember her with a bottle of Absolut vodka in her purse."

Many questions. As I answer them, it strikes me that I sound like a hard case, a daily drinker from a family of screwups. By the time I'm done I feel as if I've talked myself into inpatient rehab. They'll ship me off to Hazelden, the Minnesota mecca where high-profile drunks always seem to be going. Not that I'm delighted with the idea. I just came home yesterday. On the other hand, the Chapman Center just doesn't come off as being exactly state-of-the-art. Walking in the hall, returning to the waiting room with Sally, I can't help pointing out, "You know, not to be critical, but I have to wonder if you guys know what you're doing. I'm supposed to be this alcoholic wife beater just released from jail. And you walk alone with me back into your office there. What if I went berserk?"

"There's a panic button," she says. "Six people would come running."

There don't seem to be six people on the entire floor. The corridors are empty.

I'm ushered in to see the nurse, in a little infirmary that resembles something you would find in an elementary school—nutrition posters, jars of cotton balls and supplies, a small window out to the hall screened with venetian blinds. The nurse—Helen—takes my blood pressure and is alarmed: one ninety over eighty-five. She asks me if that is normal and I say no, usually it's low.

She sends me in to meet the center's director, Dr. Manozzi, who has dark eyes, with limp dark brown hair cut short and combed to the side. There's something unsettling about her plain face, and it takes me a while to figure out what: a rag doll's face with shoe button eyes, a child's face stuck on a woman's body. As if to compensate, she wears a gorgeously rich green and gold jacket.

Dr. Manozzi sits quietly typing, her hands on a computer keyboard, hidden below a ledge on her desk. She asks more questions. Are my parents alive? Was I sexually abused as a child?

"No," I say. "But isn't believing you weren't the giveaway that you really were?" I smile. She doesn't register that I'm making a joke—she has a very brisk manner.

I wonder if they've decided whether I'll be sent away or not. "The routine is to begin with the most minimally invasive program and work up," she says. "We'd like to start you with the program here, and if it's not working, we'll send you somewhere else."

"Maybe I should start somewhere else," I say, surprising myself, worrying about wasting time at some suburban playpen. "I'm not going through this to have it fail." In my mind, I equate inpatient treatment with serious treatment, while outpatient seems more recreational, a sop to the courts. But she assures me that the only advantage in-house rehab has is that its participants don't have the opportunity to drink because they're locked in a facility. If outpatient doesn't work—if I slip up—they can always send me inside somewhere.

In other words, after careful consideration, our professional opinion is that your insurance company should give its money to . . . *us.*

The next day is Rosh Hashanah, the Jewish New Year, so we decide I'll begin my twenty-eight days at Chapman the day after. I'm about to leave when Helen comes back in and says, basically, the more she thinks about it, the more my blood pressure seems dangerously high. I might have a heart attack and die at any moment. Why don't I head over to this doctor and get myself checked out. She hands me a piece of paper.

"Okay," I say.

———————

Tuesday morning I wake up in a bad way. Sweating. Anxious. My legs pedal spastically under the covers. The alcohol has been out of my system for forty-eight hours and my body doesn't like it. I wait for the boys to come running in, like yesterday, but they don't. Edie opens the door to see if I'm alive, and I turn toward her.

"I'm awake," I croak. She closes the door again, silently.

I lay in bed, trembling. "Ross?" I call. "Kent? Boys?" Nothing. They're playing computer games in the office and Dad being home is no longer new. I get up, my T-shirt damp, and shuffle into the bathroom. My hair is matted down, my face, red and swollen. I go downstairs to the kitchen. Edie is at the sink, her back to me, washing chicken. We are having twenty people over for dinner later. Her mother, Dorothy, always made the holiday meals, but Irv died last January and she isn't up to doing it anymore. My wife has taken over the duty and her husband having some kind of complete alcoholic breakdown isn't about to interfere. She doesn't turn around.

"This happened almost a week ago," I say hotly to her back. "Where's my help? Where's my help? I could have died in the night and you didn't even check on me."

Edie turns.

"I was up all night," she says, haggard. "I didn't hear you moving around." The water is still running in the sink. I turn and go back upstairs and climb under the covers in the guest room, twisting and flopping about. I can't go to Rosh Hashanah services. Impossible. I can't stay home alone—who knows what could happen—and I can't go. I feel it genuinely, maybe with a bit of vindictiveness: I'm not going to services with you. Nyah, nyah-nyah, nyah.

After a few minutes, I get up, stick my head in the office doorway, tell one of the boys—always at the damn computer— to go get Mom. Edie comes into the bedroom, holding a dish towel.

"I can't go," I say. "I'm sorry. It's impossible."

She shuts the door.

"You're going," she says, her voice low and firm. "We have to keep things normal for the boys. Ross is playing viola at the service." We look at each other for a moment. I start to get out of bed. Keep things normal for the boys. That's enough to get me showered and into a suit. I check myself in the mirror: damp, crazed, and miserable. A fresh corpse in a blue suit.

We arrive in the sun-dazzled parking lot, warm for autumn, hot almost, and see the rabbi getting out of his car. Rabbi Eitan Weiner-Kaplow plays the guitar, has round glasses, a brush mustache, and a bouncy manner. In honor of the high holiday, he is wearing a suit of white. The rabbi glances at Edie, but she looks away, and he doesn't come over.

Our congregation is new and does not have its own building—services this year are held in the banquet room of the Highland Park Country Club. Rosh Hashanah, the Jewish New Year, is one of Judaism's most important holidays, and it flushes out the closet Jews, blinking into the glare of their loosely held faith. We arrive early so Ross can rehearse with the other musicians, and have our choice of seats in a wide, low room with large windows overlooking the impeccable golf course. Edie picks the third row from the back, on the aisle.

"In case you have to leave," she says

The service begins with the familiar, keening songs. We stand with the congregation. Edie starts to cry, hard. This is the first Rosh Hashanah since her father died. I fish a fresh folded handkerchief out of my pocket and hand it to her.

"I miss my father," she says, weeping.

I put my arm around her. People are turning to look at us. She continues crying.

"They don't know that," I whisper. "They think you're crying because you're a battered wife."

The service grinds on. The lure of the festive meal, with its bottles of kosher wine—real wine nowadays, zinfandels and merlots and cabernets, not the thick, cloying Manischewitz of old—always got me through the obligations of my faith, the pot of booze at the end of the rainbow. Impossible to imagine how I can endure it otherwise. But I do.

Rabbi Eitan's sermon is on caregivers, on husbands and wives tending to their ailing spouses. The rabbi goes down the list—wives with cancer, husbands with Alzheimer's. As he ticks off the chronic ailments, I brace myself for the inevitable gut punch of "alcoholism," perhaps driven home with the slightest glance in our direction.

But he doesn't. Thank you, Rabbi.

I turn my attention to my wife. She has stopped crying and is listening attentively, her face neutral. *She's lapping this up,* I think, suddenly angry. The impulse grips me to lean in low to her and hiss, "Just because you called the cops, honey, doesn't make you a caregiver."

I don't say that, but hold back, managing to not pull the trigger on this bit of sarcasm. I'm in the soup as it is; why make things worse than they already are? My restraint is rewarded moments later, when the rabbi holds up his prayer shawl, arms raised high over his head.

"How many couples," he asks, "look back to the day when they first stood under the chuppah"—the traditional marriage canopy—"and then look at their lives today, and think: 'We never imagined it would be like *this*!' "

Edie and I burst out laughing. No shit, Rabbi. We never imagined it would be like *this*. We laugh and don't stop. Not discreet, into-the-fist giggling. But big guffaws that draw curious looks. I don't care. We keep going, the chuckles beginning to ebb, until we glance at each other and then erupt again. We never imagined it would be like *this*.

I haven't laughed in nearly a week, and it is such a relief that I'm almost ready to credit divine intervention. Something stopped me from making the nasty remark that would have spoiled the moment before it happened.

Afterward we walk with the congregation to a nearby pond— a water hazard at the golf course—to cast our sins upon the waters, the traditional end to the service, the unburdening of our wrongs in preparation for the wrongs we'll commit in the new year. Traditionally you use bread crusts as a stand-in for sins. Members of the congregation are waiting by the water with big bags. I take a handful—of garlic croutons, for some strange reason—and throw them into the green water, one by one, with vigor. You are supposed to speak aloud the sins you are trying to repudiate.

"Drinking!" I mutter loudly, flinging a crouton, hard.

"Thinking about drinking!" I say, tossing another.

"Planning to drink!" Another cube flies.

"Resisting treatment for drink!"

There, I think, walking away, wiping my greasy palm on a handkerchief. *That was easy.*

———————

Back home, we set the table, getting ready for Edie's family— my brother doesn't come to this kind of thing. Edie sets out bottles of grape juice.

"I feel bad," I say, "denying people wine. I hope they don't hold it against me."

"Nobody cares," says Edie. "Only you care."

The house is filled with people. I jump up to help Edie. Opening the garbage drawer to throw something away, I see, in the recycling bin, the bottle of Dubouche cherry-flavored brandy that Edie bought to make the fondue a week ago Saturday and poured out after my arrest. There is still residue in it—a teaspoon maybe. I consider downing it right there in the kitchen, with everyone in the next room. But that seems like a bad idea.

After dinner, I go for a walk with my sister-in-law, Janice. I have a bottomless need to talk—so long as I am parsing my situation, it is bearable, almost.

"I hate this I hate this I hate this I hate this," I say to Jan, and just want to say it over and over. "I hate this. Hate hate hate it. I really do." She is kind and just listens.

Back home, I hear from people. Mel Morton, a venerable Chicago lawyer, phones. He has the clipped, confident manner of the self-made man, and is calling to make sure I'm going to Alcoholics Anonymous.

"The program saved my life," he says. "Saved my life. I've been going for twenty-seven years. It's all very simple, a very simple program. All you have to do is two simple things. Don't drink, and go to meetings. That's it. Don't drink, and go to meetings."

I can't help myself.

"If you do the first," I say, "then why do you need to bother with the second?"

Frank Brohn, a magazine writer in Chicago, in the program a few years, e-mails me with congratulations—this will be the start of a new life, he assures me. It may look bleak now, but someday I will look back and be glad it happened. He gives me his phone number and says to call him anytime, day or night.

Friends reach me at home, while those calling to leave messages on my voice mail at the newspaper are casual acquaintances, with one big exception:

"Hi, Neil," my mother says, in that tentative, I'm-talking-to-a-machine voice. "This is Mom and Dad. I just wanted to tell you before we left that we heard about the incident, ah, with you and Edie."

Damn! One of their friends must have tipped them off.

"We sort of read it over the Internet and we are so sorry that this has happened and we want to support you and your family and just tell you that we love you and we're here for you and we're leaving tomorrow."

My father breaks in.

"We're both here for you and your family. We want to tell you, and support you both. Don't worry about us."

"So for the next two weeks you know we are thinking of you and wanting for you the best of strength for what you have to go through," continues my mother. "We really understand what you are going through and hope the best for you. That's it. We'll still be here for tomorrow if you want to say anything to us. If not, we'll talk to you when we get back."

I don't return the call.

———

That evening, with Edie in the bedroom, I creep down to the kitchen and drink the teaspoonful of cherry brandy that remains in the bottle in the recycling bin, tipping my head back and tapping the bottle to get the very last drop. It feels wonderful, though I am instantly aware of just how debased this is. Drinking out of the garbage.

Still, even that little bit must embolden me, because I go into the bedroom—first stopping in the bathroom to wash my face, put a dab of toothpaste on my finger, and then lick it off and rinse my mouth.

"Please," I beg. "I can't do this. Don't make me do this. I'm a drinker. Drinking is my life. Drinking is what I do. Can't we go back? Give me some kind of hope. I'll go through the twenty-eight days. I'll recalibrate myself. I'll only drink on holidays. Only for Passover. Only with you. Please."

"No," she says. "No, no, no."

"I have all the rational arguments lined up fine, but they only last for a while—they just fade away and I want to drink again. I can say: 'Okay, I don't look at my childhood as fifteen years wasted because I didn't drink.' And that two months I didn't drink in 1997, I don't regret that. And last week, I didn't drink on Monday, and at the end of the day I was proud."

"You could be proud every day," Edie says. She could always turn a phrase. The knot in my stomach loosens a notch. Proud every day. An idea a guy can cling to.

II

Detox Mansion

Chapter Five

Highland Park Hospital has valet service. Under a wide semicir-
cular entryway, black-vested valets wait. Which seems out of
place, since nothing else about the hospital is particularly
elegant—a sprawling modern brown brick structure, higher in
some spots, longer in others, but of no discernible shape and
not really looking like anything.

Edie is driving. We pull up in our van, wave off the valet—no
need, thanks, just dropping off. I kiss her, screw a pair of iPod
earpieces into my ears, grab my black ring binder, and set out
for my first day of rehab. Music seems important—something
to give me strength and underscore the moment. I really should
have hired a bagpiper to usher me in, I think, but that would at-
tract attention and smack of a sarcasm I don't really feel. What
I am trying to do is maintain a kind of resigned, realistic courage. A court is ordering that I do this; there's no point sulking
and wasting it. Might as well go in with an open mind and see
what happens.

There must be a rebellious nerve in me somewhere, however, because I pipe myself through the low hospital halls—so
low that I can stand at certain places with my feet flat on the
floor and touch the prickly white ceiling—not with bagpipes,

but with Warren Zevon's snide recovery anthem, "Detox Mansion," which I once listened to as I hotfooted to the bar, snubbing my nose to the rehab world. Fuzzy guitar, then:

> *Well, I'm gone to Detox Mansion*
> *Way down on Last Breath Farm . . .*

Even as I'm striding in, it strikes me that this bit of defiance is exactly what makes me drink in the first place. My way to flip off normalcy. To say, I'm special, this moment is special. I'm not here doing the dishes in my suburban house while my wife goes to Costco to buy toilet paper. I'm having a drink, doing the dishes in my suburban house while my wife goes to Costco to buy toilet paper, and that makes all the difference.

I'm on time. Wednesday morning—one week, tonight, since the slap. As I go through the day, I keep thinking of what I was doing a week ago—now we were having lunch, now I was back at the office—wishing I could yell, "Stop! Don't!" But I can't. "Even God," Aristophanes writes, "cannot change the past."

The receptionist sends me to the nurse's office. Sitting next to Helen is a young woman in her mid-twenties, wearing a large Mardi Gras–colored purple and green knit scarf, red high-top tennis shoes, and fingerless brown gloves from her elbows to her knuckles. She is very petite, and her mod black frame eyeglasses make her seem somewhat serious and medical. For a moment I assume she is my therapist, waiting with the nurse to meet me, and I think: *Hey, maybe this isn't going to be so bad. . . .*

Her name is Leslie and we both have paperwork to fill out. She's another patient—a cocaine addict from California—and this is her first day too. We're starting the program together. We busy ourselves with forms.

"Here's a *black* pen," Helen says, and I tuck away my blue one a little grudgingly. I have entered a world where people think this sort of thing matters.

Helen has her own notebook, and she reads aloud various aspects of the program.

"Addiction is a chronic, progressive, and potentially lethal disease," she reads, as if for the first time. "It is a family disease—not just your disease."

Edie will be relieved to hear that.

Helen tells me I will be expected to be at the sessions on time every day and, in addition, must attend four or five Alcoholics Anonymous meetings a week. I will be expected to participate, to speak openly and honestly about my disease.

She sends me to Dr. Manozzi's office to meet with her again. I notice Dr. Manozzi has one of those little scooters that people who have trouble walking use to get around—in my eyes it gives her a slightly ominous mien, like the professor in *X-Men*.

Dr. Manozzi tells me we have more questions to go over. Her fingers tip tap at the computer.

"You say you drink ten cups of coffee a day. You probably shouldn't do that."

"One vice at a time," I say.

"Why do you drink coffee?" she asks, genuinely curious, as if it were an unusual practice.

"To help me focus."

"And?"

"To do work at four o'clock in the morning. I need to wake up and work."

"Do you find yourself hyperfocused? Compulsive?"

"I'm a writer," I say. "I need to notice things."

Sally sticks her head in the office. "It's 10:32," she says. "Everybody should go in at the beginning."

She walks me down the hall and opens the door into a large room—a double classroom, with an accordion section that could divide the room in half, if need be. There is a small upright piano at one end and a whiteboard at the other, and chairs arranged along the walls. Eleven people—young, old, men, women—sit in a big oval. I zero in on an empty brown fauxleather chair, cross the room, and drop into it.

"Everybody, this is Neil," Sally says, standing at the doorway.

"Hey, Neil!" the group says, turning bright smiles on me.

From the chair, I survey the room. On the whiteboard is written: NAME, DOC, FEELING, NEW AND CHALLENGING and RECOVERY TOPIC. A mobile of vaguely human shapes hangs in the corner, the white cardboard figures labeled ADDICT and ENABLER and PERFECT CHILD.

At the front of the room is a woman who introduces herself as Cindy—late twenties, pretty in a freshly married, young bride sort of way. Speaking directly to me, she says we are going to begin the way we always do, by going around the room and—briefly, please—checking in, using the instruction requested on the board.

"My name is Ron," a thin young man with a scraggly beard begins. "My drug of choice"—that's what DOC stands for—"is alcohol. I'm feeling . . . uncertain."

Each speaks in turn. Brent—handsome, square-shouldered, the physique and shaved head of a swimmer—says his drug of choice is marijuana. Luke, a tall kid with a Vicodin addiction, is feeling "morose and quiet."

Emily is an older woman, mid-sixties, gray hair pulled back and tied in a ponytail, wearing a zip plastic jacket and pedal pushers that reveal emaciated, spotty, veined, elderly woman legs. She speaks in a Southern accent, and as she does I think: *bag lady*.

Oh great. I'm in among bag ladies.

Leslie, the California coke addict, jumps in right away, wanting to talk about the whole higher-power business. The bedrock of Alcoholics Anonymous is God, often referred to as a "higher power" to make the pill go down easier. It's as if a church said you could believe in Jesus or, if you prefer, you could believe in the man on a cross. Your choice.

"My higher power is myself," Leslie says.

Catherine is a round-faced twenty-one-year-old with straight black hair. She surprises me by saying her drug of choice is heroin. "I'm not feeling good about myself," she says.

As they work their way around the room, I mull what to do when it's my turn. I'm inclined to say my drug of choice is Jack Daniel's—irreverent, funny, true—but when they actually get to me I simply say, "Drug of choice, alcohol."

My recovery topic is how any of this is supposed to help me.

"I don't see how a group like this helps me not drink at the first opportunity," I say. "These groups offer God and the support of other people, and those are the two things I am most armored against."

After we introduce ourselves, Cindy leads a conversation. We are learning new ways to live, she says. Rehab—Chapman plus Alcoholics Anonymous—provides us with the support we need to find new lives outside of our addictions. We need to think about what our using is doing to our lives, how it affects ourselves and our loved ones. We must reflect and consider the choices we have made while under the control of our addictions.

I find myself thinking of a particular Saturday morning, the year before, when I wake up needing a drink and suggest to Ross that we go to the library, which is just north of our house, practically in our backyard. The library is large, white, spaceshiplike. We walk there together, and I leave him browsing in the children's book section.

"Wait here," I say. "I'll be right back."

I quickstep a block over to Sunset Foods and buy a $2.32 half-pint of Popov vodka. Hurrying back with the plastic bottle in its brown paper bag in my back pocket, I sense how reckless and awful this is, and walk faster. Back inside the library, before I even look for him, I duck into the bathroom, down half the vodka, then go to locate my son. He isn't in the children's section where I left him. Growing panic, racing through the stacks, looking left and right down each aisle of books. Ross, kidnapped and killed while I run off to get vodka. You'd think that would be a warning sign. But it isn't. I find him, he's okay, and the incident recedes.

We break for lunch. I head down the elevator, through the claustrophobic basement hallways to the hospital's small cafeteria—arrays of sandwiches, containers of yogurt, plates of pie, a few ladies in white ladling out Chinese food and slicing pizza.

Drinking impairs your judgment, I think grimly, trying to figure out what I want to eat. First your judgment is clouded only while you're drinking. Then, if you become an alcoholic, your judgment is off even when you're not drinking. My judgment was clouded when I left Ross in the library. Even now, trying to find something appetizing, my judgment is shaky still. It is a scary thought, one I've never had before: the realization that my thoughts aren't right, my reasoning is off.

Feeling scattered, I select a turkey wrap and tomato soup,

the only things half appealing, and head over to the area with the tables. There is Ron, the guy with the scraggly beard, sitting by himself. I join him.

He tells me this is his third time going through rehab.

"You like it that much?" I say, then ask him what he learned from his first two stints.

"Your life can hinge on every decision you make," he says. "That one drink can be one drink or can lead to ten years of drinking."

We return after lunch with our coffees and bottled waters.

"This afternoon we've got a movie—*Dual Diagnosis*," Cindy announces, to a collective groan. Some have seen this movie before. The twenty-eight-day program at Chapman is like a carousel—it doesn't begin or end, just cycles through, with people leaping on and hopping off as they join the program or leave it. Nor are there twenty-eight different days of unique programming—some days repeat.

I don't see the movie anyway. I'm pulled out of the room and introduced to Linda, who will be my therapist. Linda is in her early thirties, tall, with a kind of sturdiness that suggests she might have been good at volleyball once. We repair to her office—as small as Sally's and completely unadorned. As if she just showed up this morning and dropped her papers on the desk.

More questions, more click clacking of the keyboard. She expects me to go to four AA meetings a week—I don't have to bring proof; she'll trust me, but I must go.

"You're going to have to learn to hang out with recovering alcoholics," she says, with a little smile that strikes me as reflecting a kind of low-grade malice. She enjoys shearing these drunks of their illusions.

Perhaps trying to put a little distance between myself and her world, I tell her about the bottle of 1960 Scapa in the basement.

"Sell it on eBay," she says immediately—not the answer I expected, for some reason.

What if I have some on my eightieth birthday? I want to know. Would that be so bad?

What would be *bad*, she says, is to cling to the mind-set of being a person who drinks—or a drinking person who's not drinking. "We call them dry drunks," she says dismissively. "Which is just waiting for your next relapse."

She says relapses are natural. "We're not going to throw you out for it—we're not drill sergeants—but we expect you to tell us about it immediately."

To me, that almost sounds like permission, though I don't say so. I file it away. We end on what she obviously feels is an upbeat, hopeful note—that together we will build this new sober life for me. I limp out of Linda's office depressed—"sober," what an awful word—thinking of all the wine-tasting tours of Marin County that Edie and I won't be taking in the future. This new future, one where I will be spending an eternity in church basements listening to drunks talk about their feelings.

Linda has arranged outside counseling for me. She is just monitoring my progress here; my treatment will be handled by a really sharp psychologist.

"He's perfect for a guy like you; he'll help you," Linda says, and gives me the name of a Dr. Steve Frisch. I'm to report there right now. This is encouraging. I like the thought of someone private, away from the group, a specialist in addiction, a really sharp psychologist focusing just on me. I also like the thought of "help." I'm being quick-marched through this desert of sobriety, with the bayonet of the legal system poking in the small of my back, and if I don't want to end up back in jail, I'd better get someone to take my hand and guide me through this. I'll take all the help I can get.

Dr. Frisch's office is in a small boxy building in an industrial complex nowhere facing the highway, one of those places almost impossible to find unless you already know where it is. Dr. Frisch is burly, wears a golf shirt, and has a ponytail that I hope is not ideological. The same mobile of the white family figurines from Chapman hangs in one corner of his office.

Frisch doesn't say much the first half hour—he hands me a cold bottle of water. I sit in a chair, drink the ice water, and begin to talk.

Sure, I always liked to drink. In high school. In college. I was proud of how much I could drink—I would walk around parties, holding a half gallon of gin in my hand, fingers slipped through the glass handle, drinking from the bottle. Occasionally I'd drink too much, but I didn't invent that. Drinking wasn't an issue then.

So why is it an issue now? How did this happen? I wasn't an alcoholic in my twenties. In my thirties I got married, had kids, became a columnist at a big-city newspaper, wrote books.

"I wasn't an alcoholic then," I say plaintively. "What happened?"

Frisch says that alcoholism is like any other illness—you don't have it until you do.

"This isn't science," he admits. "But there is a circuit that controls drinking in your head, and CAT scans do detect a mechanism in the brain."

I tell Frisch that I'm supposed to start going to AA meetings and I'm dreading them. I know what they're all about.

"They say that God will help you if you believe in a higher power—the old bargain," I say. "Why doesn't he help you anyway, whether you believe or not? Seems kinda cruel of Him, like the folks at the Pacific Garden Mission giving you your hot dog stew only *after* you sit through the church service. No service, no stew. If we're going to drag God into this, why doesn't He let me drink again, moderately? He's God, right? He can do it."

I'm willing to change, I tell Frisch. I know there's a problem. I'd be a fool not to. But the advice they're offering isn't helpful. The tools they're giving me either don't work or are merely obvious. I describe a *New Yorker* cartoon where the catcher and the pitcher are conferring on the mound. The catcher says: "Strike him out."

Frisch doesn't get my point.

"The big AA revelation is don't drink and go to meetings. They tell you don't drink and offer you this solution—go to meetings, where you tell each other not to drink. Well gee, thanks for the fucking epiphany. Don't drink. Strike him out."

Frisch begins to tell me the flood metaphor. It's actually one of my favorite jokes. Flood waters rise around the home of a pious man, and his wife suggests they flee. No, he says, I've been a pious man all my life and God will provide. The waters keep rising, and they take shelter on the second floor. A boat comes by. "Hop in the boat," the guy on the boat says. "No," says the pious man, "I put my faith in God—he'll see after me." His family leaves in the boat. A second boat arrives, a canoe—as many watercraft as the teller likes. In the end, the man is on the peak of the roof—a helicopter lowers a rope ladder. "Grab the rope!" someone shouts.

"No," says the pious man. "I will trust in the Lord. . . ."

The waters rise and the man drowns. Facing God at Judgment, the man, aggrieved by his terrible death, says, "My Lord, I was a devout man all my life, how could you let me drown like that?"

"*Let* you drown?" says the Lord, affronted. "I sent you two boats, a canoe, and a helicopter. . . ."

But I never let him get that far. I cut him off. "Yeah, yeah, I've heard it—the moral is that God sends us the help we need, if we take it."

"God . . . or whatever," says Frisch. "Your fear and desperation could be your higher power."

I draw back at "fear and desperation"—that might be overstating the case. My life has been upended, and suddenly the grease that gives happiness and lubrication to my day is being rudely removed. I'm not so much afraid as disoriented, unsure of whether I can embrace this sobriety they keep talking about, whether I even want to, whether it's possible for me, and whether anything they're suggesting might work to bring it about. And angry—at myself, for letting this happen; at Edie, for drop-kicking me into jail and rehab; and at this shabby world of recovery I've been exiled to, so far removed from my beloved bars and fancy restaurants.

At least Frisch is someone I can talk to. I've never had a high opinion of the helping professions. But something about Frisch—a Buddha calm, maybe—I find appealing, despite his roundness, his ponytail, his self-published line of "Alive and Well Publications." There is a certain confidence he radiates, a sense that he knows this stuff. He isn't trying to force any particular worldview on me, just help me through this nightmare, offering the support I need at the moment.

"You're making the right choices," he says. "Having Edie drive . . ."

"You're a week from a traumatic event," he says. "Be kind to yourself."

I smile. Being kind to myself conjures up the image of kicking back with a big tumbler of bourbon. Not anytime soon.

When I wake up I don't know who or where I am. A moment of vacant calm before the cold wave of my current life sloshes over me: I'm a drunk sleeping in the guest room of his own home, getting ready for another day of rehab. It's four thirty a.m.—four hours to kill. At least the shakes and sweats are gone.

My mind begins grinding through the situation yet again—there's got to be something authoritative about alcoholism, some wisdom that isn't printed on a cardboard mobile hanging in a classroom. I roll out of bed and pad over to the darkened office to wake up the computer with a nudge of the mouse.

Into Nexis, the newspaper database. I plug in "New York Times" and "Brody"—Jane Brody, the oracle of health wisdom—and "alcoholism" and "disease."

Up pop thirty-seven articles, and I choose one from ten years ago with the promising title: "Alcoholism: Brain Disease Not Moral Failing." Brody basically says that 15 percent of the population, through a combination of genetics and personal disposition, has faulty brain mechanisms that are supposed to tell them they have drunk enough, and these balky switches tend to be ground down further by alcohol abuse. Sounds right.

I notice a disconnect between what Brody presents as the problem—an organic, partially genetic brain disease—and the solution being offered, which involves addicts sitting in a room talking to one another. The cure seems primitive, like a shaman treating cancer by singing to the tumor.

One wall of my office is all books, and on a top shelf, twenty years' worth of journals. I pull down the volume for 2003, two years previous. I began the year weighing 224.5—disgusted with myself and on the Atkins Diet. There is nothing in the first month about drinking, since I'm not drinking. "You can't lose weight and drink," I tell everybody cheerily. No withdrawal. No nothing. I obviously wasn't a drunk then.

Or was I? On February 4 that year Edie and I go to a dinner at the swank restaurant Tru, where my friend Gale Gand, the co-owner and pastry chef, is honoring Wisconsin master cheesemakers. Going doesn't seem a bad idea because I'm not drinking and, indeed, I carry around my glass of champagne but don't touch it. Nor do I touch the opening whites. An hour passes. We eat things like "Celeriac Ravioli and Walnut Oil Cured Baja Sea Scallop with Mindoro Gorgonzola Cream." The reds arrive. This is fabulous, Edie says, and I reach for her delicate goblet and take a sip. Indeed very good. After the meal the thirty-year-old Ramos Pinto tawny port appears, accompanying our fig and walnut tart with cheddar cheese ice cream.

"That was sleeping in an oak barrel when you and I were in grade school," I say and, as if overwhelmed by its sacrifice on our behalf, take a few deep swigs. I end up finishing mine and part of hers too. Mustn't waste this.

I turn the pages in the journal. No drinks the next day; I can tell because I'm counting calories. Unlike the AA warnings, I do not immediately plunge into the gutter. One day. Two days. Three. Nothing. I spend that Friday night at an Indian Guides program, where Ross and I sleep in the Museum of Science and Industry, next to the giant beating heart, an activity that sounds more fun than it actually is. The floor is hard, and it is wonderful to go home the next morning, shower, nap. That evening Edie orders takeout from a place on Skokie Boulevard and, on the way, I stop by a liquor store and buy a bottle of Jack Daniel's. I crack it open in the car, driving with dinner in a bag on the seat next to me. *Rock and roll in the suburbs,* I tell myself happily, swallowing big swallows.

Sitting in my predawn bedroom, I flip through the journal pages. Every day after that I'm drinking. Every single day. The diet fizzles out and is forgotten. The not-drinking mind-set, so lightly entered into to mark the first of the year, just as easily vanishes.

Chapter Six

By now Edie is awake and she beckons me into the bedroom.

"I went through your black book last night," she says and I freeze, wondering, *Black book? Black book?* She reads my face. "The notebook from your program," she explains. "Have you looked at it?"

I shake my head. It's like the owner's manual for your car—one glance and into the glove compartment.

"You should, because there's a lot of good stuff in it," she says. "They have a checklist of stages of alcoholism: one, two, three, and . . ."

"I know, I know, I'm at the bottom."

"No, the bottom's death. But you're down there."

She says she wants this program to work and, knowing me, the odds of a spiritual rebirth are slim.

"The twelve steps are fine, until you get to the God part, and that stops you cold," she says. "So I went online and I plugged in 'twelve steps' and 'atheist' and I found this."

"I'm not an atheist," I say. "They're zealots too. They make nonbelief into a religion. I'm an agnostic. . . ."

"Whatever," she says, handing me a sheet of paper, sort of a secular translation of the twelve steps. "I printed this out in the night."

I glance at the sheaf—"The Humanist's Twelve Steps." No mention of God, but much seeking out of other people and having the courage to change. I set it down on the nightstand.

"I'll look at it."

She follows me around to my side of the bed, praising the secular steps, reading them aloud. I draw back, crowded, overwhelmed.

"You can take this and share it with people, print out copies for them," she says, then stops, reading the unease on my face.

She kisses me hard.

"Diabetes is a disease," she says. "Parkinson's is a disease. They don't talk to you about curing it with a higher power. AA says alcoholism's a moral defect and it is not a moral defect."

She is practically glowing.

"It's probably unconstitutional for the court to mandate this . . . *religious program*," she says. "I want you take this and share it with people at Chapman. You can take this and form your own program for people to come to. You can help other people!"

I've had enough.

"I don't want to help people!" I say hotly. "I can't even help myself."

Not the most noble sentiment, but there you are.

"But you *will* help yourself," says Edie, not letting go of her intensity. "I'm so proud of you."

She tucks the revised twelve steps into the notebook.

"I'll put this in your black folder like everybody else," she says, referring to the folders Ross and Kent use to transport notes and homework to and from school, nudging me with a wing back into her brood of boys.

———

Kent is ready for school. "Let's play catch," he says. I automatically stand up and grab a football—he's been suggesting catch a lot, unusually so, though whether he's doing it as a kindness to me, because he knows I like it, or for himself, to prove that everything is back to normal, I'm not sure. Either way jabs at my heart. A lovely scene—the big sugar maple, the morning sun strobing through the leaves, the brave little boy. I set the pads of my fingertips against the football's laces, to throw the proper spiral. Kent catches the ball against his shoulder. A car turns down the street and passes, and I suddenly see the tableau from their eyes. A Hallmark movie with a horror twist—the alcoholic enjoying a moment with his son, a respite from rehab. I stiff arm that thought and we throw the ball.

———

Like characters assembling in some mediocre play, we wander in, gathering in the third-floor meeting room at Highland Park Hospital. Leslie is in black capri pants and white strap T-shirt and the same long brown gloves, from elbow to knuckles. She sits with her shoes off and her legs tucked under her bottom. She says hi, and I say hi and sit next to her.

We all say how we're feeling—okay or bad or angry or whatever; Shirley, a housewife with a deep tan, is excited because she found a sponsor last night—a sponsor is your AA big brother or sister who talks to you every day and rides herd on you to make sure you aren't screwing up. I need a sponsor, too, but can't even consider coping with that yet.

"I'm feeling rested," Leslie says brightly. "Actually, I haven't felt that way in a long, long while."

The morning session reviews the physical effects of alcohol. Cirrhosis and dementia and throat varices, which is when the veins in your throat break down by you pouring so much alcohol down your gullet that you start to bleed inside your throat.

Scary stuff. Instruction is being done by Cassie—the other nurse, Helen, must be off today. Cassie is in her mid-fifties, with big square glasses and a slightly confused look.

She talks about tolerance—your body gets used to alcohol, so you need more and more to get the same effect. Check. She talks about withdrawal—your body is accustomed to alcohol and doesn't feel right when it's not there. Double check.

"If you have tolerance and withdrawal, you definitely have the disease," she says. I point out to her that whenever I visit my doctor in recent years, I mention drinking and have him test my liver, but the liver is always fine and the doctor never seems particularly concerned.

"A lot of medical doctors, they don't know about addiction," she says.

I think of visiting Dr. Ling, telling him I'm worried I'm drinking too much. "How many drinks a day do you estimate you have?" he asks, tapping away at his open laptop.

"On average? I don't know. Three. Five."

"Then you should cut down," he says matter-of-factly and never mentions the subject again.

"So why do they treat this organic, physiological, genetic disease with psychological cures?" I ask. "You don't sit people with sickle cell anemia in a room and get them to talk about it."

Her answer is a hash that boils down to: Medical science doesn't know what else to do.

True, we have a variety of medications—antidepressants, anticraving medications, stuff like Antabuse, which will make you vomit if you drink alcohol. But they're aids, not cures. The bottom line regarding AA is what I already suspect: It's the only show in town. It's like Churchill's line about democracy being the worst form of government except for all the others that have been tried. Alcoholics Anonymous is the most unscientific, ineffective way to treat alcoholism, except for anything else available—the moderation programs and rational recovery systems whose track records are even worse.

"We're going to move on to the medical complications of alcoholism," says Cassie. "If you continue to use alcohol, every cell in your body will be compromised. Your heart muscle deteriorates. Your liver, of course. Your brain. Your sexual organs.

"Eight percent of alcoholics get cirrhosis. Thirty thousand Americans die of liver failure. Esophageal varices. Even knowing that if they ever drink again, their varices could rupture, some people drink anyway."

Shirley puts up her hand and says, "Panic attack."

Cassie scowls and checks her notes. "That's way down the list," she says.

"No, she's having one now," Brent says, and we all laugh.

"Again, now that we've talked about all this gloom and doom, if you stop, your body tends to regenerate, even with cirrhosis," says Cassie. "There are some diseases that have no cure, and this has no cure, but if you stop, you have a chance to live."

As dire as all this is, it mostly glances off me, like that *Wheels of Tragedy* movie from the Ohio State Highway Patrol that we watched in driver's ed in tenth grade. Gross, but nothing that would actually make a sixteen-year-old drive more carefully. Ditto for the grave alcohol ailments. These are things that happen to winos living under trestles. The only permanent physical effect of drinking hand over fist that I've noticed in myself is a smattering of broken blood vessels—gin blossoms—in my right cheek. I remember the first time I discovered them, in the mirror at the bathroom at work, staring at my face with a growing horror that I immediately suppressed. I try not to think about my little red badge of courage, and nobody has ever mentioned it, not even Edie.

We go around talking about physical effects of drinking and drug taking. My liver's fine, as far as I know, and the blood pressure, well, that should go back down if I keep with this. I find myself telling the room a story I haven't thought about in a long time:

I am at my desk at the newspaper, working away, and the phone rings; it's Bill Granger, a local columnist who made a name for himself writing detective novels.

"Neil? Hey, I read cher cahlum today and I staught it wash *great!*" he slurs. *This guy is drunk,* I think, looking at the clock: ten thirty a.m. Plastered at ten thirty in the morning. We talk a bit and I get him off the phone. Sad.

A half hour later, the phone rings again. "Neil?" the same voice says. "I read shure cahlum this morning and want to tell you it was *great!*" Bill again. Almost the same words. Obviously forgetting that we had just spoken. I get him off the phone, but cold horror settles in my gut. It's frightening, I tell the group, like something out of an Oliver Sacks book.

A short time later Granger has a stroke—he's only in his fifties—and ends up in a nursing home, unable to write, his mind wandering uncontrollably through the distant past or stuck in the immediate present. I can't think of a worse doom for a writer. Lots of drinkers stroke out. Royko was sixty-four; of course he, like Granger, also smoked cigarettes. But he was strong—he shook your hand, he tried to crush it. Royko should have lived to be ninety. The night I returned home, I went around my office, checking the biographies of my heroes, reminding myself how they went: F. Scott Fitzgerald is forty-three, making fudge with his fat mistress to soothe his ruined stomach. Robert Benchley is fifty-six, sitting around the Garden of Allah drinking all day with some forgotten third-rate actor. Hemingway blows his head off at sixty-one. Thurber is sixty-seven, wetting himself at parties and bitching because he hasn't won the Nobel Prize. It's a bad end.

After a break, we return. Cindy runs the counseling session, brisk, efficient, with a key fluttering on a curly purple lanyard around her left bicep.

Catherine speaks about heroin in a barely audible voice, head bowed. "All the people . . . I used to go out with . . . spend time with . . . I don't spend time with . . . anymore."

"I'm jealous," I say, trying to fill one of her long pauses. "If booze was as tough to get as heroin, I'd be home free."

The group leaps to disagree.

"Those dealers want to keep you," says Shirley, with pink, gemlike toenails and a wildly colored Chinese jacket.

"I had to change my phone number to keep them from calling," says Catherine placidly, her arms folded across her belly, hands disappearing within her sleeves.

"You all earned your places here," Cindy says, wrapping up the conversation. "While the past is helpful, to teach us lessons, try to stay in *today*. You don't have to keep fighting the past battles. Those are over. Do what you need to do to be in sobriety *today*."

The session concludes and I head for the elevator. I haven't been so grateful for lunch since elementary school—the challenges and crises in the lives of my fellow addicts, rather than assisting me in understanding my own struggles, seem distant and only faintly interesting, like those old elementary school filmstrips about volcanoes. Stepping into the hall is a relief.

The elevator door opens and five anorexic girls float out—there is also an eating disorders center on the third floor. Each girl holds a plastic tray at hip level, her twig arms straight down and locked at the elbow, as if pressing the food as far away from her mouth as possible. I examine the plastic-covered meals on the red trays. Oranges and slices of bread and little pots of cottage cheese and dinner salads. Not a big sloppy cheeseburger or a brownie to be found. The girls drift by, spectral, sexless, serene, almost preternatural. Angelic. The ideal that drives them to do this is instantly obvious. Their faces glow.

So easy to go off the rails in life, I think. You'd assume that being a teenage girl in twenty-first-century America would be simple and fun. Boys and homework, makeup and music. Then again, other people's lives always look easy. The anorexic girls are somehow comforting: for their wraithlike beauty, their strangeness. The youthful nightmare they are enduring puts my own situation into perspective. At least I managed to keep things together until I was forty-five. I didn't fall apart at fifteen. In the real world, that might not be much of a reason for pride—feeling superior to teenage girls with eating disorders. But in here, it's something to grasp at.

———

I'm shaky after lunch—my blood pressure is one eighty over seventy-six. I sit on the bench in front of the hospital. It feels strange, not being at work, to sit there with a cell phone in my hand and nobody to call. I phone Edie—she's going to Costco. "They have some nice flannel shirts," she says. "I saw them Friday, but I didn't get them because I was mad at you. I'm going back to get one now."

In the afternoon session Emily—the elderly bag lady—tells her story. She wears half-glasses, with jeans rolled up almost to her knee and her brown hair pulled back.

"When I was *drinking* I would feel really *good,*" she says in a soft Southern drawl. "But then I would feel guilty and it would bum me out. I was always hiding bottles, minimizing how much I was drinking. I'd sneak drinks. I didn't use a glass. I'd use a coffee cup with a top on it, and for a while that worked. I'd only take two drinks a day—so you can imagine the size of that coffee cup. Always just wine, no hard liquor—I can't stand it. I wasn't ever stumbling drunk. I thought my family didn't know, but of course they did. I went to the twenty-eight-day at Hazelden—'the Haze,' we called it—and was abstinent for a year. Then I started again, and now my family doesn't trust me anymore. They're starting to again now, but they didn't for a while. I slipped on a rug, and my daughter ran over and said, 'Mom, you didn't . . .' and I said, 'No, of course not,' and she believes me, which is wonderful, because she can be a snippy little thing. And I have a wonderful meeting, on Thursday nights at the Wilmette Community Center, that I can walk to."

Wilmette. Hazelden. The woman I pegged as a bag lady, condemned for her North Carolina accent and her old woman's legs, is actually a North Shore society matron. My judgment is not only skewed, it's hair-triggered. I'm so hot to dismiss these people as being beneath me that I can hardly see what's right in front of my eyes.

––––––––

At home that evening, on the couch, under a blanket—I'm cold; I get cold a lot, though it isn't cold outside—watching *The Price Is Right* with Ross. Not my habit, but by suppertime that's about all I'm good for. The phone rings.

Edie walks in with the phone. "Baker," she says icily.

Peter Baker, a bluff Brit, was my boss and friend at the *Sun-Times*; now he's editor in chief at the New York *Daily News*. I couldn't begin to count the lavish lunches we've shared, the bars we've crawled through together. He's all bluster and good cheer, phoning from New York. Just checking up.

"Tell me everything," he says. "I want the lot. Leave nothing out."

I tell him about the day, the film, and the talk about addiction. He seems very interested—almost *too* interested.

"Are you worried you might be following me?" I ask.

"No!" he says heartily. "Had a bottle and a half of wine last night followed by a few rum and cokes and I couldn't feel better. No, no, mate, it's *you* who've got the problem. *You* who have gone and ruined it for yourself."

Yes, I have, I think glumly.

"So are you really in this program *sincerely*, trying to make it work?" Baker asks, incredulous, as if it's the most amazing and perhaps also the most stupid thing in the world.

"What am I supposed to do, Peter?" I say, shifting on the couch. "Given that I could lose my house, lose my job, lose my kids, lose my wife, and go to jail, yeah, I thought I would give it a go."

Why mope and tune it out? What am I worried about losing? The right to drink a half pint of Jack Daniel's on the way to pick up Ross from his Saturday-morning chess lesson?

That seems to rock him back a bit.

"Sure, lots of people don't drink and enjoy life . . ." he muses, grasping for an example. "The Muslims . . ."

That hangs in the air. I'm not sure what to say.

"Are you taunting me?" I finally ask.

"No, no, of course not," he says. "The Muslims, well, they have their fun, don't they?"

———

That evening I have my first Alcoholics Anonymous meeting— first, that is, discounting the previous handful of misfires done to placate Edie. The first meeting as a guy in court-ordered rehab, the first check in the four checks a week I need to keep from getting into hot water at Chapman.

I select the meeting from a pink booklet listing meetings in the area. In a city like Chicago there are meetings almost every hour, somewhere, dawn to dark. That itself is a comfort; it's not just me. I choose the meeting closest to my house. Three blocks away, at a Methodist church, though I ask Edie to drive because I'm not sure, if I leave the house by myself, where I'll go.

Memories of the two or three AA meetings I've been to over the years, at Edie's insistence after a bender, make me hesitant to go now. Because in the past, rather than encourage sobriety, AA meetings prompt me to want to drink *right now*, if only to separate myself from all the bulbous-nosed navy vets grumpily announcing that they've gone 14,323 days without a drink. Particularly one meeting the previous summer. A windowless room in the Michigan Avenue AA headquarters, crowded with broken, bleary men jammed around a table, reading some kind of religious doctrine from yellowed pages stuck behind dusty glass in old wooden frames.

"I'd rather die of alcoholism," I say on more than one occasion, "than go to AA."

The program stresses anonymity—important, certainly to reassure people who don't want to be there in the first place that news of their presence isn't going to be blabbed at the next PTA meeting. But for me the anonymity, which is supposed to be a comfort, somehow makes AA even worse. It seems something of a fixation, a fetish that goes beyond merely shielding the identity of individual members. At the meeting on Michigan Avenue the previous summer, they use "Alcoholic" as a last name, as in "Hi, my name is Steve Alcoholic." It seems so strange, like those black bandit's masks people wear in old-time dirty pictures. Anonymity is fine, but "Neil Alcoholic" is shooting your identity in the back of the neck and dumping it into a pit. I couldn't get out of there quickly enough, and never went back.

Until now.

They stress anonymity and shun publicity. You're not even supposed to refer to Alcoholics Anonymous by name in print. It's the "program," the way *Macbeth* is the "Scottish play." The idea is that your eventual failure should not reflect poorly on AA, which makes sense, given the 90 percent relapse rate. Nevertheless, it sometimes strikes me as Masonic secrecy.

We drive the three blocks in silence, the boys in the backseat, taken along lest they kill each other in the four minutes Edie would be gone.

I'm dumped off at the United Methodist Church just before eight p.m.—men stand in knots in front of the door, smoking cigarettes in the gathering darkness. I nod to them as I hurry inside, feeling like I am entering a hidden male world, of watch caps and work boots and longshoremen hiring halls. We troop down into the basement: low ceiling, fluorescent lights, chairs stacked against one wall, an open kitchen of battered white metal cabinets at one end where the coffee is being brewed.

Everyone seems to know one another, except me of course, and we take chairs around a big square made up of four rectangular tables. Around the tables are maybe fifteen people, from a teenage kid in a baseball cap to Lee, who must be eighty.

These meetings have a set order, like church. The leader, a bearded man named William, welcomes us and selects people to read various items of the liturgy. I am given a laminated blue page with HOW IT WORKS on the top and asked to read it out loud. I haven't the strength to protest. I leave the page flat on the table and, at the proper moment, with a nod from William, lean over and start reading:

Rarely have we seen a person fail who has thoroughly followed our path. Those who do not recover are people who cannot or will not completely give themselves to this simple program, usually men and women who are constitutionally incapable of being honest with themselves. There are such unfortunates. They are not at fault; they seem to have been born that way. They are naturally incapable of grasping and developing a manner of living which demands rigorous honesty. Their chances are less than average. There are those, too, who suffer from grave emotional and mental disorders, but many of them do recover if they have the capacity to be honest.

Such a strange way to begin your catechism: This'll work, unless of course you are a liar, or crazy. An odd way to start your statement of purpose. Mean, almost. I press on. Very quickly I get to:

Remember that we deal with alcohol—cunning, baffling, powerful! Without help it is too much for us. But there is One who has all power—that One is God. May you find him now.

The God stuff already. I look around, feeling trapped. Not only is drink being dashed from my hand, but my entire personality—the detached wiseass sitting in the back of class whispering jokes about the teacher—is being assaulted, forced to at least feign the motions of a joyless 1930s cultlike faith, a weird branch of Christianity where Jesus is surgically removed and replaced by a sobriety fetish.

But what else to do? Stop reading? Make a joke? Argue? Flee? Jog to a bar? This is the hand I am dealt.

The famous twelve steps and seven—more than half—refer to God, a higher power or a spiritual reawakening. Leave the driving to God. The old bargain—once you believe, He takes care of everything. God strikes the batter out. We don't get sober; God does it.

"How it Works" takes a while to read, but eventually I near the end of the laminated page. "No one among us has been able to maintain anything like perfect adherence." My mind detects a loophole: Practically "Bottoms up!" Tucking away that revelation for future use I read the last lines:

> Our description of the alcoholic, the chapter of the agnostic, and our personal adventures before and after make clear three pertinent ideas:
>
> (a) That we were alcoholic and could not manage our own lives.
>
> (b) That probably no human power could have relieved our alcoholism.
>
> (c) That God could and would if He were sought.

The group echoes the final sentence as I read it. I feel chilled. As if staying sober weren't difficult enough, now I am told that also I must flush out the ineffable divine presence hidden somewhere in the universe.

They ask if anybody is here for their very first AA meeting and, discarding my previous meetings as trial runs, I raise my hand, even though this will bring attention to me. The group agrees—on my behalf—to focus on the first step, admitting that one is powerless over alcohol. We read the beginning of the *Big Book*, the AA bible.

Then we go around the table and introduce ourselves. This

is the dramatic high point in the movies—how the story ends, the camera pulling back to show that the drunkard, after his life of dissipation, is now rescued. It always seems a lousy, unsatisfying way to end a story. I don't feel rescued, don't feel safe, and blow my big speech:

"Hi, I'm Neil. I'm an alcoholic," I say, staring at the tabletop. "I've been going to the Chapman Center at Highland Park Hospital, and I've been sober for five days, the longest I've been sober in almost three years. That's all."

We count off by threes and break into three groups. My group grabs chairs and sets up in one corner of the basement, in a makeshift chapel area. The guys tell their stories, tales that have a tang of the 1970s to them, of high times and business lunches and wives drawing the line. I tell mine briefly, the drinking, the slap, jail, the publicity. I explain I have trouble with the God thing. Not hostility, though the entire AA philosophy seems to assume—a tad too eagerly—that resistance is due to feverish anti-God animosity. Not in my case. I don't bear the Big Fellow ill will. It's just I don't think He's going to come over the hill, flags flying, to save the day. Because He never does. The methodology of AA strikes me as being like a health insurance plan based on Christian Science.

"I've tried this before and it just didn't stick," I say. "I don't think AA is going to cure me."

We break up. Several men come up to me and give me their phone numbers—call them, they say. I'll be needing a sponsor—the implication is that they'll be that sponsor, but I don't even want to think about it.

One guy—Stan, late fifties, handsome once, now petrified, an advertising executive gone to seed, sidles up and says almost in a whisper. "Maybe *you* didn't stick." I look at him and he leers at me, eyebrows up, nodding his head. It takes me a moment to process what he's saying. Don't fault the program, pal, fault yourself.

I flee into the night.

Edie shows up in the Camry with the kids in the back—the worst part, the boys pulled outside into the night at bedtime to collect their alcoholic dad. I get in, thank her for coming, and we drive the sixty seconds home. She is strained—a long day—tired, not at all the enthusiastic woman who urged me this morning to start my own program.

The boys ask about what happened at the meeting. I say we talked about drinking. Ross says something like: Well, it's not a problem because you won't be drinking for two years—the court order says no booze sin the house for two years. I say, that's right; let's worry about it in two years. Edie seems to bristle, as if I'm tossing ahead cushions to ease my future drinking. Maybe I am.

Chapter Seven

"Dad, do you want to play Monopoly?"

Friday morning. I'm in my former bedroom, quickly dressing, trying to get my new green plaid flannel Costco shirt off its hanger.

"Sure, just a second!" I yell down.

"Dad, do you want to play Monopoly?" he shouts again. My younger son, Kent.

"I'm coming!" I say, agitated, buttoning the shirt, my fingers fumbling.

"Dad," he says, "do you want to play Monopoly?" I can hear him fine.

"In a sec!" I yell.

"Dad!" he shouts louder. "Do . . . you . . . want . . . to—"

"I'm *COMING*!!!" I scream as loud as I can, stepping into the hallway, suddenly falling apart. "I'm coming!" My voice rasps, hoarse and stripped and crazy and unrecognizable. "I'm coming as fast as I can! I can't come any faster!" I'm practically crying.

———————

The morning had started so well, with a hand on the doorknob. "Who's there?" I ask. In a rush it's Ross, scooting under the covers with me.

"How are you doing?" I ask.

"Great!" he says, and I look at his round and shining face and see that he is indeed doing great. Beaming, not a care in the world—nine years old. "How are *you* doing?" he asks.

"Worried . . .," I say, wanting to shield him, failing, ". . . about things." I stop there. He nestles. The furnace hasn't been turned on yet this year. I wrap the blanket tighter around us.

"We have a cold house," he says.

"You tell your mother that," I say deviously.

He has an extra-credit math assignment from school. Take the digits one through nine and group them, inserting addition, subtraction, multiplication, or division signs, or brackets, so the result is exactly one hundred. Something like $(12 \times 3) + 45 - 6 \ldots$

"There has to be a method to this, like Kepler's shortcut," I say, and begin working on it in pencil on the bottom of a Kleenex box. Ross busies himself with a piece of paper. We work in silence. For a while I always end up with 101, but I eventually find a solution, through trial and error, and Ross, I'm pleased to note, rather than demanding to see my answer, is inspired that it can be done and figures out his own, different solution. For a few minutes, doing the math problem, my personal problem recedes, and it is wonderful until I realize it is gone and it returns. We write up the answer for his teacher, with "Ross' solution" and "Dad's solution" boldly labeled.

After that, it's hard to find distraction. I check e-mails, but not the news. The headlines seem so beside the point, almost meaningless: "Bleep seeps to meep the freep."

Getting dressed, it all blows apart in five seconds. I'm screaming downstairs at a little boy who wants to play Monopoly. Anger is contagious, and Edie catches it from me and chews me out in the car. "Why do you drink?" she says. "Why did you continue to drink, even when you saw it was causing trouble? I can't have this. I can't have you in the house yelling at the boys."

"Fine," I say. "I won't be in the house. I won't yell at the boys. I'll divorce you and you can go out and find a job and see what it's like."

I'm delivered, seething, to Chapman. I take my seat. The therapist at the front of the room is somebody new. A woman with an olive complexion, deep-set black eyes, lipless, long straight brown hair, wearing a green fleece pullover and gray cords. She looks as if she were soaked in tea, or dug out of a bog.

"Hi and welcome," she says, mellow rolling off her like mist. "This is Balanced Lifestyles and Recreation. The purpose of this group is to think about leisure activities during the recovery process. My name is Rona and I am a recreational therapist."

We go around the room, introducing ourselves and our drug of choice and how we're feeling. I say, "Distressed."

"Did you say 'distressed'?" Rona asks, as if it were an exotic word.

"Distressed, stressed, disturbed," I say. "I had a fight with my wife." I'm eager to get into the details, to make them understand the difficulty of having no job, no workplace to go to, nothing to do but live in a house with a woman who, having recently sent you to jail and then into rehab, still doesn't like you and has no prospect of liking you in the foreseeable future, not until you somehow magically morph, with the help of the Lord God Almighty, apparently, into a person you have never been nor ever wanted to be.

"Well, we'll get back to that," Rona says. First we have to play Imagine If. A game where we finish thoughts such as, "If I were a cable channel, I would be . . ." We write down our channel, then view everybody's answers and try to match the response with the person who wrote it.

"In this way," Rona says, "not only do we learn how to have fun without mind-altering chemicals, but we also get a chance to learn more about other people in the group."

We play for a while: If you could get free tickets, what concert would you like to see? If you were a historic disaster, which would it be? What color would you be? What country? It quickly stops being fun, particularly with the argument gnawing a hole in my gut. I'm in no mood for cocktail party games without the cocktail party.

"Oh, interesting . . ." purrs Rona, when it is revealed that Luke, the Vicodin addict, would be Noah's flood.

For the first time in rehab I feel truly damaged, one of eight addicts playing party games in a suburban hospital room in the middle of the day. They yank me out to have my blood pressure checked and I'm grateful—flashing to the coolness of the hallway at Fairwood School, delivered from the boredom of a cursive lesson. Recovering drunks should be parachuted into the deep woods with a pocketknife and a single match. They should be forced to flee down slick hillsides with packs of dogs chasing them in the rain. Something distracting, exciting, meaningful. They shouldn't have their faces ground into the very boredom that pushed them toward drink in the first place.

That afternoon Linda has us do pie charts—the pie represents twenty-four hours, and we're to divide the typical day of doing our drug of choice into sober, using, and being under the influence. Sober is white, using is dark red, under the influence is light red.

My pie looks like one of those red-and-white-striped hard candy mints. It's white from six a.m. to noon, then back and forth, deep red and light, for the rest of the day. Drinks at lunch. Drinks before dinner. Drinks before bed. Drinks in the middle of the night. Drinks, drinks, drinks. Not every day. But most days.

I'm not sure when the drinking went from something I did with other people, socially after work, to something I did by myself, by force of habit. Maybe during the years I worked the night shift—I was the last seven p.m. to three a.m. reporter at the paper. I'd take dinner at nine p.m., slide over to the Billy Goat—the original Goat—to see who's there, have a drink with them, or, if nobody was around, just a drink by myself, passing the time, watching the TV.

Eventually I come to prefer not drinking with other people, because their indifferent sips at their beers only emphasize how quickly I'm pounding back my hard liquor. Richard is three sips into his Red Stripe, and I'm ordering my next round. It's embarrassing.

Drinking was not something you thought about, it was something you *did*, whenever you could. I'd be having dinner with Edie, nursing a glass of red wine, excuse myself to go to the bathroom and pause at the bar to down a glass of Jack, just because I was passing by, just to keep the tank topped. Because the opportunity presented itself. It was not a practice I chose to dwell upon.

The pie chart cannot be ignored, however. The chart seems stark, clinical, compared to the patty-cake of the morning.

Rehab is not soft and gauzy, not the touchy-feely process that people smirk at, I think. *Rehab is attending the autopsy of someone you love.*

We go around the room. Name, drug of choice, feeling. I say, "Flayed," and Shirley grabs the arms of her chair as if to get up.

"Ooh, let me get a dictionary," she says sarcastically. I'm too spent to be offended; I have been enduring this sort of thing my entire life.

"It means, 'Having the skin stripped off your body,'" I say mechanically. "It's a metaphor."

Since today is Friday, we have to say how many AA meetings we attended this week. Some people went to five.

"One," I say, my face hot as I talk about it. "They made me read, 'How It Works.' I felt like Galileo, forced to kneel before the Inquisition and recant his heresies."

"Well," says Linda, unsure what to do with *that*. "The first meeting doesn't always go well. Where are you going tonight?"

"There's a church around the corner," I say. "They're having an eight p.m. meeting."

"Great."

I worry going to only one meeting will put me at the bottom, but others didn't go to any.

"Zero meetings," says Catherine, her voice tiny, her hands hidden.

"None," says Ron.

"Guys, you have to go to meetings," says Linda. "It's part of your agreement. We expect it of you. It only works if you work it."

Luke has been to seven meetings.

"Wow," says Linda. "That's impressive. Now—just to give you a subliminal hint—how many meetings does everybody plan to go to over the weekend?"

"I'm going to five this weekend," says Luke. "One tonight, two tomorrow, two Sunday."

I expect Linda to say that's too many—give yourself room to live—but apparently there is no such thing as too many meetings. She smiles and nods approvingly. I briefly consider whether next week I should report that I've been to fourteen meetings, just to test Linda's reaction. But that would involve either going to two meetings a day or lying, and I'm not yet willing to do either.

Some say they plan to go to three. Catherine says one. They get to me. "Two," I say, squirming.

Shirley says she's having trouble going to meetings.

"You don't need to believe; just show up," says Linda.

"Fake it till you make it," chimes in Ron.

There is one final piece of business this morning. It is Shirley's last day. Sally and Cassie come in, and there is a "coin ceremony." Linda produces what she calls a gold coin—a big brass slug with the emblem of a butterfly and some AA jargon, and we pass it around the room, imparting our karma upon it, apparently.

"Get the Kleenex out," says Linda.

Everybody holds the coin and talks about the impact Shirley has had on their lives.

"You haven't really said much since you've been here, but everything you've said has been very smart," Catherine says, gazing meaningfully at the older woman.

Even Leslie—who only met her Wednesday, two days earlier, along with me—speaks with this deep warmth that strikes me as false, or would, if she weren't so intense and seemingly genuine.

"I want to know more," she says, her arms spread out. "Who is Shirley, and why is she such a sweet, loving, wonderful woman? I want to know more about you."

My turn. "I don't know you and won't miss you" seems bad form, though that is what comes to mind. I take the coin, contemplate it for a moment, and say what a pleasure it was to meet her and how sorry I am that I didn't get a chance to know her better, then pass it on. The coin works its way to Linda.

"What I've been so privileged to see is you're reaching inside yourself and realizing: There isn't a big empty void there I have to fill with alcohol," says Linda.

At the end, Shirley has her say.

"The road I was going down was leading nowhere *fast*," she

says, wiping away tears. "God, I'm going to miss you all . . . I'm just so happy you gave me my life back, my kids, my friends, my husband, everybody I pushed out of my life."

The ceremony ends and everybody is still hugging one another while I slip out of the room to go to lunch.

————

During the break, I sit in the lobby of the hospital with my cell phone in my hand. I can't call Edie, because of our fight. I can't call my parents because they're in Greece. My brother is busy, my agent is out, my friend Cate doesn't answer. That's the limit of the phone numbers I have memorized—I never learned to program numbers into the phone. I almost wish I had taken some of those AA numbers, to reach out to my new drunk pals.

Drifting back to the afternoon session, I run into Emily in the hall.

"So you were at Hazelden," I say. "What was it like?"

"It was like a prison," she says. "You spend all your time doing chores, sweeping up cigarette butts. This is one hundred times better."

That helps my spirits—I'm in a good place. Better than Hazelden. Better than Detox Mansion.

I get pulled out of the afternoon session for my "Psycho-Social Assessment" with Linda in her office. This is my anger evaluation, to satisfy the court, to make sure I'm not dangerous. There is a certain small pleasure in answering questions, a rhythm, like playing a slot machine. In with the nickel, pull the handle, see what comes up.

Linda sits at her keyboard. I muster my response, gazing at the weave in her red sweater.

"Your usual occupation?"

"I'm a writer."

We go over the boys, the house, how long I've been married.

"Does Edie use drugs?"

"Sadly, no," I say, and she gives a little laugh. If she did, I wouldn't be in this mess. We'd be wacked out together, happy.

How do I deal with anger? How did I deal with it when I was small? I tell her I used to punch walls. I remember being sent to my room, as a little boy, and pounding my head against the door. Once I punched the glass out of a window—cut my hand all up. I was small, maybe four. My mother went to the neighbor's house for a moment and didn't tell me. I couldn't find her. I still remember wandering the house, looking for her. "Mom? Mom! Mommmmmmmm!!!"

Linda has a little seen-it-all smirk that I've already begun to dislike.

"Surrender is a tough thing," she says philosophically. "For a smarty-pants like you, that's got to be hard."

No kidding. It's hard, and I'm glad. Being reluctant to casually hand yourself over to somebody else, to let them drive while you close your eyes, is usually the same thing as being intelligent. You close your eyes and do that trust drop backward into the wrong arms, you end up sending money to Nigerian scams. Every corner church, every newborn cult, every half-baked crackpot and rip-off artist starts his spiel by cooing how you should trust them, how you must learn to surrender, to let go of your previous hang-ups and misconceptions and bathe in the golden glow of whatever they're selling.

I'm loath to do that. Loath to let go of myself. Myself is about all I've got nowadays.

I must look injured, because Linda tries to be comforting. "Let me tell you the thought for the day: You should know that you are tailor-made for this disease. Tailor-made. It was unavoidable. You may think that you're unique. You obviously fancy yourself the Special Boy. All alcoholics do."

This kind of session demands a plan, and she leaves me with one. I am to "socialize with AA members" and "to be open to developing a conceptual framework of a higher power."

Yes, fine, I say, eager to end it. The session over, I feel boxed in, heartsick. As someone who is selective about friends, I will now be pals with any random omnium-gatherum of losers who have screwed up their lives as badly as I have. As someone who dislikes hospitals, I'm to spend six hours in one every day. And, just in case the whole thing doesn't seem enough of a wasted exercise, I'm to pretend to reach out to the God who isn't there and in whom I don't believe.

Just delightful. The only positive aspect is that there is no choice whatsoever. Oh, I suppose I could sleepwalk through the twenty-eight days, then move out, flip off my wife and children, and go back to drinking. Surrender to Booze Triumphant. And that does sound appealing. But whenever I squint into the future and try to imagine actually doing that, it seems impossible. As bleak as this path is, I'm on it and I can walk it, for now.

———

That night, just before the meeting at Fourth Presbyterian Church, I slip upstairs to my home office to check my e-mail. I sit in the chair, the computer in front of me. Behind me, the walnut rolltop desk I bought with five years' worth of paper route money when I was fourteen because I was going to be a writer someday and a writer needs a rolltop desk.

Dropping my arms, thinking, *I really need a drink*, I turn and reflexively pull open the desk's file drawer—that's where the bottle of Jack was always stashed. I tried to keep one there, though of course it had a habit of going empty. Vastly comforting, to reach into the drawer in the evenings, the day done, the family elsewhere, to take out the bottle, admire it, and pour a slug into the shot glass I kept next to my keyboard, tucked away, hidden in the little computer drawer. The drink always felt warm and wonderful.

Of course there is nothing in the drawer. I practically paw the empty space, then proceed to carefully open each of the eleven drawers in the desk, to poke in each cubbyhole. There, to the right in a tiny pencil drawer, a plastic half pint of Dmitri—cheap vodka—and two little Smirnoff airline bottles, leftovers from some frantic trip to Sunset Foods over the summer. All empty, but a residue inside. A few condensed drops. Not enough to drink . . .

I impulsively uncap one of the airline minis and insert the neck into one nostril, clamping the other nostril closed with my finger and inhaling deeply. I hold the alcohol vapor in my lungs, then exhale and repeat the procedure with the other nostril.

The anxiety ratchets down as the alcohol hits my brain. Just a little. Ahhh . . . I smile. Not technically a drink. I've never heard of anyone snorting booze, and wonder if I could have invented some kind of new and unique depravity. Is that possible? I'm too amused by that thought and too relieved by whatever vapors reach my brain to even feel reproach.

It's time to go to the meeting, and I clomp downstairs. The boys are roughhousing with each other, and immediately the tension begins winding in my head again.

"Boys, please" is all I can say, just above a whisper. "Boys, please." They scramble over the couch. The phone rings. Edie picks it up in the kitchen.

"Jonathan," she says. She hands me the phone. It's my neighbor from down the block. He's in the program, too—a fact I discovered the week before when he showed up at my door with a bag of chips and a couple of cans of soda. He read about me in the paper, he says, adding that not only is he also an alcoholic, but he is in rehab at this very moment, over at Illinois Masonic. I never suspected. Jonathan. A guy I've known for five years and never seen drunk, not once. Tall, lanky, a runner.

The idea that there are other people in the same boat with me doesn't generally help, just as the fact that one hundred and fifty thousand people die every day doesn't make death any more attractive. But he's here, he's going through a similar ordeal, and he's someone to talk with.

That first evening he came over, we sat on the front porch for the first time in the five years we've lived on the same block. His drinking threatened his marriage, he says. No big incident occurred. He checked himself in, relapsed, and is now trying again, going to a hospital program in the evenings and of course to Alcoholics Anonymous meetings. Jonathan is a big fan of Alcoholics Anonymous meetings.

"Sure, they take time," he says, "but you have to balance time spent at meetings against time you used to spend drinking, or thinking about drinking, or fighting about it."

At the end of that first conversation, when we stood up, I went to shake his hand, but Jonathan stepped in and hugged me. That was unexpected. We had never hugged before, I thought, my face against the plaid fabric of his shirt. When we weren't alcoholics, we never hugged. Why are we hugging now?

Still, I'm glad he's here, on his cell phone in his car in front of our house, going to the same meeting I am. Would I like to go with him? Sure. Somehow, this makes it a whole lot easier. I don't have to drag my wife and family around the corner. I feel like I'm in high school again, out for the evening with an older pal who already has his license. We drive a few blocks, park, walk into the same church common room I had been to last

time. There at a table is Hal, seventy-three, with his Glenview
Air Station hat, his wide-set eyes and frog's mouth and white
hair. I met him the year before, when I went to a meeting or two
and gave it up.

Maybe because Jonathan is at the meeting, the stress of the
night before is gone. The same "How It Works" is read, but not
by me, which also helps. We go around the table—when it
comes my turn, I pick up on something someone said about
how difficult this is.

"To me, this being so hard is a comfort, because it helps
soothe the remorse I would otherwise feel," I say. "When I came
here over the summer, Hal was kind enough to take me under
his wing"—I figure, butter the old guy up—"and had I stuck
with it I would be in a far better position today. But I didn't. I
didn't find anything here for me, and soon I was back to my old
ways. And when I wonder why, I quickly remind myself that
even now—when I stand to lose so much—I can hardly do it.
So how could I have possibly done it before, if I can hardly do it
now? If it takes every ounce I have? I'm so there with the powerlessness stuff. I've got powerless down pat. It's the higher
power that is causing me trouble. But you can substitute your
own higher power, they say. I try to find stand-ins until I can
understand."

After we've gone around, Hal addresses his remarks again to
me directly. "Neil, I'm the only one in my family to inherit my
uncle's gene." He tells of the people he knows who have died,
and that death is the only end, "wrapping your car around a
lamppost or in the hospital with an exploded liver."

The meeting ends. Jonathan and I walk out into the night in
our quiet little town and get in his car, an old Cadillac he inher-
ited from an aunt. My head doesn't feel tense anymore. I am, if
not quite happy, then at least not frantic, which feels pretty

much the same. Jonathan says he is going to a big open meeting in Wilmette the next day.

"Can I come with you?" I ask. He says sure. He pulls into his driveway. We shake hands, and I place my other hand on his forearm—no hug, to my relief. When I am halfway down the driveway he thanks me for coming with him and I turn and thank him for going with me, and I think we were both just grateful to have each other for company.

Walking along our block, under the black trees, I marvel that I have licked drinking in three days. It seems a waste to go through the remaining twenty-five days of rehab, but I suppose I have to humor them.

Chapter Eight

The boys want French toast. I make it special, with challah, cinnamon, and imported Madagascar vanilla. Linda says I have to get rid of the vanilla, because it has alcohol in it, a suggestion I use as proof that rehab doesn't always know what it's talking about.

"It isn't as if I'm going to drink the vanilla," I say.

So we have vanilla, but no eggs. The old refrigerator is in our dark, sour-smelling basement. Going downstairs, I flash on the brown bottles of cold Sam Adams once waiting patiently for me there. I grab a Styrofoam package of a dozen eggs and go back to the kitchen.

French toast made, Edie takes Ross to a chess tournament. Another cue to drink. I trained myself so well that if Edie announced she's going to the store, I would automatically think: *Drink!* The car would pull out of the driveway and I would reflexively reach for whatever was lying around the house, tucked somewhere, or else trot off to Otis & Lee Liquors for something to pass the day. "Bye, honey, see ya later!" Not this time. Not today. Not anymore.

A big limb from a catalpa tree is lying in the yard, having cracked away in the rainstorm while I was at my brother's house.

I grab a pruning saw and start taking the limb apart. After a half hour or so, Kent begins calling my name from somewhere on the other side of the house.

"Dad!" he shouts. "Dad! Dad!" I open my mouth to answer, but don't. I don't have the energy to yell, don't want to light that fuse within me by yelling, and don't want the spectacle of the town drunk and his youngest shouting at each other in their yard. I put down the saw and walk around the house.

He's on the front porch, a cordless phone in his hands.

"Someone named David Rosen called," he says. "I didn't know where you were."

David is my first cousin, battling colon cancer in Boston.

The last time I saw David was over the summer, when I went to Boston for the weekend to sit with him during his chemo at Mass General. Despite the somber purpose of my mission, we had a great time talking, laughing, sharing stories about our mothers, who are sisters. I'm closer with him than anybody else in my extended family. But I haven't told him about the arrest and the rehab. I figure he has enough to worry about.

The news is mixed. The cancer has spread to his liver, and while doctors at first thought they would operate, now they aren't so sure. They are going to bombard the cancer with millions of microscopic radioactive spheres and see what happens.

"So I won't need a night-light," David jokes bravely, a line he has obviously used before. His prognosis, which had been looking up—the cancer had shrunk by a quarter last time we spoke—is now not as positive. David is in his late thirties, has two daughters, one and three, and is struggling to squeeze out every day he can with them.

"I want to hold on until Anna can remember me," he says, of his younger girl.

Compared to David's situation, my own little crisis seems minor, self-imposed. He is coping with a far grimmer ordeal with a lot more class than I am coping with mine.

Halfway through the conversation, I realize that not telling him is a mistake. When my mother gets back from Greece, she'll tell his mother and he'll feel out of the loop. I wince and dive in.

"I have a bit of bad news myself," I say, and tell him the story: slap, jail, twenty-eight-day rehab.

"I'm shocked," he says.

"So now I can't drink anymore," I say, then realize that we're in the same boat. "Of course, you can't either."

"Not a huge loss."

"You're not an alcoholic," I say, asking him how long it had been since he had a drink.

"Since May." Five months. "I miss the wine," he continues, "because it goes with food. Now meals seem less eventlike. Sometimes we'll be at a friend's place and he'll have an interesting bottle and I'll miss it. But it's not a huge thing for me, not a huge loss. I'm too terrified by everything else."

He suggests I replace drinking with some other habit or hobby: cigars perhaps. I've heard that before—it seems naive, like telling a suffocating man that he should replace breathing air with a pastime, like knitting. Imagine, I tell David, battling to stay alive while at the same time trying to undermine yourself.

"At least you don't have to worry about wanting to drink bottles of cancer," I say.

"You'll do it," he says. "You're strong-willed."

I point out that a strong will cuts both ways. A strong will can straight-arm drinking, or it can thwart all the forces that would keep a person from drinking.

"You'll beat it," he says. "One thing I noticed about you is that drinking was an affectation—the hard-drinking reporter. You'll reinvent yourself, you'll do it, you'll become a better person. Just take it one day at a time. One day this will be a blessing. You're lucky that Edie loves you that much."

"And lucky for you," I say, "that you have Kim." David's wife.

"She's been incredible," he says

"Hang in there," says David.

"Hang in there," I respond.

"One day at a time," he says.

"One day at a time," I answer, with sincerity.

————

Edie comes back home with Ross. I'm in the kitchen, doing the dishes. I expect her to be happy: husband home, sober, tree chopped up, dishes being done. Instead she is flinty, scrutinizing.

"What's wrong?" I ask.

"I'm just tired," she says.

"Well, it's Saturday afternoon—a perfect time to rest," I say, smiling expansively, bobbing my head, looking for a smile in return. No dice. *Okay,* I think, *just let it go.* A few minutes pass. The dishes are almost done. Edie is back in the kitchen.

"Were you in the basement?" Edie asks. "The cat's mewing down there."

I think hard.

"Eggs," I say finally. "I made French toast for the boys. Went downstairs to get eggs." She looks at me.

"Eggs," I say again. She turns away. I go to let the cat out.

An hour later, I'm upstairs in the office, at my desk. Edie bursts in.

"I want to know where that bottle of Scapa is," she demands. "I'm making an inventory of what we have to sell on eBay." The two bottles of nice champagne and a bottle of single-malt scotch, the 1960 Scapa.

A wave of panic.

"Don't sell that bottle," I implore.

"Where is it?"

"Don't sell that bottle."

"I want to see it."

"I drank it," I lie, "a long time ago."

"No, you didn't. I saw it."

"Okay, I moved it. I didn't drink it."

She turns away, her face a mask of disgust.

"Booey, don't do this," I say, my good feeling draining away. I follow her.

"Show it to me."

"You won't sell it?"

"Show it to me."

"Promise me."

"No, why should it be important anymore?"

The conversation has moved downstairs, into the kitchen. I step over to the wooden block holding cutlery, remove a carving knife, and jam the tip against my throat.

"It's important because if you get rid of it I'm going to slit my throat in front of you, that's why."

That gesture catches her attention and she agrees to keep the bottle. We go down into the basement among the metal shelves we put up five years earlier, hammering them together using a black rubber mallet, a late newlywed moment, building our new nest together. I open a cardboard box of clippings and hand her a bottle-size gift box, sealed, with the bottle in it.

"I didn't even drink it during my worst moments," I say. "I never opened it. I never will. But I have to have it around. It means something to me."

She puts it back with the champagne in the fruit cellar. I follow her up to the kitchen.

"Promise me you won't sell it," I say.

"I won't sell it."

That was too easy. There must be a lawyerly equivocation.

"Or get rid of it."

"Why?" she says. "Why do you care?"

"It's part of my self-image, my *new* self-image, who I am." She looks even more revolted. I glance over at the knives again and, for one split second, consider running over, grabbing one, and driving it into my heart to demonstrate to her that I actually am sincere. The feeling passes.

"I'm not a guy who doesn't drink because his wife has gotten rid of all the booze. I'm not a guy who thirty years from now will be violently struggling to keep from taking a drink. . . ." I make a grasping claw with one hand and hold it back with the other, as if pulling it back from a glass. "I don't drink because I don't want to. I could have drank that anytime. I still can. I choose not to—I *choose* not to, because it isn't in my self-interest to do so. Because I don't want to. Promise me you won't get rid of it. I need it."

She looks at me.

"Promise me or I'll divorce you."

"You're going to divorce me anyway," she says flatly.

"No, I'm not. I'm sorry. But I need to keep that. I'm going to have that on the shelf of my office someday, as a symbol of my victory, and if in my heart I'm planning to drink it on my fiftieth birthday, well, if it gets me through the next four years, is that so bad? We'll worry about it then. Don't get rid of that bottle."

She makes a noise that sounds enough like "okay" to let me calm down.

"I'm not divorcing you," I say. "We're going to grow old together."

I truly feel as if my life depends on that bottle being around, and am anxious that it is now exposed to Edie's caprice—so much so that I go back down and make her promise again.

"I'm a patsy," she says.

"Why?" I ask. "You think I want it there so I can drink it whenever I want? Guess what? There's a bar around the corner. There's a liquor store down the street. I can drink whenever I want, but I don't want to, and that bottle is going to be the symbol of that. It's going to be my trophy, okay? Let me put it somewhere I know it's safe and I'll show it to you whenever you want."

"No, I want to see it," she says.

"Promise me," I say.

"Tell Kent that his turkey and cheese sandwich is ready," she says.

At lunch, we have a calmer conversation. I apologize for lying about the bottle in a moment of panic. She seems brighter, smiling.

"Take this to the garage, would you?" she says. "We have enough things cluttering up the counters." She hands me an empty square cardboard peach basket from Bergman Orchards in Port Clinton, Ohio, a rectangular box with a wire handle. It had been filled with peaches when we bought it coming back from Put-in-Bay after Labor Day. I drum the box ruminatively, walking out the back door, saddened to be reminded of anything before the Fall. Back when I could drink. Then I remember . . .

Before we stop at Bergman's, we stop at the Cheese Haven. Another touristy spot—aged cheddar, meat sticks, flavored taffy, sweet Ohio wines, crusty clerks. "Let's take refuge in the Haven," my private joke, made while swinging the car into the parking lot. Edie goes off to ring up some cheese and crackers and such for lunch. I take the opportunity to tuck into our groceries a little airline bottle of a vile rum drink—Passion Harbor, some such thing. Putting the bag in the car, I pocket the bottle, and at Bergman I slip past a grouping of yard-tall decorative wooden lighthouses on the margin of the parking lot and duck into a brown port-a-potty. Standing inside the cramped fiberglass coffin, over the open crap hole filled with odiferous sogged toilet paper, I unscrew the cap, tilt my head back, and quickly drain the coconut-scented liquor.

This, *this* is the life of comradeship and sophistication I am so desperate to preserve.

The sky darkens. Time for me to get to the dry cleaners before it closes, the day's final chore. Because it's closed on Sunday and I'll need clean shirts come Monday morning. The place is three blocks away, but I wouldn't go there myself—I don't want to walk by the Landmark Inn unsupervised. So I mobilize the brood out of their Saturday-afternoon languor. Shoes on, coats on, the sky is suddenly leaden, wintry, the boys already outside. I step out the door, into an ambush. The boys have gathered berries and throw them at me. I'm so shell-shocked I stand there and let them pelt me, arms up over my face, defensively.

"Boys," I say weakly. "Now, boys."

We walk to the park, the boys conspiring behind us gleefully about future berry attacks. Kent is carrying a football, and we all play catch in the little downtown park, clumsily tossing the ball around, Edie and the boys and me, our Kennedy family moment. I find myself glancing at the road whenever anyone misses, the ball skittering mockingly away, to see if we're observed. I throw and catch, but am mulling the situation over and over in my head, cycling in an endless loop, from pillar to post. Is this how it's going to be? I think, in the chill, under dense gray skies. Sleepwalking through my family life while dreaming of drink? On the way back, dry cleaning over my shoulder, just as we approach the railroad tracks, the lights start to flash and the gates come down. An Amtrak express. My gaze tracks its approach, as it nears, nears, then blasts by at seventy miles an hour.

"Bam," I whisper under my breath as I watch it flash past. After it passes, and before the gates rise, I hazard a glance into my wife's eyes and she looks steadily back into mine. "Don't even think about it," she says.

———————

At home again, we sit at the island in the kitchen, exhausted, drinking jasmine tea. Pondering booze in the park reminds me of Archy, the journalistic cockroach who leapt upon Don Marquis' typewriter at night, producing a chronicle of the yearnings of his insect heart, all in lowercase because the little guy couldn't work the shift, the practical touch that every good fantasy needs.

"Marquis was once the most famous columnist in the country," I tell Edie. "Now nobody knows who he is." Including her. I run up to my office and, after a search, lay my hands on an old anthology. I show her the column I have in mind—they're almost poems—where Archy interviews the mummy of a pharaoh, who tells him:

> i am as dry as the heart
> of a sand storm
> at high noon in hell
> i have been lying here
> and there

for four thousand years
with silicon in my esophagus
and gravel in my gizzard
thinking
thinking
thinking
of beer

Before I even finish reading I realize she'll suspect that I'm lobbying for drink, and maybe I am. She barely reacts anyway. We sit and sip our tea and listen to Ross practice the viola—the music rich, low, an apt soundtrack for regret. The new kitchen—done last year, all blond wood and polished granite, a rough-hewn pale green limestone floor and stainless-steel appliances—surrounds us like a brightly lit stage set.

"I wish I had put the time I spent thinking about this kitchen into thinking about my life," I say.

"You're doing that now," she says.

"It's too late, now. I'm an"—and I put a sneer into the word—"*alcoholic.*"

"You were an alcoholic before," she says.

Chapter Nine

Monday morning, my first full week of rehab begins and everything is feeling normal. I wake up in my own bed—last night
Edie gives me a hug and a kiss and decrees that ten days in the
guest room are enough. The boys are delighted to wake up and
find Dad back where he belongs and so am I. In the car we talk
about when we'll go to Six Flags Great America next and who'll
ride which rides. The happy negotiations of family life.

Dad gets dropped off—almost like school—and hurries to
the third floor.

"Hi, I'm Rona, and this is Balanced Lifestyles," she begins.
"A time to focus on leisure planning and try to come up with
healthy alternatives to meet your recreation needs in creative
ways."

Rona is back—recreational therapy is Mondays and
Fridays—but because I'm not upset, this time she's a welcome
triviality. Rona addresses the room as if she had not just spoken
to us on Friday, as if none of us has ever seen one another
before.

While we're playing Apples to Apples, Dr. Manozzi calls
me away from the fun and into her office. She wants to know
how I'm doing. I tell her my moods are all over the place. The

Saturday-afternoon dread, the moment with the train. Now that I feel seminormal, the frozen tide has gone out, it seems hardly worth mentioning. But I know that it is just gone temporarily, and the anxiety about not drinking will spill over into mind again, a chill back surge.

"I could give you something . . ." she begins, in such a way that I automatically add the "but" in my mind and begin speculating over her reasons for denying me.

No "but" comes. She could and she will give me something. A drug called Zyprexa. It's usually used to treat psychosis in schizophrenics, she tells me. Heavy-duty stuff, but a minuscule dose will be just the ticket for a guy like me. She takes out her prescription pad, then realizes there are samples and goes off searching for them.

"This'll take the edge off," she says, walking out of the room, on foot, not using her scooter, and I nod, thinking: *Taking the edge off is good. Taking the edge off sounds fine by me.*

She returns empty-handed.

"The only doses they have are large enough to put you out for a night and part of the next day too," she says.

I'm tempted to shoot my hand out and say, "Any port in a storm." But I don't. I arrange my face into a serious look and nod grimly. Oh no no no, we don't want that.

She writes a prescription.

"I want you to take two a day, but I'm prescribing three a day, so you'll have extra," she says. Extra is good too. Maybe I was too quick to judge her. Maybe Dr. Manozzi is my kind of doctor after all. I take the prescription and return to Balanced Lifestyles.

The late-morning session is taken up by Ron—the guy I had lunch with on the first day—who drank over the weekend and is now a shaky, sobbing wreck. Earlier, describing his pie chart, he describes his average day as: "Drink every waking moment, pass out, do it again the next day." He says he's been that way for twelve years, only drinking beer with occasional shots. He'd always be late for work, so his boss took to scheduling him an hour earlier, so he'd be there when he needed him. Ron came here, strangely enough, not for booze, but for his Internet gambling addiction. "There was nothing left to gamble away," he says.

His lapse comes, he says, when a friend who was supposed to go with him to an AA meeting backs out at the last moment. So he got drunk instead. Alcoholic logic. Ron is yanked out to meet with Dr. Manozzi with a definite sense of "off to the principal's office."

After Chapman, I stop by Walgreens to fill the prescription. The pharmacist gives me a bag containing my Zyprexa—tiny little pills. "Your insurance saved you $582.49," it says on the bag. Down the hatch.

That evening Jim calls. I've known him since junior high school. Solid guy. Soft-spoken. Bearded. A civil engineer. He still lives in my hometown of Berea, a couple blocks from where we went to high school. Our families get together once or twice a year—we go stay at their lakefront cottage at Put-in-Bay, his family visits relatives in Illinois at Thanksgiving and swings up for a Chicago weekend with us. He is my oldest friend—we have never argued, never been on bad terms.

I thought of calling him, but couldn't. "Hi, Jim, guess what: I hit my wife and now I'm in rehab. What's new with you?" Not a call I'm eager to make. Now there's no choice. He's on the phone. Edie takes the call, talks a bit, then tells Jim that something terrible has happened and I'll fill him in about it. She hands me the phone. I take it, go in the office, close the door.

Jim says he noticed my column hasn't been in the paper for the past few weeks—he reads it online—and he's wondering what's up.

For the first time I have difficulty saying the words. I stammer out the situation.

"I'm always leading the party," I tell him, subdued. "I worry that, without that, there won't be much to me." Why would he possibly want me around?

Jim's family has a cottage on Lake Erie. Ever since I was seventeen, I've been escaping with Jim to his place on Put-in-Bay, first as part of a crew of his high school pals, then with my girlfriend, then with my wife, now with my family. You drop your bags, crack a beer, and the weekend melts happily away.

Say good-bye to all that.

Jim says there's a lot more to me than drinking, and we'll still have fun at the island, even if we're not holding up the bar at Frosty's.

"You won't take me downtown, and I won't take you on the kayak," he says, referring to the previous summer, where I flipped myself in his wife's kayak on Lake Erie and came as close to drowning as I ever wish to come. We laugh at that. Hanging up, Jim says, "We love you a lot, Neil."

In the darkened office, gazing at the silent telephone, I feel genuinely bad. I made Jim Sayler say he loves me. I must really be in sad shape. Must really be pathetic. We are never going to be invited back to Put-in-Bay.

Returning to our bedroom, I'm ready to recount the phone conversation to Edie, who is under the covers, reading. "It felt good to have you in bed last night," she says, "but now I don't know . . . Jim calling made me relive that night. You said such awful things. You never said you were sorry. You never took responsibility for your actions."

I get out of bed. "I said I was sorry several times. I stood in open court and admitted I'm an alcoholic. I could have hired a lawyer and fought it. I didn't. I'm in rehab. That's taking responsibility aplenty."

Removing my wedding ring, I set it on the base of the lamp, leave the room, and trudge upstairs to confront the jumbled guest room, with the skewed bedframe and nest of piled covers. I literally can't lie down. Instead I go back to our bedroom and we go over it all again, one more time, with feeling.

"You're going to grind my face in this for the rest of my life," I say.

"We were always so close," she says, turning to face the wall.

————————

The good news is that I wake up in my own room the next morning and don't feel that old cold dread. The bad news is I don't feel anything at all. Zyprexa. I lie there, trying to figure out what's going on in my head—as if somebody placed an empty shoe box inside my skull. "Take the edge off"—what if it is the edge that allows me to think? To write? How can I write a column if I can't form a thought? The entire edifice is endangered.

Edie drives me to Chapman. I don't say a word—I sit looking out the window, my fist against my lips, rooting around in the empty box for a comment while she floats a couple of conversation openers. But there aren't any comments. There is nothing to say. Eventually a scattered thought does show up in the empty box, like lint, and I scoop it together, make a little ball out of it, roll it around with my fingers. She didn't like me . . . she didn't like me sometimes coming home drunk . . . and being uncommunicative . . . and now . . . now I'll be that way . . . all the time.

I smile. But don't say anything. My secret.

Catherine finally makes an AA meeting, and is lauded with applause. Today is her first step—the part where she tells her story—and she explains her journey through heroin addiction. It isn't a very long or involved tale. She's twenty-one. She fell in with a group of friends who took heroin. It took her less than a year to become an addict.

"I would make sure to save a little bit just in case I couldn't find any the next day," she says. "Just going to get it wasn't the safest thing. We'd go to the West Side of Chicago. I told myself that it was fine, that it wasn't a problem. I was pulled over once, trying to buy drugs. But they didn't do anything."

It is almost impossible for me to imagine Catherine, with her smooth pie plate face and vanishing hands, prowling the blasted streets of the West Side, searching for smack.

While Catherine is speaking, a new drunk comes in— Howard, a chunky man in his mid-fifties, with glasses, a bushy mustache, and gray hair. He plops into a chair.

Catherine says she pushed her friends away to hang out with fellow users. "The people I was getting high with, it's not that we didn't care for each other. But we didn't. Getting high was more important."

Like the host of some unimaginable public television show— *Addict Theater*—Linda wraps up Catherine's comments and puts them in perspective for us.

"As you go along in recovery you become more comfortable with the idea that you're not a together person," says Linda.

That's it exactly! I think, an idea pushing through the Zyprexa like a bubble rising in warm honey. That's the problem, or one of the problems. Recovery seems to be a commitment to being a fuckup for the rest of your life. I am together. I am. A together person who just so happens, at this particular moment, to also be a drunk.

Time to meet the new patient.

"Howard, drug of choice, alcohol," he says in a phlegmy voice. Then a long pause. Then a rush of words, as if he's said it before and is bored with the story himself and just wants to get it out: "Been doing it a long time, been through a couple de-toxes, lost an eighteen-year job because of drinking. Giving up drinking lifted a weight off me."

He sits, slope-shouldered, bloated and exhausted. Howard says his liver is ruined, he was hooked up to a ventilator earlier in the year, almost died. As he talks, I look at him closely. His skin indeed is a sickly shade of light-yellowish orange.

———

"This is like a date," Edie says, kissing me. We are in the van, heading off to Family Night at Chapman, which is every Tues-day. I'm still quiet, groping for something to say. But I just can't find the words. Zyprexa. Edie fills the spaces, remembering, as she parks, how her mother parked her big-finned Cadillac in two spaces, to have more room on either side.

At a stoplight, we pull alongside a Ferrari, red and perfect. I study the driver—about my age, head shaved, sunglasses, hockey puck watch. A cell phone pressed against his bald head, he darts me the briefest glance, his face registering nothing. Some guys have life by the balls. And some guys are being driven to rehab by their wives in a Honda van. I gape at him dully, like a cow in a field.

"You always said you wanted to have a breakdown," Edie says, accurately enough. "To sit on the front porch with a plaid lap rug over your knees and stare at the tree. And now you have your chance."

We plunge through the bowels of Highland Park Hospital, into a small room. There is a pitcher of water in the back, and coffee. We watch a filmed lecture entitled *The Biopsychosocial*

Disease. A lot of talk of the brain healing, of it taking six to eighteen months to repair the damage wrought by drugs or alcohol—not so you can go back to drinking, of course. But no citations. This is not, apparently, science, or if it is, it is science by declaration. We know this stuff—trust us.

Family Night has three parts—first the film, then we break up into two groups, the addicts trooping upstairs for a regular therapy session while the families talk about what an ordeal it is to live with us. Finally, both groups are reunited in a circle downstairs. During the middle session, I talk about my concern for backsliding—as things grow "normal" I start wanting to get my life back where it was and that means drinking. I can't get my mind around never drinking again.

"Why not think about never sleeping in your wife's bed again? Or not seeing your children again," says Pat, a chatty lady about my age, offering probably the most helpful concept yet. "Why not concentrate on that?"

Leah is running Family Night. Apple cheeks, wire-frame glasses, she is a stocky woman in khaki pants, her hair close cut and going gray, her manner brisk and efficient.

"Denial is the primary symptom of addiction," says Leah, before our movie, *Denial: Breaking the Defense Symptom.* "It's the disease that tells you it isn't one."

A thought fights its way through the Zyprexa. Tamping down a grin, I lean toward Edie. "They say that alcoholism is a disease of denial," I whisper. "But I think that's a bunch of crap." I pull back and raise my eyebrows, waiting for her smile, but there isn't one. She shoots me a "this isn't funny" look. Of course it's not funny, dear. Nothing is funny. My old world, of jokes and loosened ties, of old friends with their feet on a rail, drinking bourbon whiskey, laughing and sharing intimacy and understanding, is blown to hell. This is my world now, and I can't even joke about it.

During the session, while Deborah—a new patient, a former nurse, and Benzedrine addict—is prattling on about herself, a rehab ballerina twirling in the spotlight of attention, I do something I have never done in my life. As she talks and talks, her voice a handsaw through sheet metal, I close my eyes tight, and turn my head hard to the left, trying to tune it all out, just for a moment. Like a prisoner turning his face to the dungeon wall in despair.

Eight days after the Jewish New Year, Yom Kippur arrives, dreaded by Jews for its long services, fasting, and generally downbeat tone. But for a newly recovering alcoholic, Yom Kippur is the perfect holiday. The evening Kol Nidre prayer is a haunting, sorrowful lament, a dirge that chills you like an ancient tomb and sets the tone for introspection. The prayer renounces any vows and oaths you might make, a practice thought to have originated in late-1400s Spain, when Jews were forced to swear allegiance to Christianity in public, and thus had reason to privately retract their vows.

Still, being who I am, I can't help but draw Edie's attention to the translation of the opening lines. "All solemn vows, all promises of abstinence, and formulas of prohibition, and declarations of austerity, and oaths which bear a name of God, and pledges to ourselves . . . from all of them, we now request release."

"That's not what they mean," she says, unamused.

Prayer feels good. Not because God suddenly pulls the clouds apart and give me a big wink. But because the words are right. Pounding on my chest and begging forgiveness meshes with my mood, and I enunciate the prayers boldly and loudly.

"For on this day, atonement shall be made for you, to make you clean from all of your wrongdoings," we pray. "Before the Font of Mercy, you shall all be clean."

————

The next day, Edie wants to go to the daytime Yom Kippur services, but if I go, I'll miss a day of rehab and be reported to the court, and God wouldn't want that. Which means I'm driving myself to Chapman for the first time.

The idea of picking up booze passes across my mind like a shadow, but I brush it away. A thought, never a possibility. The idea of failing, of being shipped off to a locked, in-house facility, of following Ron, crying the day before as he was drummed out of Chapman, is an impossibility. No way. And the bottom line, if I'm even thinking of doing that, then they're absolutely right.

When it's time to leave, Kent comes over for his kiss on the head, but Ross won't get up—he's playing a video game—so I bend over, carefully placing my hand against his head to hold it still as I deliver a gentle peck. The boys have been known, historically, to leap up just as I lean in to kiss them, and it takes a skull cracking against your mouth only once or twice to inculcate years of caution in a man.

"A ghoul tried to take my cards, but I wouldn't let him," Ross is saying to his brother as I head out the door.

I'm surprised and disappointed that the boys play computer games so much—can't they see it's fruitless, an addiction, a time-wasting sinkhole that avails them nothing?

I should talk, I think, getting behind the wheel for the first time in more than two weeks. It feels good to drive again, though on my way to the hospital, I have to swerve to avoid a woman who has pushed her baby carriage into the street, crossing against a green light. "You're crazy, lady!" I shout at her back as my car passes. Deep breath, and an inward smile: screaming at pedestrians. A sign my old self is coming back.

Did I say that I abandoned Zyprexa after two days? It's supposed to even out after a few weeks, but I couldn't risk that when it did I'd be left a dullard. It's too Orwellian, taking a drug that Dr. Manozzi and half the staff have emblazoned on their freebie clipboards. And Edie has a friend who took Zyprexa and gained about fifty pounds. But the bottom line is, I'd rather retain the capacity for thought and be anxious, sometimes, than be a placid zombie.

———

The session is another movie—a man in a purple sweater is talking in the energetic, prowling-evangelist style I begin to suspect is required for therapist lectures. He has a salt-and-pepper beard, and hard, coal-like eyes.

"Children *idealize* their parents," he says. "They can't not do it. It's a survival tool."

Behind him is a huge orange book with TOXIC SHAME written in six-inch letters across its cover.

Purple Sweater uses his own dysfunctional family as a template for teaching, which raises my standard qualm as I watch: Those leading recovery seem to have been screwed up themselves. Maybe they have to be. It wouldn't do to have survivors of normal, loving families try to give guidance to alcoholics. "Of course you love your parents; why wouldn't you?" they'd say, with a look of bewilderment. "Unless you're an ingrate."

He also hits on codependency. "Shame-based people marry shame-based people," he says. "You go into a room, you aren't going to be drawn to the healthy person."

Ahem. Not in every case; I almost feel foolish now for marrying a strong woman from a solid family such as Edie. She has always been good sense itself. I can't think of a reckless, irresponsible thing Edie ever did. Not one. Edie wouldn't throw away an aluminum can, not when it's supposed to be recycled. I don't think she could physically do it.

It is Edie, when I start downloading songs on Napster, who scowls over my shoulder and berates me. "That's *stealing!*" she says. "I cannot believe you're stealing music!"

The song is "(I Can't Get No) Satisfaction" by the Rolling Stones.

"So I'll send Mick Jagger a check," I say.

The day before, Leslie had brought back a spicy-smelling pint of Chinese food for lunch, and I ask her where she got it. Jade, a restaurant over in Highland Park. She's going again today—do I wanna come with her? Yes, I do.

She drives a powder-blue PT Cruiser, the kind of car a well-to-do dad would bestow on his little girl. The restaurant is plain beige stucco, but inside is elegant and empty.

"We could sit down," she says. "Do we have time?" Forty minutes—that should do it. We walk in, and confront a wall of bottles.

"They have a bar," she says. "I hope that's all right."

It'll have to be.

"Sure, sure," I say, taking a seat looking out the window. "I'll just face away from it."

Leslie asks for pot stickers. I order the beef and broccoli lunch.

She is a chef at Persimmon, in Los Angeles. The fingerless gloves that I assumed were hiding needle marks were actually hiding burns. Chefs at fancy restaurants put in long hours—up early in the morning scouring farmer's markets, hours of prep, dinner that stretches from five p.m. until one a.m., cleanup. Drugs are part of the life.

"I thought I could do it recreationally," she says.

My back dutifully to the bottles, I trot out my pet idea that at least she doesn't have to see cocaine everywhere she looks.

"I can get coke as easily as alcohol," she says, adding that her drug dealers have been very understanding about recovery.

"They've been wonderful," she says, toying with a pot sticker. "My main guy told me: 'I'm glad you're getting help, Leslie, because I don't want you to die.'"

"That's sweet of him."

We sit and talk—she might go back to drinking wine, she says, but never drugs, and I envy her that opportunity, envy her the lack of a wife who has appointed herself as life's hall monitor.

Well, this is going very nicely, I tell myself, digging into my Chinese chow. I consider suggesting we order some of that wine right now—but that's probably a bad idea. *Oh, well, at least I have this recovery buddy to go to lunch with. Perhaps we can make the most of it. . . .*

———

That afternoon, several in the group give their "chemical histories"—the story of their lives told through their addictions. You could just as easily, I think, tell the story without mentioning booze or drugs at all. That's how it's usually done—alcohol is a stage convention, like the curtains opening and closing or the lights going down. It's assumed, unspoken. There's something impolite in drawing attention to the drink. Certainly rude, almost naive, like standing up at a musical and wondering aloud why the main character keeps breaking into song.

But that's what we do here.

Howard sits hunched forward, his folder down on his knees, staring down at it, reading. "I was in the hospital for ten days in January," he says. "I was on a ventilator and nearly died." His description is stripped down and dispassionate, as if he were describing somebody else.

"Alcohol just takes a toll on your body," he says. "My kids have been very loving and supportive. To be an alcoholic, to know you're an alcoholic, and to blow it off and keep drinking anyway—that's sick behavior. I've been hospitalized three times. This really is my last shot."

"You were right at the bottom," says Linda. "I heard it affecting your emotions and self-esteem. I heard minimizing and denial in your story. I'm not trying to jump on you, but you worry me. You have on paper powerlessness and unmanageability, but do you feel it here?" she says, placing both palms on her stomach.

We get into a discussion over how much Howard truly understands his own predicament, with Howard sometimes jumping in to defend himself. I have to admire Linda's observation. She picked up on the resignation in Howard's voice; it floated him, surrendered, into treatment, but it could just as easily float him back to a bar and death.

Now it's Luke's turn—he's twenty-four but sounds fourteen—angry with his folks, languid, and marinated in grandeur.

"My general thoughts will drive me mad," he says airily, like a character from Rimbaud, outlining his self-hatred, boredom, and a "general sense of inadequacy," which of course is the fault of his parents. I'm uninterested in his petulant self-regard, until he lights into rehab.

"This program, it's so kindergarten," he sneers, with a dismissive wave of the hand, "with your movies and your trite slogans. All those little sayings. 'Stinkin' thinkin'' is the statement I hate the most. You should have songs and, like, a bear costume. 'It's stinkin' thinkin'! You know, it rhymes!' Yes, yes it does."

He's right of course. Rehab has more slogans than the army—"one day at a time" and "easy does it" and "stinkin' thinkin'," which refers to the alcoholic mind's genius for rationalizing the need to drink. Some days the phrases seem worn, empty, and meaningless. Other days they just seem true.

Then it's Leslie's turn. She wears salmon pedal pushers and a green tank top under a black jacket and blue tennis shoes.

"I was a privileged child," she begins. The daughter of upper-class, liberal Jewish parents who basically sat back and smiled while she did whatever she pleased.

"I was eleven, twirling at Grateful Dead concerts," she recalls, spooling out a steady progress from there: Ritalin, pot—at thirteen, the age she discovered oral sex—mushrooms, opium, travel through Thailand, Mongolia, Australia, then, four years ago, cooking in California.

"My career took off and I lost my sense of self," she says. "Cocaine was the one drug I swore I'd never touch, because I liked it too much. I saw what it did to people. I went into it with my eyes open. Before I knew it, cocaine was my best friend and we went everywhere together. Until I came here, I didn't realize I have been using drugs for thirteen years. I thought I was so together, so in control, but cocaine, it kicked my ass. It really took me to my knees. I was in control of everything else. I thought I was having a good time. I really was. But cocaine took me to my knees."

I study her carefully while she's talking. It dawns on me that she does not look petite; she looks wizened. Not Audrey Hepburn, but Yoda. Her skin is tight, her face lined. Put her in a Chanel suit and she could pass as Luke's mother. She looks forty-seven, but she is twenty-six and has been using drugs, by her account, exactly half her life.

She finishes up. My turn.

"Well, I was born . . ." I begin, glancing around the room, gathering my thoughts. Linda cuts me off.

"You haven't written it out?" she asks.

"No," I say. "Events intruded. I thought I'd wing it." In truth, with the court case in the morning, I forgot.

"It's supposed to be written out—writing it is part of the process. You of all people should know that," chides Linda. I can do my chemical history next time.

After the session, I take Linda aside and talk privately with her. Ross' tenth birthday is Tuesday, the same day as Family Night. We're having a small party at home—just his *bubbie*, his aunts and uncles, a few cousins. I was sort of hoping that maybe I could be there, instead of going to Family Night. She says she'll look into it.

———

The first court hearing is a humiliating disaster. I mistakenly assume Jeanne Bishop, my college friend, will represent me—no, the judge lectures; public defenders are for the indigent. Get a lawyer and come back in a month. I come off as an inept cheapskate.

"You know my role model for this?" Edie says that evening, after dinner, as she gets dressed to do some volunteer work at the school. "Bill and Hillary Clinton. He could hold his head high and he was getting blow jobs under the desk. You have to hold your head high and go about your business. I know this has been a hard day and I'm proud of you."

Perhaps this emboldens me.

"I know you're glad about the rehab part," I say, "but are you sorry about the humiliation part?"

"I'm sorry about the humiliation but . . ."

"Thank you," I say, trying to end it there.

"If you're asking would I do it again . . ."

"No, I'm not asking you if you would do it again. I'm asking if you're sorry about the humiliation I'm being put through."

"I am—and you?"

"Yes," I say. "I am."

And then she's gone for three hours, volunteering at the school book fair. *How much can she really care,* I think, *sashaying off like that?* How worried can she be? My mood deepens and sours while she's gone. Edie leaving was always a sign that the coast was clear to have a drink or three. The bell goes off, a muffled, distant *clang clang clang.* I drink cup after cup of coffee, put the boys to bed, and then of course can't sleep myself, though I try.

Edie is back. I look down the stairs. She's on the couch, petting our elderly cat, Vronsky.

"Tuck me in," I say, as if I'm six.

"Come down here and pet the cat."

"Tuck me in."

She comes upstairs, perches tentatively on the bed, gives my head a pat, and says good night. I see her sitting there, in the dark, body turned away from me. I take her hand by the wrist and stroke my hair with it. "There there, baby, everything's going to be all right," I say, providing the lines for her. She lets this continue for a few seconds, then pulls her hand away.

"I'm done with this. It's too much. I'm finished."

"What do you mean?"

She gets up and walks out of the room.

————

Hope does not come with the morning. Instead, a bleak numbness. Numb, I get in the car. Numb, I race the engine at the stoplight, gazing at the pole, musing numbly that I could jam the accelerator when the light changes and power the van into the pole.

I don't. Instead I drive to the hospital, a few notches shy of crazy, and lurch toward the morning session, feeling empty, vacant. Upstairs at Chapman, as I pass the nurse's office, Helen calls to me, hands me a Ziploc bag with a clear plastic cup inside. I look at it, uncomprehendingly for a moment. Of course— the drug test. I carry the bag into the meeting room, toss it onto the chair next to mine. I stare at my feet, thinking: *I've lost my mind. I've gone insane. . . .*

"Good morning, everybody!" enthuses Rona, popping up like a jack-in-the-box, in a zip pullover made from a red Navajo blanket.

"This is Balanced Lifestyles," she begins. "I'm a recreational therapist. The purpose of this program is to make your life more satisfying without the need to resort to mind-altering substances. Whenever you take away something you need to replace it, and recreational activities are a perfect substitute. The idea is to present alternatives, to think about alternatives in terms of leisure activities. You have things to look forward to, things that are meaningful to you, scheduled in, that are predictable and fun."

We play Loaded Questions, which for a moment I think must be a drinking game dragged, like the human participants, unwilling into a sober setting. No, just more fun. We pick our favorite breakfast cereals, athletic activities, types of potato.

I pick hash browns, thinking, *You just have to endure. Just hold on.*

Linda pulls me out of the group, apologizing for making me miss out on Recreational Therapy. I tell her it's okay. In her tiny office, I relate how I am turning to Edie for comfort and it just isn't there. She tells me I need to not expect anything from Edie and instead reach out to my fellows at the program and at AA for support, because they understand what's going on. I just don't think that will work.

"I've been isolated all my life," I tell her. "If the solution is my crying on some alkie's knee at AA, that's not going to happen."

I'm not going to rush to make new friends in rehab. What would be the point? I don't like most people I meet, and the ones I do like inevitably drift off—I can never figure out why. The people I care about most shrug and vanish, and the more I clutch at them, the faster they seem to disappear. Edie is unique, in that, for some unfathomable reason, she wants to stick around. At least she did prior to all this.

On my way back from Linda's office, Helen grabs me for a checkup. My blood pressure is one sixty over one hundred.

"My sleep wasn't that good," I say. "I had eight cups of coffee last night."

She asks why, and I say that my wife went out for three hours. She was gone, I felt an urge to go get a drink—the opportunity was there. So I made coffee instead.

Group session begins. I'm staring at my foot. When we get to me, I say I feel unmoored and as for discussion issues I'm fine with whatever people want to talk about. Linda says she's not going to let me get away with that, and we'll get back to me.

Dr. Manozzi sticks her head in the room and beckons to me. I'm so out of it—focused on a spot on the floor, ignoring everything—that I miss my name and several of the others have to call me to get my attention. I stand up and mechanically follow her to her office.

"You can't drink!" Dr. Manozzi exclaims, shutting the door. This shocks me so much for a moment I worry I've been caught in some lapse.

"I didn't drink," I sputter, waking up.

"You can't drink!" she repeats.

"I didn't."

"But you were tempted." She pulls over a prescription pad and begins writing. "I'm going to put you on Campral. Three times a day. Breakfast, lunch, dinner."

"Look, my wife went to volunteer at the book fair for three hours. I looked ridiculous in court. The thought of popping over to the Sunset Foods and buying something crossed my mind—I wouldn't be much of an alcoholic if it didn't. So I made eight cups of coffee and drank them instead. I didn't do anything wrong."

I tell her I feel as if I'm being punished for being honest about what is going on.

"We were talking about doing this days ago," she says, referring to herself and her fellow therapists. "This isn't a punishment. It isn't because of yesterday. This will reduce your cravings for alcohol."

I put the prescription in my wallet and return to the morning session.

"Do you cook with wine?" Linda is asking Howard. "It doesn't all burn out. It takes something like ten hours for it to cook away. Don't assume because you flambé something it cooks off. Even then, you might get triggered if you taste it and have the flavor."

I suppress incredulity. She's telling a guy with cirrhosis, who probably was pounding back a fifth a day for years, not to cook with wine. That's like telling him not to eat rum-raisin ice cream. Or use vanilla in French toast. Linda would be unhappy if I wore a burgundy shirt, the kind of absolutism that tends to indict the rest of the program. That makes me want to sprinkle red wine vinaigrette on my salad at lunch, just to see if I really end up in the gutter by dinner. My bet is I won't.

Luke is leaving. We pass around the coin, imparting our psychic energy into it, part of the healing process that our insurance companies, or parents, or selves, are paying four hundred dollars a day to experience.

"The sacred in me honors the sacred in you," begins Linda intently, launching into lengthy praise of Luke's humor and courage. They get to me and I stare at the coin for a few seconds, trying to muster up something to say that is both honest and addresses Luke. "AA may be the only way to stay sober," I begin. "But it is a Procrustean bed—where they stretch you to fit if you're too short and chop you down to size if you're too tall. This can be painful to those of us who feel we are too big for the program and, Luke, your resistance has been a great comfort to me, to realize there is room to react to the flaws while still getting benefit from it. I've already been quoting your line about the bear suit and stinkin' thinkin'—I only wish I had said it myself."

We break for lunch. People are gathering around Luke, getting his phone number, giving him hugs. I shake his hand, wish him well, but somehow never stick to the group, and it moves off for the celebratory lunch without me. I stand there a moment before loping after them. I slow down as we reach the parking lot, vaguely hoping that somebody will turn around, beckon me. But nobody does. I could jog up, bluffly announce, "Where're we going?" But I don't. They get in their cars and go. I get in mine.

I'm tired. I feel as if I could drive into a distant corner of the parking lot, put my seat back, and go to sleep. That's a plan. But no spot looks amicable, and I end up driving out of the parking lot, through a different exit than I usually use. There is a park directly across the street, so I drive straight in and angle the car into a space.

Sunset Park. How apt is that? In fiction it would be hokey, but life has no qualms about grinding your face in your own mess. Sunset Park. The weather—which has been mocking from the start, with its gorgeousness, is prancing around me in circles of autumnal joy, the leaves yellow and orange and red, quivering on their branches, holding their little leaf thumbs up to their leaf lips, wiggling their leaf fingers and going *Pthblthblllll!*

Suburbs are built around children, so rather than erect statues of heroes at their center, suburban parks highlight playground equipment—welcoming, warm, ergonomically designed for safety. Walking across the park, I see a dad helping his little girl play on the climbing structure ahead of me, and veer away. I don't want to alarm them, don't want to seem like Peter Lorre, the scary stranger eyeing children in *M*. I give the playground a wide berth. On the far side of the park there is a bench waiting for me, and I head for that.

I sit on the bench, watching the dad and the girl from a distance, the only other person in the park, the solitary man, the alcoholic, the pariah. There is something depraved about being alone in a park at noon on a weekday. Sitting on a park bench . . .

Opening rock guitar chords—*DAHNT,* dun-nah. A drum flourish. Then, "Sitting on a park bench . . ." *Bamp,* bamp-bamp. "Eyeing little girls, with bad intent . . ."

I'm "Aqualung," I think. *I've become "Aqualung."* The old Jethro Tull song. Not the bad intent part, thank God. But the broken-down loser sitting in a park all by himself. I take out my cell phone and hold it loosely in my hand and gaze at it, like it's a dead baby bird. Who's left? I dial my brother's number—nothing. I dial my work voice mail number. Some oblivious PR flack calling to invite me to a tasting of Spanish wines. How perfect is that? I dial Dr. Frisch's number—he picks up. He has appointments—there are patients other than myself—but could see me at three thirty. I think of just going and not telling Edie, but picture her calling Chapman, worried. "He's gone!" I phone her, telling myself, *Be detached. Do not engage.*

"Hello, Edie," I say. "I'm phoning to tell you that I will be seeing Dr. Frisch at three thirty so I probably won't be home until after five."

"Okay," she says. There is silence.

"That's all," I finally say. "Good-bye."

I sit on the bench. Time passes. The phone does not ring. I call her back.

"I thought you'd call me back," I say.

"You were so hostile," she says.

"I wasn't being hostile; I was being aloof. Trying to be aloof," I say, realizing how lame that is. I try another tack. "I love you," I say.

There is another silence.

"I love you too," she answers, unconvincingly.

"See? That's what I mean. What's with the pause?"

"I'm sorry," she says. "I was daydreaming, looking at a bit of fluff on the floor from the cats."

I return to Chapman because I'm supposed to and have nowhere else to go. It is Friday, and we are listing our goals for the next week, writing them on big sheets of newsprint. Mine are:

1) **Stay sober**

2) **Shadow box**

3) **Clean office**

4) **Buy clothes**

5) **Call lawyer**

6) Go to new meeting

7) Four brisk walks

8) Look for sponsor

"Shadow box" refers to Ross' tenth-birthday gift. I collected items the day he was born—newspapers, calendar pages, and such—and kept them in a file for the past decade, and plan to arrange them in one of those deep frames. A tenth birthday should be a big deal—when the successful father lavishes his son with something wonderful to show him how welcoming the world is. A Patek Philippe watch. A salmon fishing weekend. I'm not that dad, especially not now, and probably never will be. A homemade shadow box will have to do.

———————

That evening Baker calls from New York.

"I just wanted you to know that I'm thinking about you," he says, and I start to outline my lonely, desperate day. I'm looking for sympathy, but I don't get it.

"It's still all about you, isn't it?" he says. "Maybe you should dedicate the next two years to the boys. It seems to be all about you, Neil, until you can make it about someone else."

Strike him out.

"You know the success rate of rehab?" I say. "Seventeen percent. The chances of succeeding are not good. I feel like I'm playing patty-cake while time is running out. This is like one of those nightmares where you run up to people and grab them by the shirtfront and scream, 'Help me, help me!' and they smile at you and suggest something meaningless."

Chapter Ten

Jonathan suggests we walk to the meeting at the Presbyterian Church. Downtown Northbrook is quiet and fairly deserted, even on a pleasant Friday night. We walk past four restaurants. A woman in the window of Oliverii's holds a glass of red wine. I quickly look away and wonder what I'd do if Jonathan suggests we slide into the Landmark next door to pass an hour at a bar instead of going to the meeting. Refuse, I hope.

The Presbyterian Church's Fireside Room is paneled wood with a large refractory table and stone hearth in one corner— elegant, particularly compared to the cinder block and stacked folding chair ambience of the usual church basement.

This meeting is led by Arnie, solid, sixtyish, in the standard plaid flannel shirt. We go through the regular opening catechism. I try to tune out "How It Works," but notice that two people seem to be repeating it like a prayer, one woman clasping her hands against her forehead and a man closing his eyes and murmuring fervently along with the words. Maybe it's just me, but I find this stuff just doesn't bind my soul to sobriety, though I flatter myself that I'm neither crazy nor dishonest.

Today's reading is the second step: God and/or a higher

power will restore our sobriety. Last week it was a deal breaker for me; now it just seems irrelevant.

We count off by threes and break into groups; a smart stratagem that makes confession more intimate and shortens the meetings. There are six guys at my table—myself; Arnie; two ponytailed bikerish men who mumble their names; Ralph, an addict trembling as with palsy; and Gordon, a small man, firmly grasping his shoulder and forearm, as if holding himself together, as if he stopped drinking yesterday and not, as he tells us, exactly two and a half years ago.

We go around the table. Gordon begins by saying he's sort of an agnostic, but has gradually come to see that somebody up there is helping him out. Arnie talks about waking up one day in the psych ward at Evanston Hospital. When it gets to me, I say that, like Gordon, I have trouble with this higher power business. But obviously I couldn't do it on my own—that's what I kept saying to my wife. "I can't do this. I can't do this."

But gradually, over the past week, I have begun to suspect that maybe I *can* do this, somehow, and while I'm not ready to suspect that God has paused from spinning the cosmos like a plate on His finger and is rushing to my aid, the fact remains that I have never been able to do it before, so perhaps something is afoot.

"I compare it to television," I tell everyone. "I was interested in the mechanics of TV, even read a book about the development of TV. But I just couldn't grasp, intuitively, how it works. And I finally realized, the beauty is, I don't have to. I can turn on TV and enjoy it, and see that it obviously works, without understanding the technology at all. That's my view of a higher power."

I finish, slightly embarrassed, and not because I am endorsing a God I don't believe in. Publicly admitting I am an alcoholic yearning for the Lord's care is easy; saying I enjoy TV brings a pang of shame.

We stand, form a circle, hold hands, recite Psalm 23, and are done.

My group leaves; I linger, waiting for Jonathan to finish with his.

"Did you notice that guy was wasted?" he says, explaining that one of the ponytailed bikers was blitzed. Completely. As if in proof, we pass the man Jonathan is referring to, swaying at the church entrance, prattling on drunkenly to his companion as they both smoke cigarettes.

I tell Jonathan I didn't notice.

"I thought it was fervor," I say. "And I'm supposed to be the journalist. At least he was at the meeting."

Jonathan suggests we take an alternate route home, past the supermarket and the library, and I agree, noting that then we wouldn't have to go by the four, count 'em, four bars we passed on our way to the church, half a mile from our homes.

"I hadn't noticed," he says.

"Then you're not as bad as me. I have bar radar. I always know they're there." I tell him how Ross and Kent once had a Cub Scout meeting in the basement of the church we just left, and while they were busy with some group activity, I snuck out and hotfooted across the street to Francesca's for a drink.

Not the prettiest image. Though not one I'm particularly ashamed to recount either. Going for the drink wasn't some bored, casual indulgence. Alcoholism is, I'm slowly beginning to grasp, at its essence a motivation. An urge. You're moved to do this stuff with near desperation. Not compelled—not a marionette on strings, forced to dance across the road to Francesca's against your will. But it seems a good idea, a very good idea, of pressing importance, and you take one lingering look at the scouts, happily racing around in the church hall, and then leap to your urgent task.

Grim though the compulsion might be, memory of it prompts us to contemplate the aridity of our future lives as suburban alcoholics, a bleak desert stretching dryly before us. Where will our fun be? From whence our comfort? A gut punch I have already begun to try to ward off by cobbling together a thin armor of logic. I proudly display my most recent effort.

"Have you ever looked back on a period in your life—a year, a week, an hour—and said, 'I wish I drank more'? Have you ever looked back at an event and said, 'You know, that was fun, but I just didn't drink enough'?"

Jonathan laughs, shaking his head. "Never."

"Exactly. So why look forward and despair at all the drinks we're not going to have in the future when the truth is, once we've lived through it, we won't miss them at all?"

Why fixate on the celebrations that may or may not be dampened, when we could just as easily look at all the messes we won't get into? However much New Year's Eve might be lessened if I hold up a glass of sparkling cider at midnight, I also won't ever wake up on the train in Grayslake at midnight either, and that's not a bad trade.

We pass the library, lit up, gleaming white. Jonathan is also fretting over this higher power business.

"I can't understand it," he says. "I was raised religiously. I believe in God, believe in a higher power, but have no idea what it might be."

"Jonathan," I say, turning to face him, "if we could understand it, it wouldn't be much of a higher power, would it?"

We both laugh; we're in a good mood. Somehow, trying to keep up Jonathan's spirits inspires me more than just trying to keep up my own. Talking things out is often more effective than merely thinking them through. "Reason all you like," he says. "But existence just doesn't seem appealing without drinking. Life loses its appeal."

"I feel the same way," I say. "But okay, let's go with that thought. Drinking is the most important thing in the world. Everything else is a distant second. There is drinking, and there is the meaningless sleepwalk through life we must endure before we drink again. Do we want to sign onto that? Is that our credo? Do we want that on our tombstones? 'Neil Steinberg: Liquor Was His Life.' If Wendy"—Jonathan's little daughter, a beautiful girl, huge blue eyes, a year older than Kent—"came to you someday and said, 'Daddy, drinking is the most important thing in my world and nothing else matters,' would you go 'All right! That's my girl, because I feel exactly the same way!' "

———

Saturday morning. As I rake leaves in the front yard, a trim man in a blue Nike T-shirt comes jogging down the street.

"Hey, Neil," he says, pulling up short. "I've been in the program seven years."

"Small world," I say, gazing at his face, trying to figure out who he is. Sunglasses. Thinning hair. About my age. No idea. Never saw him before. It must show in my expression.

"I read about you in the paper," he explains, shaking his head sympathetically.

His name is Henry and he lives down the street, not five houses from mine. With Jonathan, that makes three alcoholics within one suburban block. Obviously, I didn't invent the problem. Henry sings the praises of the program. "It was the best thing that ever happened to me," he says. "Jennifer was going to take the kids and leave me. She told me to stop drinking for six months, and then I could drink socially."

He grins, as if amused by the naïveté of the idea. "That lasted twenty-seven days."

I ask him if there are any meetings he can recommend—I'm going because I have to, but I really don't like them. I feel hunted by Stan, the guy at the first meeting who said, "Maybe *you* didn't stick," and now likes to drift over, leer, and ask, "Cured yet, Neil?" as punishment for my saying I don't think the program is going to cure me.

Henry says his home meeting is on Wednesday at Techny Towers, the imposing edifice a few miles east that an order of Catholic monks built in the 1920s. He tells me I need to go to a *Bill's Book* meeting and to a step meeting and to a discussion meeting. *Bill's Book* is the AA handbook, a collection of stories of people struggling with drink. Step meetings focus on the twelve steps, while discussion meetings encourage conversation. I am still only vaguely aware there are different types. I tell him I'll stop by Techny Towers this Wednesday. He jogs off.

Kent and the boys from across the street are playing at our place and, with lunchtime approaching, I send Tommy back home to ask his mother if macaroni and cheese is okay; now is not the time to kill a neighbor child with a milk allergy. His mom, Samantha—a fit, compact woman with warm brown eyes— walks over, smiling, and quickly delivers the freighted "How's it going?"

After I give her the basics—not drinking, going to rehab— she tells me how her father and her husband's father were both alcoholics.

"We're adult children of alcoholics," she says. "Though there was such a culture of drinking then, we didn't notice it until my father had his triple bypass. The doctor came out and said, 'You know your dad's an alcoholic. He has an alcoholic's heart—I know them in a minute.' I always think of it as affecting the liver, but it affects your heart too."

The exchange is bracing—not only because of Samantha's frank, unembarrassed curiosity or because she volunteers that she is proud of me, but for her comment about the heart. I could feel my heart flutter sometimes, drinking. My blood pressure was one ninety over eighty-five when I entered rehab. This isn't something I could keep doing forever if only I masked it better from Edie. It would, eventually, break my heart. Maybe it already has.

"Hello, everybody!" chirps Rona, wearing chinos and a short, Indian blanket shirt. It's Monday morning. Balanced Lifestyles!

But first we have to check in. I'm "relieved and spun around." Edie and I had another fight, but I phoned her during the drive in and now things are better.

"I got on the cell and poured oil on the waters so . . ." I say, shifting into my best approximation of perkiness, "I'm relieved to be in that happy, quasinormal postfight place." Each patient in the group describes his or her state in a few words.

"I'm feeling rested," Rona confides, joining in, as if she were just one of the gang. "The fall is such good sleeping weather. I slept so heartily."

Then it's time to launch into the game.

"Any time you take a behavior away you have to replace it with something else," she begins.

We play Scruples. "For those of you unfamiliar, it's kind of an eighties game, each card has a moral or ethical question on it. . . ."

The movies shown in recovery do not have snappy titles. Thus we get, not *Days of Wine and Roses* or *The Lost Weekend* but mouthfuls such as today's *Healing the Addicted Brain Part III: Relapse and Recovery.* The idea is that no matter how long you've been sober or how strong your will, you are exactly one sip away from lying facedown in the gutter. It is the old Salvation Army warning given a veneer of science.

Nor are the production values tremendous. A moderator—an old guy in glasses with gray hair and a mustache—leads a panel of addicts and alkies through a discussion of the various triggers that caused them to slip back into their old ways. The only special effect consists of a large rat trap, which the old guy holds and periodically snaps jarringly to show just how quickly these triggers can drop us back in the quicksand.

"The brain is like a steel trap," he says, snapping. *Whap! Whap!* "The brain of the addict isn't functioning the way it is supposed to." No kidding.

The film ends on the requisite high note—the huge boosts in self-respect and natural pleasure you will find when you stop taking drugs, stop getting yourself sent to prison or, as one panelist did, stop seeing your wife touting herself on the *Jerry Springer Show.*

When the lights are brought back up, Linda goes around the room asking us what we thought of the movie. Everybody murmurs the usual approval until we get to Leslie, nestled in a big leather chair, who replies with unexpected vehemence.

"That film made me want to use drugs!" she gushes, pointing out a scene where a recovering addict, illustrating the need to avoid old acquaintances, spoke of a friend describing the sight and smell of cocaine.

"When she talked about that pound of cocaine I could *feel* it," Leslie says. "I've been in this pink cloud from being clean for fifteen days, but it's fading, and I think: *I want cocaine! I want cocaine so fucking bad it kills me!*"

Linda gingerly steers the group into talking about other cues that might send us back to our old ways. She tells us that many "return visitors" slap themselves back into rehab by deciding that they've cured their woes and can now safely drink. "Folks who just wanted to have a glass of wine at their daughter's wedding," she says. "It's so much easier if you just close the door to all mood-altering substances."

Sure it is. "Strike him out." But how?

Foremost among the triggers that cause relapse is random opportunity—one addict in the film reported walking down the street and noticing a plastic bag on the ground. Suddenly he had the bag in his hand and was checking inside for drugs.

Deborah, the nurse/Benzedrine addict with a grating voice, says how she was once in an office where somebody tipped over a hole punch, and all the little round circles of paper tumbled out. They seemed to her, for a breathless instant, like pills.

"For me it was the shiny surfaces in public bathrooms," chimes in Leslie. "You run your finger over those and lick it to see if anybody has done drugs on them."

"*No!*" I interject, amazed. Really? She didn't really lick the surfaces of public toilets?

Leslie laughs.

"Are you fucking kidding me?" she says brightly. "I have licked every bathroom in Los Angeles, with the stuff in my pocket, because why use mine if I can use somebody else's?"

Emboldened by Leslie's confession, I tell the group something I haven't even been able to tell Edie yet.

"She has a bottle of olive oil that's shaped like a wine bottle," I say. "And every time she puts it on the table, for pasta or whatever, there's a giddy moment when I see the green glass and think: 'Oh wine, thank God, this nightmare's finally over!' Which is crazy, but there you are. I've wanted to ask her to get rid of it, or get a cruet, but I can't do it—it's too embarrassing."

Linda tells the group that it would be good to let our significant others in on things like that, to make sure they understand the depth of what they're dealing with. I'm not sure I *want* Edie to understand. Before the slap knocked everything out into the open, I was able to drink the way I did, in part because I hid the scope of it from her and in part because she learned to avert her eyes. And while this is obviously a big problem, and Edie is obviously aware of it, now, part of me still somehow believes—hopes, yearns—that if I can only keep the full immensity of the situation from her, then perhaps someday we can go back to how things used to be.

Rehab falls into a pattern. Movies and lectures, questions and confession, coffee breaks and cigarettes. The fellow addicts and alcoholics you have become familiar with vanish one by one, plucked out as their twenty-eight days expire.

Or because they quit. Or are thrown out. They show up drunk and blow their Breathalyzer test. A check bounces. Sometimes you get the explanation; sometimes you don't.

Meanwhile newcomers arrive, each one bumping me ahead, and I go from trainee to cast member to old-timer.

Amber is out. Problems with her insurance, or so we are told. And Matt—a compact man with tiny eyes, coal black and lost in a gaunt red face the color of the center of filet mignon—is in. He wears dark blue thermal underwear as a shirt and has the casual manner of a plumber and surprises me by telling the group he is addicted to crack cocaine.

We've got the second-string nurse, Cassie, again this morning. With maximum discomfort, she launches into a spiel about venereal disease.

"The population you are a part of—people who abuse alcohol and drugs—are at a higher risk than the general population for sexually transmitted diseases." She licks her lips and looks around the room, shifting in her chair. "Even if you aren't in the part of your life where you believe this information is applicable, you might someday sponsor someone and need this kind of information."

She asks us if we've participated in any risky behavior.

"I had unsafe sex with multiple partners on various occasions," Matt happily volunteers, straight out of the box, using a formal argot I've come to think of as "therapy speak." Cassie seizes on it.

"When you are using, you're disinhibited and make choices you probably wouldn't make if you weren't using," she says. "When you are in that state of mind, your higher decision-making processes are taken over by your primitive brain."

"Who has hepatitis?" Cassie asks, as if offering it. Half the room flops their hands up.

Catherine demurely enters the room—black headband, zipped black sweatshirt, black pants trailing three inches behind her heels on the floor.

"We're talking about sexually transmitted diseases!" Deborah squawks.

Catherine sits next to me.

"We're all going around the room and talking about our sexual diseases and exactly how we got them," I tell her. "Now it's your turn."

Catherine gives a musical little laugh. We've taken to smoking cigarettes together during breaks. I've never been a smoker, which is astounding, because I love the habit. Sometimes in the spring, when Edie and I were dating, we'd be at an outdoor café, and she would say she wants a cigarette and I would trot off to buy a pack of Marlboro Lights. She would smoke one cigarette, and I would smoke the other nineteen, one after another. Maybe that's why I never took up the habit, because one feels lousy the day after a tobacco orgy like that.

But a daily cigarette break with my fellow addicts is a near necessity, and the fact that it is with shy, quiet, heroin addict Catherine makes it almost sweet, like something out of high school. A little midmorning date.

"If we can think back to that simple person you were in childhood," says Cassie, "the ideal situation would be to get back where we were at the beginning. But people change, drinking or not. You get married at twenty, and now you're fifty."

Cassie looks toward the end of the room where Catherine and I are sitting.

"Any of you guys have any comment on your relationships and how alcohol has affected you?"

Catherine gives her head a brief shake. Cassie looks directly at me.

"No," I say.

Bad enough that every celebratory moment of my life has now been cast under the harsh light of disease and dysfunction. Bad enough that even the possibility of any future revelry is now firmly established as a slide into damnation. I'm not willing to also surrender every romantic encounter I've ever had, and refuse to publicly denounce the result of every candlelit dinner as some regrettable alcohol-fueled lapse.

I truly have nothing to say. Talking seems pointless. I look around the room. Of the eleven people here, the therapist and I are the only two who have jobs, assuming mine will still be there when I get back. I don't belong here, I tell myself. I'm better than this.

We're talking about our relationships—the need to tell others what we need. As if that would work. Yet another bad fight with Edie this morning—sitting there, in the room, a few hours later, I can't even articulate what it was about, which is fine, because fights are never about anything—an argument set off by an egg, a stick, the molecules in the air. A steady escalation. A question, a look, a glance, and we're yelling at each other. Over nothing. They're all about us wanting things we don't get, mistiming each other, the dancer leaps into the air and falls hard upon the floor. Did she jump at the wrong moment or did her partner fail to catch her? Or both? Does it matter in the end?

"What if they *don't* rise to the occasion?" I ask Linda, with surprising intensity, cutting off the vague happy talk about the value of communication. Earnest, almost demanding. "What if you communicate, if you state your needs honestly and plainly, and it doesn't work? Life isn't the movies. 'Please do the laundry because the house looks bleak otherwise'—I say that, but it doesn't lead to laundry being done; it leads to accusations that I don't help out around the house enough. The smallest thing.

"Other moms bring their children to meet their husbands on the train. I've asked Edie to do it, over and over, but she doesn't. Not once in five years. We live a block away from the station. The train arrives at the same time every day. It would take her ten minutes. But she doesn't do it, even though she knows I would like her to, even though she knows it would mean something to me—heck, I've told her I pretend that other parents' kids are mine and they're meeting me at the train. Not once."

"It's no picnic to be with an alcoholic when you are active in your disease," says Linda, which I interpret as: It's your fault; cope with whatever you get.

"I've changed," I say. "I've given up the thing I loved, and she doesn't have to change at all. It's like I'm fighting to preserve my job so I can keep you living in the style to which you've become accustomed and you can't do the *laundry*?"

Looking around the room I can tell that I've lost them. I'm the angry husband slurring his wife.

"I know I'm not coming off in the best way," I say, deflating. "I just want the laundry done."

Linda's advice is to not engage, to go about my business and not expect Edie to lend a hand—not to expect her to say the right thing, not to expect her to do the right thing. Not to expect anything at all from her. Focus on myself.

———

After dinner I head to Techny Towers—a pair of twenty-story square towers forming a kind of cathedral. The meeting is down a sweeping staircase, in a Chinese-themed dining room— bamboo, red ceiling, a bright, tiki bar effect. Everyone talks about how grateful we are for God and AA. I sit next to Henry, the guy down the street who jogged by and told me about this particular meeting. He chews gum like a squirrel nibbling on a nut. He smiles at me.

"Do I realize that I do not know how much time I have left?" someone reads from a book of daily AA homilies. "Do I know that I am living on borrowed time and that I would not have even this time left without AA and the grace of God? Am I going to make what time I have left count for AA?"

I'm supposed to help AA? That seems ass-backward. I thought AA is supposed to help *me*.

———

Jonathan is upset—he drank earlier in the day. He found an old half pint stashed in the basement, half full, and automatically drained it, then panicked, and told everyone—his mother, his sponsor, his wife, and now me.

"The moment I drank it I thought, 'What have you done?'"

he says, remorseful, in his car on the way to the big open meeting in Wilmette. "Stupid! Stupid! Stupid! I used to be able to say that every day I went to an AA meeting was a sober day. Now I can't say that anymore."

"Should we not go?" I say.

He laughs, and I almost add, "Maybe we should go to a bar instead." But I sincerely don't want to drink—not now, anyway. I want to get through my twenty-eight days, to give it a try. Though if I *do* relapse, I think, looking at him pityingly, I'm sure not going to run around telling everybody about it.

The meeting is at a Catholic high school. There must be several hundred people filling the low-ceilinged cafeteria, which has that weird, school-building-at-night feel. The first speaker, a woman, smolders with dysfunction and paranoia.

"My apartment's been broken into, my identity has been stolen, my social security number was taken when I was deposed," she says, during a rambling iteration of marital and legal woes; a scattered monologue that I can hardly follow. "I don't have to drink over these things today. My life is about showing up for my boys every week even though I've been blocked access to them for five years."

I turn in my seat and scan the crowd to see how this is going over, hoping to see a few sadly shaking heads. But people are smiling, supportive, rapt. She gets hearty applause and a big embrace.

Back in the car, I try to buck Jonathan up. "The next meeting is in thirteen hours," I say. "How much trouble could we get into?" We muse a bit on our predicaments. I somehow feel better—not quite the confidence of the day before, but not bad either. And I say something about drinking that surprises me.

"If you don't need it, why bother? And if you *do* need it, well, then you better take care of that." That sounds like sense to me.

At home, Edie is already asleep. Ross comes downstairs when he hears the door, and I tuck him in, sing to him—"Rock-a-Bye and Good-night" and "My Bonnie Lies Over the Ocean" and "Amazing Grace." He asks me about favorite authors. I sit on the edge of his bed in the dark room and tell him about Hemingway and *The Sun Also Rises*.

"What's it about?" he asks.

"Well," I say. "There's a group of friends, in France, in the 1920s, and a man who was hurt in the war, and they all go down to Pamplona, Spain, for the running of the bulls. They let a herd of angry bulls race through the street and people tie red sashes around their waists and run just ahead of the racing bulls. . . ."

"And people do that *because* . . . ?" he asks.

"Well," I say, groping. "I suppose they find it a thrill."

"Do people get hurt?" he says.

"Yes."

"Do they get killed?"

"Yes. Sometimes."

"Would you do that?"

I chew on this a moment. It seems an important question. Honesty is always a good fallback.

"At one point in my life I would have, yes, if I had the chance," I say. "I would have loved to. But probably not anymore."

I kiss him. "Hug," he says, reaching up. I hug him, and walk out of the room, filing away that bit of good sense for future use: "And people do that *because* . . . ?"

Chapter Eleven

Sukkoth is the Jewish harvest festival. We aren't the farmers we once were, generally, but we still set up little booths called Sukkahs in our backyards. Then we sit in the Sukkah and sip schnapps. I used to love that. But obviously schnapps sipping isn't on the schedule this year.

Driving the kids back from Sunday school, groceries in the trunk, I think toward the afternoon and Janice's party. It seems so unfair that I can't just park myself at the booze table on the porch, as usual, and lap it up. I remember standing in the kitchen, just last year, pouring a big glass of wine and talking to Janice. All sweetness and light. Not this time. Not ever. I want to scream with the unfairness. I want to scream in general. Maybe, I think, brushing those thoughts away, I ought to fill that Campral prescription.

At the party, sitting by myself on a couch, eating cellophane-wrapped squares of nougat, trying not to listen to the toasting on the porch. My niece, mid-twenties, walks over.

"Your son is trying to take booze," she informs me in a monotone. I hurry into the kitchen and find Ross standing by the bottles. I grab him by the upper arm, hard, hoisting him to his toes.

"Are you out of your mind?" I hiss.

"I was just looking at them," he says. Jerking his arm free, he wanders off. The bottles are not in the Sukkah this year, but set out by the refrigerator. I reach out and touch one, laying my fingertip atop the cap of a squat bottle of Crown Royal. Hiya, buddy.

"The game I brought today is a *thinking* kind of game," says Rona, eyes wide. "It's a modified version of Scattergories, which is my favorite game."

She gazes around the group—we are spread out, as far away as can be and still be in the same room with her. She tries to tighten our circle.

"Howard, you may want to scootchie closer to Neil, and Neil, scootchie closer to Howard," she says. He gets up, moving slowly, as if underwater, protecting his dying liver. We nudge our chairs a few inches closer to each other.

I pass the morning watching the others talk. My worries are all centered around work. They expected my case to be over by now. Uncertainty about the job makes it hard to focus on therapy. Leah, with her steely close-cropped hair and rosy cheeks, takes over for the late-morning session. We all check in again. She is the meeting cop, and wants to know how many we hit over the past week.

"I'm Neil, drug of choice, alcohol, number of meetings, four, it would have been five, but an old friend was in from out of town and he and another college classmate asked me to dinner Saturday night. I know we're meetings *über alles*. But I thought it more important to live life and see old friends. As it was, we were in a couple of bars, but I wasn't tempted—I could go to the john without being tempted to stop at the bar and get a shot of Jack. So that was something."

No, in fact, it wasn't.

"Your progress has got to come first—that's the overarching principle," says Leah. "You can't trust your brain—if your friends ask you to come to dinner, then plan to go to a meeting earlier."

That doesn't make sense to me—if you're feeling good, and not drinking, and not worried about drinking or planning to drink, then why not live your life, why not hang out with your actual friends and talk about normal things instead of running off to huddle with a group of random strangers to talk about drinking and God for an hour?

Not that I say that.

———

Back at home, Linda phones—which is unusual; she has never done that before. She meant to catch me at Chapman. "I talked to the staff . . ." she begins. The upshot is I need to go to Family Night tomorrow because otherwise I won't be in compliance and they'll report me to the court. I can't make up the lost session at the end—I'd have to put in another week. She implies it was wrong of me to even suggest missing a night, wrong to even conceive of it.

"Well, that's why I asked," I say, feeling galled and devastated. My life is not my own. Other people are in control. There are rules and, however nonsensical, I have to obey them. I have to miss my son's tenth birthday party, modest though it may be. I'm required to skip out on a night with my family in order to attend Family Night alone.

———

On the morning of his birthday, Ross wakes us up at 4:25, wanting presents. Not the best judgment in the world, but we know whom he gets that from. It's tough not to view the boys through the lens of my own problems. Impulse control. I try to fall back asleep. Now Kent is up, and Ross is whistling. I want to scream at him, but don't. Edie is awake, telling him, "Happy birthday, Ross, but you're going to have a grumpy mommy all day."

I wait until Edie's up to call Ross over and give him his shadow box. He seems to like it, but of course it isn't something a ten-year-old would get excited about. Downstairs, he gets the PlayStation game he wants—plus a birthday letter, written by Edie.

"Where's Dad's letter?" he asks, and I realize that Edie tucked the note into his gift without inviting me to write anything—her payback for the shadow box, I suppose, which I made without consulting her.

I have my own letter, however, one I wrote to him the night he was born. I run upstairs, dig it out of my files, and read it to the family, glancing over to Edie when I mention, in the letter, that I came home from the hospital and had a couple of Ballantine ales and some Suntory whiskey to celebrate his birth.

I wasn't an alcoholic then, I think.

Edie doesn't react, but something strikes me. I picked up that little round bottle of Suntory—about the size and shape of a large grapefruit—visiting my brother in Tokyo, where he lived at the time, six years before Ross was born. The bottle looked cute and I saved it for something special. That bottle sat on my shelf, unopened, from 1989 to 1995. Which means that something had to change, dramatically, because that never would have happened in recent years. I try to keep special bottles—the bottle of Booker's signed by Booker Noe, Jim Beam's grandson; the bottle of good port that Dick Mitchell brought to dinner—for special occasions, to be opened with a flourish among friends. But those special occasions drag their feet, they tarry, and I end up losing patience and drinking them myself, alone. There was a quarter of a bottle of Old Grand-Dad that I took from my grandparents' house after my grandmother died. It had been my grandpa Irv's, and had the old Ohio tax stamp on the neck that they used to have. I always thought my brother and I would share it someday, in some anniversary toast to our grandfather, but I ended up pouring it into a glass, standing alone in the basement, on some forgotten solitary afternoon when there was nothing else in the house to drink. The 1960 Scapa is the only bottle somehow spared from the inferno of my thirst—maybe that's one reason I am so frantic to keep it.

––––––

That afternoon at Chapman, Linda starts her session. Time for me to finally deliver my chemical history. I've scribbled a few pages of notes, and though I still mostly extemporize my comments—it isn't as if I need to be reminded of the details of my life—having the sheets in my hand is enough to satisfy Linda that I've written it out.

"I was born in Cleveland, Ohio, and grew up on the west side," I begin. "My father was a nuclear physicist, from a family of well-off New York Jews. His father owned a sign-painting company in the Bronx. My mother's parents were Polish—her father was the only member of his family to survive the Holocaust."

"A Jew on the west side," laughs Linda, who must have some knowledge of Cleveland, where all the Jews live on the east side. "No wonder you're isolated."

"I was the only Jew in my elementary school," I continue. "Every Hanukkah I'd give the little dog-and-pony show—'This is a dreidel, this is a menorah. . . .' I hated that. We lived on the west side because there is a huge NASA facility there—Lewis Research Center it was called; wind tunnels and lasers and things. I didn't have friends when I was a kid, not in the traditional sense—there were kids on my street, nice enough guys,

Ricky and Bobby and Danny, but I just didn't take to them. They'd knock on the door, ask me to come out and play, and I'd whisper, 'Mom, the guys are here. I have to go. But wait twenty minutes and call me in.' "

I wanted to play inside, alone, with blocks and army men. "Isolating" as they'd say in the program. But that's what I liked. Kickball seemed pointless, repetitive. Everybody arguing all the time.

Where does drinking come in? I begin at the beginning. I'm taking a bath with my sister, which makes me about three and her about six. Big mounds of suds: Mr. Bubble. We make beards for ourselves, make hats, balance white hillocks on our open palms and blow foam at each other. We take the big scarlet plastic cups our mother uses to rinse our hair after shampooing, raise them, our frothy steins, and slam them lustily together, like on the beer commercials on TV.

"Have a Duke!" we chant together giddily, the suds sloshing all over. "Have a Duke! Have a Duke, Duquesne!"

One of my earliest memories. It never seemed malign before, but now that detail sizzles on the brainpan, the first little red flag. Then the next year, when I am four, we drive to New York to my cousin Jeffrey's bar mitzvah. The New York Steinbergs, the rich ones, the ones with the furs, the brother who took over my grandfather's sign company while my father was studying physics at Ohio State. The bar mitzvah is held in the Waldorf-Astoria, at least in my memory. Jeffrey is brought into the room on a rickshaw. I play with my uncle's aluminum cigar tubes, and explore the recesses of the ballroom, wearing my red sports coat and clip-on tie. In a side room is a platter with an array of little chocolate cups, set on crinkled foil nests. Inside each cup, a splash of Drambuie. I start eating the cups, one after the other. The next thing I know I'm puking in a bathroom.

My mother tells the story forever, whenever the subject of the bar mitzvah comes up and sometimes when it doesn't. That Neil.

The gap of a decade and I am at the Passover seder at my grandparents' house in Cleveland. Irv, my Polish grandfather, smelling of Ludens and cigarettes, is reading prayers in his shtetl, machine-gun Hebrew, which always sounds to me like a rapid-fire babble. "Cha-ma-humma wumma chumma . . ." I go into the kitchen, where a bottle of Slivovitz—Polish plum liquor—sits on a counter. Everyone else is at the table. I screw off the cap, tip the bottle back. Why? No idea. Because it's there. The next moment I'm in the car with my folks—and my cousin David, for some reason—hanging out the window, puking down the side of the car. My mother tells that story for the rest of my life, at Passover, and sometimes when it isn't Passover. That Neil.

It goes on from there. Pitchers of beer at the Chardon Inn as a junior counselor at Camp Wise. In high school, I would swish a gulp of scotch around in my mouth before picking up my girlfriend for a date, to give my breath that air of sophistication. A cold can of beer radiated excitement and promise, and I never passed one up if I could help it.

You want to grab that sulking teenage self, shake him, scream at him. What are you doing? But the past unspools its inevitable course, a Greek tragedy, and to remember is to watch ourselves, handcuffed by habit, with the marshals of fate at each elbow, urging us forward toward our destiny.

Sure, there are bad times. As a freshman, sitting in the Hut, that greasy burger place just off the Northwestern campus, staring queasily at the cheeseburger with grilled onions I typically adore, too hungover to eat.

But what about all the parties? The confidences? The wine

arrives and the conversation flows and nobody gets hurt? My high school girlfriend and I would sit at the Chinese Palace and order the sweet drinks illustrated with little colorful pictures on the paper placemats—grasshoppers and mai tais and Singapore slings—before heading out to grope each other in some deserted corner of the Metroparks. That's not a cautionary tale about drink, heck, it's an *advertisement* for drink. I don't regret it—I wish I could go back to it right now.

Later, as an adult, drinking was the grace note of success. To travel to exotic places and drink. That's the brass ring of life. Huddling with Sam at one of the tiny Suntory Jigger Bars in Tokyo. Champagne at the Moulin Rouge in Paris, pints of ale in London at that old tavern across the street from the British Museum. Drinking homemade sorghum whiskey with Taiwanese fishermen on the island of Kinman, two thousand yards off the coast of China, quaffing *bierra hazaka*—"strong beer"—in Jerusalem, cocktails at Harry's Bar in Venice, playing chess at the bar of the Grand Hotel Olofsson in Port-au-Prince, drinking Jane Barbancourt rum neat and imagining myself a character out of a Graham Greene novel. Flying to Kentucky for dinner with Booker Noe. Five kinds of whiskey with our meal, including clear moonshine. The next day—a gorgeous day—sitting among the white oak barrels in one of the vast aging houses, looking out over the knobbish green hills, we use a long brass rod to draw his special Booker's Bourbon from its cask, and sip and admire the natural beauty spread out before us. Nobody gets hurt.

Edie and I—for her fortieth birthday—go to Tru and drink a bottle of Iron Horse champagne, then walk home together. Heck, drinking has a role in my finally asking her to marry me, after seven years of dating. We have this trip planned to Galena, a little historic town west of Chicago, an area that also makes its own fruity wine. Then we break up, but we have the reservations already paid for, so we go. We sample varieties at the winery and Edie buys a case of strawberry wine—a case. I watch her load the case into the trunk of my car, thinking, "She doesn't even drink—who's she going to drink that wine with?" I want it to be me, forever.

Ha.

As I talk, about being a reporter, putting my foot on the rail, drinking, drinking, drinking, it strikes me that I am cataloging practices, but not touching my finger to the reason at all.

Don't you see? There was an attitude, a lifestyle. You could be a civilian, a nobody, and grind away at a job and drink tea, or you could be glittering and special and an artist and drink alcohol. I try to explain. F. Scott Fitzgerald and James Thurber, Mike Royko and Hunter S. Thompson. We were just doing what we were supposed to do. What was expected of us. Just doing our jobs, and boy did drinking seem like a job at the end. A bad job, something I had to do whether I wanted to or not.

By then it was too late. I hid the problem as well as I could. Not a single close friend ever suggested that I had a drinking problem, not one, except for Edie. They may have thought it— they *must* have thought so—but were too polite to say it and, after all, so much of my personality was taken up with it. I was a drinker, a guy who owns a black silk smoking jacket and a chrome-plated martini shaker.

Nor was I alone. The standard first crisis is supposed to be trouble at work—that's what happens in the *Big Book*. Not for me—heck, half the time I was with my bosses, happily drinking away upstairs at Gene & Georgetti. Drinking never got me in trouble at work—never, not once.

Drinking never gets me in trouble at work. But Edie trying to get me to stop sure as hell does. Now I'm damaged goods, a citywide laughingstock whom they won't even let pen obituaries at home in the afternoons, not until his legal woes are resolved.

I don't tell them this, my fellows in rehab, earnestly following my drunkard's tale. None of it. No resistance, no romanticizing, no clinging to happy booze memories here. I tell them how I move to the suburbs in 2000 and start taking the Metra commuter home, which requires me to walk past the Goat on Washington, where I grow to like sharing a drink or three with Phyllis on my way to the train, which itself is like sitting in a bar. Like being forced to sit in a bar every single evening for forty-five minutes. The wonder is that all commuters don't become alcoholics. I tell them how the years go by and I shift from having a drink by myself in my office at home because it's pleasant to having a drink by myself in my office at home because I have to and never even realize that a fundamental change has taken place.

The time to stop talking approaches—a practiced speaker will feel when his audience is getting restless. And I haven't done it. An engaging story, perhaps, but the central mystery— the *reason*—is still unaddressed. As a child I could not sleep if the sheets were taut and smooth. I would yank at a neatly made bed until there was a fold, a wrinkle I could worry between my fingers and, thus comforted, fall asleep. Maybe that's it.

Comforted by a wrinkle. Then food—eating, not a single Fig Newton, but one after the other, until I ran out or someone took them away. That led right into alcoholism. Didn't it?

Lots of people are fat, but fewer are alcoholics. Children are allowed their comfort; they cling to blankies and special toys, suck on pacifiers or thumbs. They have great fears, even at this moment of greatest comfort and protection, which says something about the depth of human anxiety. While adults might gently argue—there is no monster in the closet, Mommy is not going anywhere—we do not yank their blankie away.

Maybe we should. We should take their comfort objects and destroy them, burn teddy in front of their eyes. Because that is what happens when you grow up. They take it away, your source of greatest comfort, and leave you in a room with strangers, pouring out your soul, clawing at the smooth, sealed box of an impenetrable mystery. I finish speaking, and we move to the next person.

Chapter Twelve

"The past few days I was very . . . not upset, but I had the growing suspicion that none of this was going to work," I tell Dr. Frisch that afternoon, settling into the chair in his office, uncapping my ice water. "That I was going to get through this all, and I was going to say"—I snap my fingers—" 'That's fine, but I'm going to have a drink now.'"

I tell him about Ross looking at the bottles of booze at the Sukkoth party.

"I was aghast," I explain. "But I didn't tell Edie, because I thought: He never turned me in when I had a drink between my knees when we played chess, and who knows, I might need that again . . . I'm throwing pillows ahead, keeping the alibis ready."

Fifty minutes a week with Dr. Frisch. I vastly prefer him to rehab or AA meetings, no listening to the woes of others while waiting to speak my brief piece. I tell him about missing Ross' birthday party for Family Night. How I surprised myself not only by meekly honoring Linda's decision and leaving the house after a quick rendition of "Happy Birthday," but also by not sulking at Chapman and participating as best I could.

"What else was I supposed to do?" I say. "They have the whip hand."

"Can I just interject something?" Frisch says, holding up an index finger. "A quick bullet point? I want you to understand, behaviorally and emotionally, what's going on. Your going to Family Night and not being upset about it is an act of surrender."

"I never thought of that," I say. "But you're absolutely right."

Surrender is very big in rehab. You do not call the shots—calling the shots is what got you here—but rather renounce your ego and gratefully collapse into the arms of your therapists, your fellow alcoholics, and of course, God. Maybe Frisch is right; going to Family Night was surrender. Perhaps this is significant, maybe even important, maybe even a breakthrough—if a tiny one. Maybe the enormous Steinberg ego can be overcome, if I work at it long enough.

Or maybe not, I think, seesawing from optimism to despair. People struggle for years to give up drinking. They go through rehab again and again. Is that my fate? To endure this process, cobble together a few months of sobriety, and then end up back where I started. Because that's the pattern. The next day at Chapman, a new patient, George, a compact suburban husband with glasses and a long startled face, says he did rehab here four years ago. And now he's back, red-faced and dazed, going through it all over again.

This is a Greek tragedy, I glumly tell myself, spooked by George's fate. Borne inexorably toward my doom, struggle and rail against it though I may. A Greek tragedy, but with shades of Kafka—I have help, but shabby help, threadbare help. The tools being offered are blunt, useless. Here, pound the nail with this wrench. Let's talk about God—He'll come over the hill with the cavalry any moment now. Let's play parlor games. I'm here. I've got the desire to change. And what are we doing? We're playing Scattergories.

How will it end? Do I stumble through twenty-eight days of this, only to flop face forward into a pool of booze when I'm done, there to drown? Join the repeat rehabbers and the serial losers under a trestle, while Edie and the boys head off to a new life without me.

Not a satisfying conclusion. Not satisfying at all. The story can't end like that. Blaming fate is peasant thinking, a surrender to forces greater than yourself. Certainly not the path of the hero. Calling this a Greek tragedy is just a metaphor, and certainly not the only metaphor available. Maybe there's a better one. Maybe my story isn't a Greek tragedy. Maybe it's a thriller— where the secret agent is trying to figure out which wire to cut on the whirring A-bomb while the big red LED numbers count down toward zero.

These thoughts bubbling in my mind, I try to share my insight with my fellow addicts.

"And the great thing is," I say, excitedly, to the room. "In thrillers, the bomb never goes off. The hero always cuts the right wire at the last possible moment." I pause, and look around. Blank stares and puzzled silence. "I know that sounds crazy, but I find it comforting," I say quietly, deflating. Still nothing. I can see from their expressions they aren't following me. Just Neil babbling nonsense.

———

The good news is, finally I have a sponsor. I had brushed off Linda's increasingly emphatic urgings that I had to get one. In my mind, a sponsor is a kind of personal AA grand inquisitor, a program zealot eager to peek into the cell of your soul every day and make sure you are lifting your knees high enough as you run in place to the twelve-step tempo. Who needs that? Going to meetings is bad enough.

But with Chapman moving to half days after three weeks,

my afternoons now free, and the end bobbing into sight on the horizon, a sponsor seems necessary, part of my commitment to try to do what I am asked. And there is some appeal to the idea of somebody who will stick with me when the framework of Chapman falls away. The people who talk about their failures at meetings always seem to blame lack of a sponsor. So when my pal Frank sends an e-mail, checking up, I seize the opportunity, like a needy man who, when somebody extends a hand to him to shake, grabs it and will not let go.

In my reply, I write:

The people at the farm are pressing me to find a sponsor. I haven't met anybody at meetings I want to chat with, never mind cry on their knee when need be. You, of course, seem tailor made for this assignment.... Maybe?

I half fear that Frank will brush me off—he's a busy guy—but he doesn't. "You honor and flatter me," he begins, modestly outlining his own limitations. "I'm a mere one year, nine months and three weeks. . . . Also, to the naked judging eye, I would seem to be working a very flawed program, in that my own sponsor is somebody I barely speak to and with whom I have worked no actual steps."

That sounds ideal. My sponsor will not stand over me, a marine drill sergeant of sobriety, barking slogans. Rather, he'll be good old Frank, who used to stand with me at the Drake Hotel bar, swilling martinis. He'll be on alert, ready, my sobriety buddy, poised to provide advice and counsel should it become necessary. He's perfect.

———————

My parents have returned from Greece, and Sunday morning they phone. So am I done with treatment? Half days, Ma. But I still go to those meetings? Yes, Mom. Dad is on the line too.

Why can't I write unsigned editorials? Because they don't want me to.

Mom: "This is the best thing. It might not seem like that, but it's the best thing."

"Absolutely," I say. I don't like rehashing everything for them. It renders me terse.

"This Halloween party we went to yesterday," Mom says, "they had every liquor in the world. Maker's, Maker's . . . what's that name?"

"Maker's Mark," I say, flatly. Dark, sweet, with a thick red wax seal around the cap.

"That's it," enthuses my mother. "It was like the Ritz Carlton. In honor of you . . . " and here I expect her to say she had a drink, but I'm mistaken, "we didn't drink anything."

"I'm glad my example is inspiring you, Ma."

I'm left with a lump of unease—to some, this is all I'm ever going to be: an alcoholic. The biography of the great man mentions that his father was an alcoholic—with its attendant image of some hollow-cheeked wino pressing his face against a liquor store window while the famous-person-to-be grows up ignored. It never says his father was an alcoholic who dogged his son to practice viola. Or an alcoholic who designed and built a cool cedar fort in the backyard for his boys, or who constructed elaborate clue games to occupy them when he went away on business trips. You only get one fact attached to your name—if you're lucky. Most people don't even get that. Mine is "alcoholic."

Frankly, I prefer "drunkard." "Alcoholic" is so clinical. "Drunkard" is redolent of tankards and alehouses and Falstaff in a wide leather belt. If your life is going to be wedded to a slur, it might as well be a colorful one.

Chapter Thirteen

A neuron in my brain calls out for the drum line from Iggy Pop's "Lust for Life" and I stick it on my iPod and let it drive me to Chapman, the relentless beat pumping my blood up. In four weeks of rehab, nobody has mentioned the word "music." It strikes me that somebody should. Music is a drug you can happily lose yourself in. I decide to suggest to Rona that she might want to inject a few tunes into the party games. As a bonus, the song contains a pair of lines that I never noticed before: "I'm through with slipping on the sidewalk. No more beating my brains, with liquor and drugs."

You tell 'em, Iggy!

Catherine's last day looms, so I stop at the drugstore on the way to Chapman to buy a pack of Marlboro Lights to replace all the cigarettes I've bummed from her.

The cigarette counter at the drugstore is empty. I wait for a clerk to show up. Behind the counter, a shelf of pints and half pints and a few regular bottles. *There must a lot of alcoholics,* I realize, with a trace of amusement, *because who else buys a half-pint of Seagram's vodka at an Osco in the suburbs?* I scan the shelf and find Jack Daniel's, my old friend. *I could,* I continue, in a dispassionate way, the thought quiet and far off, like a church bell in the distance, *buy that half pint right now. I could have it in my pocket this morning at the Chapman Center.* A flourish of perversity I would have savored, once.

A short, round clerk finally shows up. I make my purchase and when I step away from the counter I notice the booze a second time, and am surprised that in the moments spent paying for the cigarettes, I had forgotten about the half pints. I give the flat bottles an even more anesthetized glance, and walk away thinking: *There was a time when I would have felt a surge in the pit of my stomach to see those bottles. It would have haunted me. Now it was sort of a numb nod. This is progress. This is good.*

———

Later that morning, during my session with Linda, she tells me it is a mistake to keep barware in the house—my kitchen has glass cabinet doors, the cabinets filled with array of martini glasses, wine glasses, shot glasses, brandy snifters.

"Get rid of it," she says. "Pack it away in the basement."

"But I use shot glasses to cut the hole for Rocky Mountain toast!" I protest.

"Get rid of it."

I tell her I'm worried about relapse. "I catch myself, planning for it. I know, when Edie goes to California, I'll start drinking again while she's gone. I can fool myself and say that I won't. I can pretend I won't. But in my gut, I know I will."

Edie's brother Don has esophageal cancer. He's out of the hospital; Edie's family is taking turns going out to California to care for him, and Edie is next. I'm half worried—the part of me that has bought the program. And half excited. Party time approaches.

Talk about inconsistency. On one level I am on board, participating, discussing, hitting my four meetings a week, mouthing mantras, striving sincerely toward sobriety. And at another level it all seems ludicrous, almost crazy. I'm convinced that, when Edie goes to help Don, I'll start drinking again, and pretending it won't happen seems dishonest. I'll do it because I can, because I'm looking forward to it, and because I can't imagine denying myself when presented with the perfect opportunity. She'll never know.

———

Bob is a fat, friendly social worker from Louisiana. He first popped up observing our sessions a week or so ago at Chapman. Now he's running his debut session. He has reddish hair and a vague goatee, and wears a brown corduroy jacket over a pink shirt. You can practically feel the excitement rising off him, like steam. This isn't grad school; this is real-live therapy with real-live addicts. We have a film, he says, on toxic shame.

"Buckle up, this is my first time doing group," he says. "This is a fun one, we're going to talk about shame."

"I think I've seen this before," Howard says. So have I. No matter.

First we go around the room. "New and challenging?" Leslie says, reading the question off the whiteboard as if unfamiliar with it. She has an old purse in a closet, she says, and went to get something from it last night, then bit her fingernails afterward and they tasted like cocaine.

"What does cocaine taste like?" I ask, slipping into my reporter mode.

"Like heaven," she says, without a pause, smiling tightly. "I prayed because I realized, at that moment I would have used, no question, if I had it. I realized I have no conscience. How quickly it's gone." She seems stricken at this.

"That okay . . . " Bob says, soothingly.

"It's not okay!" Leslie says fiercely, cutting him off. "It's not okay to wake up with blood on your face, blood on your pillow, because your nose is bleeding in the night. Not okay to crawl on the floor looking for cocaine and you already HAVE cocaine but you don't want to use it." She pauses a moment, composing herself.

"It was a scary moment," she continues. "I'm not going to call people and start using drugs. But one taste. One side of my brain was ready to start using right now. And the other side of my brain said, 'Are you nuts? I've done all that work.' Part of me was, 'Wow! Is there any more in there?' I shook the bag out."

Today's film paints addiction as the result of abusive upbringing.

"Out of these broken dependencies come the sick dependencies we call addiction," our guru du jour tells us. I don't feel the lesson particularly applies to me. My parents didn't abuse us and certainly didn't drink. Oh, my father would have wine with dinner; I remember him praising a certain bottle, good stuff and only $1.99. But I never saw him drunk—he was so tightly wound, I wish I had—and he spoke with scorn of other physicists at NASA puking in the bushes during the summer lab picnics, which he stopped attending. He wouldn't go to block parties either, dismissing them as "beer-drinking affairs," a phrase whose awkwardness I marveled at. If anything, my drinking was not a legacy from him, but a reaction to him, a way to put distance between us, my doomed attempt to be sociable, easygoing, happy. Not that I blame him; the fault is mine.

————

At a quarter to twelve we have Catherine's coin ceremony. As we go around, people compliment her as best they can—they claim she has opened up and been talking more, which she really hasn't. I like Catherine, she's my cigarette buddy, but I have trouble conjuring up the expected praise. Somehow, the truth—

that I think she's cool because she is twenty-one and a heroin addict and a girl—doesn't seem the right thing to say.

"Silence can have a power," I begin, groping, gazing at the coin in my hand, the coin warm from being fondled by every-body else, "and even though you don't say much, you fill the space and get your needs met. I appreciate the way you included me—that gesture you made at break."

She had turned, going out for her final rehab smoke that morning, and given me a friendly "c'mon" gesture, the way you would pat your hip to get a dog to follow you.

"Nobody did that to me before," I say, sincerely, "and it meant the world to me."

She gets the coin. "Whoa, this is so sad," she says, brushing a strand of hair from her face. She thanks us, and that's about it.

Afterward, in the hall, Matt collars me by the nurse's office, where we are waiting for our blood pressure to be checked. His coal eyes gaze at me intently. "You know, I feel sorry for you," he confides. "You're the only one who has to be here. The rest of us made the decision to give it up. But you didn't have any choice."

I never thought of it that way.

"That's the only way it was going to happen," I say, thinking that the exact opposite of Matt's view is true—if it were my de-cision, then it really would be difficult, because I could always decide to forget it. But having no choice—having the law dan-gling over my head—is, in a way, liberating. The tough part will be when the legal clouds lifts and I have the choice again. His sympathy doesn't help; instead I find it depressing. I walk away thinking: *crack addicts pity me.*

"Well, let's get started." says Rona. "Gosh darn it, it's nine o'clock. Wooo! Wooo!"

You can, I have learned, get accustomed to anything. Besides, this is my last Friday in rehab. Monday, then Tuesday I get my coin and get out. No need to resist anymore.

"This," says Rona, "is Balanced Lifestyles. An opportunity to look at and become aware of activities you can incorporate into your daily life and replace old habits."

There is something new. She strings a blue volleyball net across the middle of the room and plays Earth, Wind, & Fire on a boom box while we bat around a pink balloon. I flatter myself this is due to my suggestion that a little music might help the process.

Chapter Fourteen

Costco. The beating heart of bottomless American consumption. An enormous white hangar, crammed with product and people. Huge cases of food, crates of electronics, pallets stacked toward the rafters, shelves jammed with gallon jars of mayonnaise, hills of toilet paper, triple boxes of breakfast cereal that seem a violation of nature.

Normally you couldn't force me into Costco. But my wife picked up a green plaid work shirt there two weeks ago. Thick fabric, brown corduroy collar and cuffs, a garment that comforts in the way only a soft flannel shirt can. Flannel is the official fabric of AA—drunks are cold a lot; I know that I am—and I want to pick up another shirt.

Hurrying past Brand X plasma TVs and rolls of cheap carpeting and walls of giant taco sauce bottles, I am brought up short: Costco has a liquor department, I remember the moment it parallaxes into view, and I change direction and beeline there, instinctively, without hesitation. To say hello. Because I am in the neighborhood.

It feels dangerous just being here, standing in the aisle, before the orderly ranks of familiar brands. I naturally find myself face-to-face with Mister Jack Daniel. One point seven five liters. I reach out, heft the big square bottle, and feel its weight. I never let myself buy these big bottles because that always struck me as something alcoholics do. But hey, the ship has sailed on that one, hasn't it? Until recently, I liked to keep a regular-sized bottle of Jack in my desk drawer at home whenever I could, and every time I cracked open a fresh bottle, I would first ceremoniously kiss it—how depraved is that?—a fervent peck on its perfect grainy black label. Hello, sweetheart.

I stand in Costco, deaf to the Saturday morning commotion around me, and furtively raise the bottle to my lips for a light, dry kiss, then quickly set it back on the shelf, glancing guiltily around. There is nothing to do after that strange ritual but grab my new flannel shirt and hurry toward the exit. I almost rush past Larry Green, an executive at Hollinger, the company that owns my newspaper. He's pushing a huge cart.

"How are you?" he asks, shaking hands.

"I'm holding up," I say.

"You've lost weight."

"The stress diet," I say. "Effective, but not recommended."

"Are you coming back soon?"

"I hope so," I say. "I hope they let me."

"Why wouldn't they let you?" he says. "Do you know how many times I went through this with Royko?"

"Yeah," I say, smiling, "but as the readers are always telling me, I'm no Royko."

"The talent's the same," he says. "The times are different. Everyone has had something like this happen. It could have been me, with one of my wives or girlfriends."

I proceed to the checkout, feeling encouraged—Larry compared me to Royko; ludicrous, of course, but at this point, barred from work, waiting for my rehab to finish and my court case to resolve itself, I'll take whatever professional ego boost I can get.

I wait to pay for my red flannel shirt—almost laughable, holding a single item in a line of groaning cartfuls of merchandise. Some shoppers have *two* carts, nudging them forward with a hand on each, like a farmer guiding oxen. Only in the car do I realize what a good thing it is that I was not carrying a big honking bottle of Jack Daniel's when I bumped into one of management's top honchos.

———

New and challenging?

I tell the morning session at Chapman about my encounter with Larry Green. "I see it as a kind of permission," I say. "This is something you're going to do a lot. It's expected. It's okay." Royko was a drunk and I'm a drunk, newspapermen are drunks and drinking is what we do, with periodic dips into treatment, as needed. Edie says she wants to meet her family in Lake Geneva—not all of us, just her. If I'm supposed to feel slighted, left out, upset, I'm not. I say, "Great idea, hon. Why don't you go?" adding, in my mind, *and I'll stay home and drink.*

Make hay while the sun shines. But writing it off to opportunism is too simple—that's like saying salmon swim upstream to spawn because the river's there. That isn't it. They're swimming because their nature dictates it; ditto for my drinking. I need to plunge into that river at the first chance I get, after this enforced absence, this necessary evil. No matter how sincerely I approach this stuff, it's alien and misguided, a system set up for other people, not me. Me, I'm a drinker, and my nature beckons me.

"I feel like I have one more relapse coming," I tell the group.

"I hear that, and I think, 'Oh no, I'm sorry he feels like

that,'" Leah says to the room, and I'm touched by how sincerely sorry she seems to be. She may spend her days tending to an endless procession of drunks, most of whom will fail. But she does care.

That afternoon I see Dr. Frisch.

"So after five weeks, what are you taking away from the program?" he asks.

I almost blurt out "Nothing." I don't feel as if they've prepared me for a life of sobriety at all. Heck, just the phrase, "life of sobriety" makes my skin crawl. But that isn't quite true.

"Before I went in . . ." I tell him, picking my words carefully, "I couldn't contemplate not drinking—it didn't seem *possible*, and now . . . though I don't think I can do it, long term, I do see that I *could*, conceivably, if I could keep my head in the right place."

———

Tuesday is my last day at Chapman. Of course I blast Warren Zevon's "Detox Mansion" as I march through the long, low corridor to the elevator, as a bookend to my time in rehab. Once more, the lurid purple-and-green portrait of a hospital benefactress by the health library. Once more, the slow elevator ride to the third floor. Leslie takes the chair next to mine—my friends, gathering around to see me off.

I have a form to fill out, on relapse prevention. I'm to tell my loved ones about the signs that I'm intending to drink again, and what they should do to stop me. I fold the form over and tuck it away in my black notebook. I don't *want* to tip them off.

"If we go to meetings but are just there in body and nothing else, if we go into a bar just to say, 'Hi,' if we go into slippery places, we have to think about what the consequences are," says Linda. "Think of the consequences if you use, and the benefits, the rewards, if you don't use."

The film, again, is *Healing the Addicted Brain*.

"If I take a drink, I know it will wake up that craving," says Laticia, in the movie. "Anything that changes the way I feel and think is lethal to me." She takes a sip from a blue coffee cup.

The film ends. Suddenly I get a tingling sensation, a swooping in my gut, as if I'm at the top of a hill on a roller coaster. The real world, life, work, the rest of my dry and miserable existence, are ahead, about to rush at me.

Linda asks me what the biggest signs of relapse are, for me.

"I guess what you said about rejectionist thinking," I say. "I use one aspect of the program to dismiss the rest. You tell me to get rid of the wineglasses or not to make French toast with vanilla, and I use that to dismiss everything, because I know I'm not going to drink the vanilla."

"Don't focus on that. Don't focus on what doesn't work for you," says Linda. "Focus on what does work. Just like you shouldn't focus on what you've lost. Focus on what you have, and what you could lose. You had a line during your chemical history that I liked—You said you could 'lose the palace' if you weren't careful. Everything you worked to build up—your career, your family, your home—could be swept away. You could lose the palace. Think about that. Write the reasons to be sober on an index card and keep it in your wallet. Before you drink, look at that."

It makes sense. And I have gotten things from the program. It forced me to look at the unexamined parts of my life, to acknowledge my deceptions and rationalizations. And I've met others—good people, smart people, in the main—who have wrecked themselves on the rocks, ruined themselves, people further along than I am, guides to my present and harbingers of my possible futures.

It all makes sense. But I know I'm not going to write the reasons to be sober on an index card and put it in my wallet. I am not going to do that.

Linda looks around the room.

"How many of you have a *Big Book* or a meditation book on their person? Hard to read the *Big Book* and think of using."

To me it's easy, I think but don't say. *I read the* Big Book *and want to drink just to distance myself from this stuff.*

Noon approaches. Almost time for the teary send-off.

"We never had lunch again," says Leslie, to my surprise. "That was fun."

"I asked you, but you couldn't that day, and I didn't want to pester you," I say, slightly flustered, thinking, *I should have asked her again.* I quit too easily.

We go downstairs for my last smoke—a whole bunch of us. After five minutes, we finish our cigarettes, flick away the butts into the parking lot, and begin trooping back in. Something seems very wrong. A voice in my head snarls indignantly, "Fine, fine, this is all very fine, but where's the *drinking*?!? When do we fucking *drink*?"

————

"All right, Mr. Neil," says Linda, addressing the coin, smiling broadly, as if amused by the very notion of me. "This is just the beginning of your journey. We have been so blessed to have you. Your originality has been a joy. I hope you're learning there is hope."

She holds the bronze coin loosely in the palm of her hand. The coins have different patterns—butterflies, praying hands, slogans. This one has a camel.

"I came up with the camel, because they are famous for being able to go and go without a drink. So can you. You don't need to think of how you're going to relapse in the future. Just think about what you're going to do today. There's no need to compare yourself to others. Just remind yourself: 'I'm no better, no worse than anybody else.' Say: 'I'll be fine if I stay with the program, if I stay outside my ego.' You need to go to meetings—they are the daily waterings your sobriety needs. Without them, your sobriety will wither and die. You are an I-can-handle-this-kind of guy. I'm going to miss you."

The coin is passed around, each person expressing a few thoughts about me, even the two ladies who arrived that morning and don't know me at all—they wish they did, politely. I try to maintain an attentive look on my face, but am too uncomfortable being addressed so directly and sincerely to retain much of what the room is saying, though they certainly aren't gushing about how special and wonderful I am.

"I don't understand some of the words you say," begins Howard, and I expect him to add a "but" though it never comes. That's about it; I'm an ass. "I've learned, if you can't impress them with reason, dazzle them with bullshit." He speaks a bit more, eventually allowing that I am "always thoughtful."

The newest people in the room have the nicest things to say, while those who have been around me longer are cooler, a common pattern. Something in me must turn people off—ego, I suppose. You see a guy stuck on himself, no matter how he struggles to hide it, to bury it under obscuring layers of false modesty, and you want to slap him down.

I'm surprised, and would be hurt if I let myself be, but manage to tune out the room, to go numb, and just wait until it's over so I can go. This isn't what I expected at all.

Leslie, who joined the same morning I did, who has been here every moment I have, who caught my attention with her bright clothes and strong views, takes the coin. My little rehab pal speaks so briefly and so tepidly that she's done almost before I realize she is talking, saying in essence that I taught her the risks of overintellectualizing and the value of shutting up. Then it is over, and I have my coin. Nobody cried.

———

There is one final bit of Chapman business. Linda ticks through my recovery plan: take your meds, make an appointment in a month with Dr. Manozzi, and, oh yeah, go to aftercare every Thursday night for the next twenty-four weeks.

That's a surprise; twenty-four weeks sounds like a lot. Like infinity. The standard is twelve weeks, and I wonder why I have to keep coming back for the next six months.

"Because that's what the team decided was right for you," says Linda, shutting off discussion by reminding me that if I don't go, they'll tell my probation officer that I'm not in compliance. The blatant threat offends me, making the whole thing seem baldly commercial—we've got you in our clutches and we're not letting you go for a long time.

Still, I am in essence free. So what does a free person do? Well, he drives home. He puts in a call to tell bosses that rehab is concluded. He looks around, tries to find some chores to do—dry cleaning to take in, library books to return—and gets into his car.

Nothing stressful at all, yet the whole thing seems overwhelming—clattering around this empty suburb alone on a Tuesday afternoon. I end up sitting behind the wheel of the car, engine off, in the parking lot of the library. I didn't have to drive there—I live half a block away. Now I need to turn the key and go to the drugstore for razors.

Only I can't. Something has me frozen, panicked. Maybe the possibilities overwhelm me, or I'm disoriented from having the routine of Chapman pulled away. I smirked at it while it was there, but now that it's gone I'm spinning. I'm on my own, my twenty-eight days are done. I could, for instance, go stand in a bar for a few hours. I'm not tempted—I'm not going to. That would be a bad idea. But I could do that. I could do anything. And while I know drinking is a bad impulse, it is an impulse nevertheless, one that slithers through my guts like a snake going through black mud. After all this, it's still there.

I phone Frank, my sponsor.

"It's a scary thing, buddy," he says, over the phone. "The framework of rehab is comforting. I know when I was released, I was freaked out."

There are constant hurdles, constant challenges to this, he says. While we are trying to process what has happened we are also trying to live our lives at that moment and face the future speeding toward us. It's a juggling act and sometimes we drop the balls.

Chapter Fifteen

Our one-hundred-year-old farmhouse has an unfinished basement—brick walls bowing out like bellies, crumbling mortar, cobwebs, dead bees, dirt. We've been tossing boxes and miscellaneous stuff down there for years, neglecting the place, except when it floods.

For the next five days I clean the basement, carefully, methodically. Cleaning a filthy basement is fun, at least compared to rehab, and the two may even be comparable tasks—getting rid of the crud that's built up unnoticed over the years. I like finding places for all the scattered possessions, piled around the steps since that is the first place to drop them. Dragging bag after bag of garbage upstairs into the light, then sweeping the fine gray dust carefully across the cracked concrete floor. As with rehab, there is something zen to the task, the great ego humbled. Napoleon on Elba. The low impact, suburban version of joining a monastery.

————————

One can't clean the basement forever. I'm outside, raking leaves, when Edie walks out with the portable phone. It's John Barron, the editor in chief.

"Here's the thing," he says. "We've decided that your being on the editorial board has too many conflicts . . ."

They're kicking me off the board. Having a drunk who some-times shows up for meetings with booze on his breath was not a problem, but a recovering alcoholic is unacceptable. It looks bad. Not that he says this. He doesn't have to.

But God bless the *Sun-Times*, they have to use every resource, squeeze every penny. They won't give you a new pencil until you hand in the stub of the old one. So they can't simply cut me from the board—that would mean lightening my workload.

"Since you won't be writing editorials," Barron continues, "we figure you can write an extra column a week, so we'll push you to four days a week."

We chat a bit about how great everything is going to be, and then he's gone. Off the editorial board—which means no more ten a.m. meetings. No more listening to Jesse Jackson—in a safari suit, his eyes half-mast, jet-lagged—bloviating for ninety minutes at a crack. No more writing generic editorials. And my column will be running four times a week—management's attempt to extract maximum mileage out of an asset will seem, to those who don't know any better, like a promotion. Any chance of my slinking back into print under a cloud of shame has vanished.

Edie comes outside to see how the call went. I can't resist delivering the news with maximum gravitas.

"They're kicking me off the board," I say, arranging my face into a mask of gloom.

But she looks so stricken I can't hold back the good news.

"And giving me an extra column a week!"

Edie breaks into a grin. "Congratulations," she says, hugging me. "That's fantastic!"

Before I turn in for the night, I e-mail Frank—how do you cope with it, almost two years in, what do you find that replaces drinking, to give life its thrill, its savor?

The next morning I have his answer.

"I've found it gratifying to seek out passions I recall were in place before drink became a priority," he writes. "Certain kinds of old movies or novels or comic books or TV shows. . . . Things that held my attention rapt. Those are things that delight me anew, since I'm able to experience them with all pistons firing. . . . Those are the things that were never boring, especially now all over again. Cast your mind backwards and see what floats to the top. (It will probably take awhile to get there, but it will come eventually . . . and it's really quite good, I promise. . . .)"

I pull my hands back from the keyboard and let them fall into my lap. Old TV shows? Comic books? Somehow I hoped for something . . . more. I sit in the morning light, rub my face, and try, as Frank said, to cast my mind backward. What did I like as a kid? Zeppelins. Mummies. Stamp collecting. That won't replace drinking. "The illusion you took from me," Horace writes, "was what I lived on." What will I live on now? I have interests. Work. Reading. The boys. Is that enough? It'll have to be. The boys—it kills me that they'll know I'm not the sophisticated dad swirling the wine in his glass and casting off confidence like a glow. They won't admire me. I'll forever be the damaged drunk, the guy with a problem, the guy at the picnic sifting through the cooler full of beer looking for a soda. My dad, the fuckup.

Then again, if I keep drinking, they will also know that I am a drunk. They will notice, eventually, if they haven't already. Drunks like to pretend it's a big secret, but it's not. Sooner or later, everybody knows.

———

Kent's voice, from the backseat of the car.

"Can I drink wine at Thanksgiving?"

We're driving to Dorothy's to drop the boys off so they can

spend the night—Edie and I have court early in the morning. I wince and say nothing. The silence hangs.

"No," says Edie.

"Sometimes you let me drink wine." That silence again.

"A sip. On religious holidays," Edie finally says. "Thanksgiving isn't a religious holiday. Wine is an adult drink."

"Wine is an adult drink . . . " Kent continues, as if trying to figure it out, "but not for Dad, right?"

My mind drifts back in time. The stuffing always came out great. Edie bought two bottles of red last year, so I wouldn't run out. Some wine for the stuffing, some wine for the cook. Playing the radio, listening to the parades, wearing an apron, dicing and toasting seven or eight loaves of challah into croutons. Plus onions and celery, chicken broth and apples, all go into the big bowl, where slowly the stuffing assumes density, richness and flavor. I carry the covered tray from the kitchen to the car and set it, warm and heavy and fragrant, into the trunk. There are no fights. The long table at Dorothy's is set, studded with wine bottles. I open the wine—my job, because I know how to do it. Gentle, slowly, lovingly pulling out the corks, so as not to mangle them. Only happy Thanksgiving memories.

We get to Dorothy's—Thanksgiving is two days away, but her table is already set. I worried there would be no wine, because of the newborn drunk in the family, but I see the wine is there, glasses even at the children's table, so now I fret about that. I'm slightly discombobulated. Of course I won't drink—not this Thanksgiving. The prudent man would lay low. There will be other Thanksgivings, I tell myself.

———

We sit, waiting, on a blond wood bench in the courtroom hallway—too wide and tall, really, for the word. "Causeway" is a better term. Planes should be taking off outside.

"Want a Life Saver?" Edie asks.

"What flavor?"

"Butter rum."

"Better not." A pause. She gets it, and laughs happily.

"Now aren't you glad you married me?" I say.

"As long as you keep making me laugh, we'll be fine," she says.

They unlock the door and we all go inside. Edie goes over to the assistant state's attorney and they talk for a long time.

They swear Edie in. She testifies that she is my wife and I am her husband, that she is asking that the case be dismissed, that she is not herself drunk or high, that she is not being forced or threatened to do so, that she doesn't fear for her safety, that she understands the police and state's attorney will happily help her if she ever has any other issues with me.

The state's attorney says, given all this, we're dropping the case. The judge says, in essence, "okay," and the whole thing is over in less than a minute.

Since we didn't have breakfast, we go to a nearby Panera Bread shop for coffee.

"You must feel relieved," Edie says.

I try to gauge myself. Relieved is not the word. "Anxious," I say. "Not relieved at all."

"Why?" says Edie.

"Well, first, there is Thanksgiving to endure. I'm not worried about drinking, but I still have to get through it. Wine tomorrow would be a bad idea."

"Wine forever would be a bad idea," she says.

"You know, let's just get through now. You know what they say, one day at a time."

"You drink again, I'm going to divorce you. I'm not going through that again."

The temptation is to say: "Go through *what* again?" A defense of my record as a husband, a good husband, a good father, despite the drinking, swirls around the pit of my battered soul.

But I don't say that; I don't have any fight left in me.

"Given the relapse rate, that doesn't bode too well for us then," I say quietly. "I just need to figure out what I need to do to get through things. I mean, we go to two seders a year. Most people go to one. Maybe one would be enough for me this year."

"You love the seders."

I want to clarify—"I love bolting back wine at seders" —but that wouldn't be helpful either, and I suppress the thought as well. Instead, I say, "I did, but things have changed."

She starts to cry. "You're just saying things to be mean."

"Don't cry," I say soothingly, stroking her arm. Does that ever work? We sit there for a miserable moment, then start picking our way back to normalcy. We have to go get the boys at Dorothy's house and take them to school.

Edie wakes up very happy. Wasn't yesterday a great day? Yes, I say, groping at a dream I was having—drinking Jack Daniel's in a red-lit bar—yes, it was.

And the stuffing! It was the best ever. Somehow, every year I make it better. Yes, honey, thanks.

My mother calls. How was Thanksgiving?

"Great, Ma, great," I say, through gritted teeth. Brace for it, here it comes.

"So they had wine at dinner . . . " she ventures.

"Yes, that's right, Ma. But I didn't."

"I'm proud of you," my dad says—he's on the line too.

"Well, it's not as if I had a whole lot of choice in the matter."

Monday morning, trying to tie my necktie in front of the mirror
in our bedroom while Ross and Kent scrabble and fight in the
hallway—one pressing a door against the other, trying to shut it
on him, while the other struggles to force his way in. Yells of
outrage, calls for help.

I close my eyes, take a long breath, afraid to enter into the
scrum, afraid I might lose control and end up pummeling them.
"Arrested for domestic battery again, his children this time, the
day he was to return to work . . ."

"Boys," I whisper. "Please. Please boys. Please. Can't you
help me out? Just a little?"

The boys are calmed and fed, and I'm projected out into the
day. The rain has passed. It isn't as cold as it looks from inside—
almost balmy, the clouds racing across the sky. Long as it was in
coming, it is surprising to get on the train, to leave the suburban
flannel world I've been inhabiting the past few months and journey downtown, in a suit and tie, walking up Wacker Drive, the
Merchandise Mart looming enormous before me.

My first column back is about what happened. It had to
be—the issue would hang over my head otherwise. The column
runs under the headline, "Hello, I'm Neil . . . " my little wink to
the program, and begins:

> Those columns I wrote about my home life over the past ten
> years were not a lie. I really live in a rambling old house with
> a pair of eager, mischievous boys and a pretty, wisecracking
> wife. We really remodeled our kitchen on a pharaonic scale.
> We really have three cats.
>
> But the stories in the newspapers (*and* on TV, *and* radio)
> last month were also true. I probably shouldn't say that. But
> you have come to expect a certain candor in this space and

now does not seem the time to change. I got drunk and slapped my wife during an argument. I immediately knew it was a mistake—I used to say that if I ever hit Edie, I would draw back a bloody stump, and that wasn't far from what happened. She called the cops, they came, clapped me into handcuffs, and hauled me off to jail. When I asked her later why she had to have me arrested, she said, "Nobody hits me, buddy." Pithy as always.

I haven't seen my office at the newspaper in two months, and except for a stack of papers and a carton of mail, nothing has changed. I pull the venetian blinds open and fire up the computer, never once looking at the top the bookshelf, where a bottle of fifteen-year-old Jane Barbancourt rum sits, a gift Baker gave me when he left for New York. Right where I left it, its box like a plinth, holding up the Russian general's hat Baker also gave me. Linda be damned, I don't want to give the bottle away. It would be agony. Frankly, I don't even want to think about it. If anyone asks, I will tell them it is there as a symbol, as a trophy. I don't stay sober because I don't know where the booze is. It's right there.

The e-mail—with a few notable exceptions—is overwhelmingly positive. Readers, friends, acquaintances are glad to have me back, and say so. Maybe I'm not quite the dick I felt like at the end of rehab. I meet Sam for lunch at Harry Caray's. No hiding; get back on the bicycle. We sit at my usual table, under the picture of my younger son, Kent, throwing out the first pitch before a Cubs game at Wrigley Field last year. I order the usual salad, but instead of the usual iced Jack, I order an iced tea.

———

It's late November, getting dark early now, and the windows of the train going home are black. I gaze at my own reflection, remembering how I would sit in the bar car with Ingrid, a blond lady from down the street, and we'd drink red wine together and laugh. There's still a bar car, but I don't dare go in it. Maybe she's in there now, drinking with a new bar car buddy. I fish around in my briefcase for something to read.

The ride home jangles me enough—I could taste the wine— I figure, time for a meeting. I call Jonathan at home, but Molly says he's over at his new sponsor's house. He has a sponsor, which is more than I can say. I mean, I have Frank, but we never get together, aside from one coffee in the city. He's very laid-back, which I like. No demands.

I check the AA brochure. There's a meeting at the North-field United Methodist Church, a place I've never been to be-fore. Yellow cinder block walls in the common room. I get there just as "How It Works" is being read and, to my surprise, Jona-than is there, sitting next to Stan, the "Are you cured yet, Neil?" guy.

After the readings, we break into small groups. I go over to join Jonathan. Stan joins us. He doesn't say it, though I keep waiting for him to. Even broken up, it's a crowd—a dozen peo-ple in my group—and they talk about matters that seem to have only a passing relationship to sobriety; traffic encounters and family spats and such. Maude, an older woman wearing what strikes me as a bathing cap with floppy plastic flowers on it, gives a protracted talk about trying to return some item at a de-partment store.

After the meeting I talk to Jonathan—we usually talk after meetings—and he tells me that Stan is his new sponsor. The guy who has been taunting me since day one is the sobriety coach and spiritual guide to my neighbor. Just lovely.

At home, Edie is in bed, reading. I open my mouth to tell her about Stan, and see she's reading an Al-Anon inspirational book.

She's one of them. It strikes me that while drinking hasn't finished us—not yet anyway—recovery just might.

—————

Peter Baker is history in New York City. Five months after he was urging me to quit the *Sun-Times* and work for him, no contract necessary, he's gone.

"Baker should have known better than to take the job," Edie says, tartly.

"I don't know why you don't like him," I say. "He's my best friend."

"He led you astray," she says. "He took you out until you couldn't stop."

"I led myself astray," I say. "And I did stop."

"Not without extreme measures," she says, standing at the sink.

"Look," I say. "You've already cost me most of my friends. They're uncomfortable talking to me. Don't go after Baker too. What do you want me to do?"

"I don't know," she says. "Don't go out with him if he comes back."

"Because I have no control over myself?" I say. "That makes it easy."

—————

The days begin to pile up. The column returns to my usual gripes, thoughts, and observations. Most colleagues at the paper never mention that I was gone. A few feel obligated to say something. Walt Decker, a former cop who now works security in the building, a trim guy with deep bags under his eyes, pokes his head into my office.

"Welcome back," he says.

"Thanks," I say, shaking hands. "I'm with the program now too." He looks puzzled. I remind him that I once asked him out for a beer and he declined, saying he doesn't drink.

"This chair expensive?" Walt says, and I gesture him into it.

"I used to drink half a fifth a day, with a dozen Miller Lites . . ." he begins.

"Miller Lite," I marvel, interrupting him. "That's foul."

". . . but in the force, people don't care about that," he continues.

"They see it as taking care of their own. . . ." I add.

"I was in narcotics, and we lived by our own code anyway. So one day we come in and our boss says, 'What are you guys hanging around here for?' which was his way of telling us to get lost. My partner says, 'I don't want to go home because I'll have to talk to my wife.' So we go to a bar. This is ten o'clock in the morning. We spend the day there, a lot of us, and by evening I'm out of it. I would get blackouts. I mean, my eyes were open, but I wasn't seeing anything.

"I go home, and now it's the next day, and I'm gassing up the car—we had these unmarked cars—and the guy who pumps the gas, colored guy, says, 'How are you doing, Officer Walt?' and I say, 'What do you mean?' and he says, 'You were in a bad way yesterday, waving your gun around,' and I look at my partner and ask, 'Why didn't you tell me when you picked me up?' and he says, 'You weren't yourself.'

"It turns out, the night before, I was sitting on the stool, out of it, and he socks me in the arm, playfully, but harder than he thought, and I fell over on the floor. But I came up mad, and chased him out of the bar, and pulled my gun on him—I carried a .44 Magnum. And I was waving it around, and they were laughing, because I couldn't hit anything, and I'm screaming, 'I'm going to kill you, you fucker.' "

That isn't what gets Walt to quit drinking, however. The next day, he tells me, he drinks again, as people tend to do, and is driving home, and another car rear-ends him and pushes the right side of his car into an abutment. He chases the guy for miles, slides off the road, and crumples the *left* side of his car.

At that he pulls off the road and sits there for a while and, yes, prays to God, and that was March 3, 1983. He drove slowly home.

"I had two hundred dollars' worth of booze at home and I start pouring it down the sink and my wife says, 'What are you doing?' and I say, 'What does it look like I'm doing? I'm getting rid of this because I'm never drinking it again.' She gave me a big hug."

"You never went to meetings?"

"I didn't have to. Just made up my mind. That's how I am. I gave up smoking the same way."

Walt pulls himself to his feet and is gone. Some guys can just give it up and never have to worry about meetings. He doesn't need therapy or the fellowship of AA—what he needs is the knowledge that he never again wants to be waving his .44 at a friend ever again. That is enough for him.

III

Too Much of a Drunk for Rehab

Chapter Sixteen

Edie, dressed in brown jeans, kisses me good-bye. It's five a.m. and she's leaving for California to tend to her sick brother. I get up to see her off because I like when she does that for me when I travel. When I *used* to travel. Neither of us is particularly warm.

"Do you have your cash card?" I ask.

"It's not going to do much good," she says. "We've only got a couple hundred in the account." The cab parks silently in front of the house. She takes her bag and is gone.

I go upstairs to the office. Now what? The tiniest urge to begin drinking right now, this very second, stirs, appearing like a light winking on in a distant window. Something small but definitely there. I sit down at my computer and check my e-mail. The first message I open begins:

Dear Neil,

I have never written or e-mailed a newspaper or a columnist before. I don't know that you'll even read this; that's probably why I don't. Anyway, I'm a thirty-five-year-old black male currently residing in Champaign, IL. I'm originally from Chicago, but moved here about five years ago. I usually read your column online and enjoy it immensely. I had been looking for your column online and was surprised when there was nothing. I checked again and again; and still nothing! Today I was able to check again after about a week or so. I was so shocked when I read your first column back from rehab.

Anyway, all I'm writing to say is that it took a lot of balls to write that column. To come clean about what happened took a lot of courage. I am also a recovering alcoholic/addict. I spent from age twenty through thirty in the midst of an addictive hell. Just about anything you can name, I did. God willing, on February 7th of 2006 I will have four years of uninterrupted clean time. It hasn't always been easy; but it hasn't been that hard either.

As with you, it also took an incident with my wife to send me on the road to recovery.... The last time, I stayed out all night drinking and getting high. When I finally did slither back into the house, I didn't have to say anything. She knew exactly what I had been doing and the look on her face as she held my son haunts me until this day. She said a lot of things that day, but the main point was that I had a decision to make. Either I wanted to be a father and a husband or I wanted to be a crackhead and an alcoholic. I couldn't have it both ways.

Right then and there I decided in my heart what I truly wanted was to get clean and I did whatever it took to stay clean after that. The point is that *I* made the decision to get and stay clean. *I* did it because *I* wanted to do it more than anything else. Nothing else could've kept me clean. Not a judge, prison, near-death experiences, nothing!

The e-mail jars me—extraordinary, the right message at the right time. I can't do it because Edie is watching over me. I have to do it for myself.

That gets me through Wednesday.

———————

With Edie gone, I decide to work at home Thursday. I get the boys off to school, turn the column in, then go to see Frisch. He's pleased I've gotten this far—not everyone does—though

he's concerned that I'm motivated not by love of AA or commitment to sobriety, but primarily by spite, in his estimation. I'm
doing this, he says, to deny satisfaction to those who want me to
fail.

Frisch suggests: Why not look for something more positive?
Why not embrace my new friends at AA and at Chapman aftercare? Perhaps I'm already warming to them and don't even realize it, he says, pointing out that today, for the first time in our
sessions, I referred to Leslie by her name instead of calling her
"the eighty-seven-pound cocaine addict at Chapman." Maybe
I'll find myself making friends after all.

That isn't going to happen. I thank Frisch and head home.
Snow begins falling. I gaze wistfully at the fat flakes, thinking
how nice it would be to be stranded indoors with a bottle of
Jack. Ross comes home, his shoulders dusted.

"I have to go to the bathroom!" he announces. "What's for
snack?"

"Cookies?" I venture.

Kent stamps in after him, covered with snow. "Help me get
my coat off," he says. I reach for his backpack straps, he sticks
his arms straight out, kicking off his boots. I depack him and
strip his coat off while he stands still, like a knight having his
armor removed by vassals.

The phone rings—Kent's friend Max. He'll be over in ten
minutes. Kent goes downstairs to play a video game. Ross takes
his cookies and follows him, to watch. I scan the suddenly
empty kitchen, a trace of sadness stealing into the room. They
blow through so quickly.

The weather keeps getting worse—big wet clumps tumbling
down from the sky. The TV news reports a plane has skidded off
the runway at Midway Airport. Right through the chain-link
fence and onto Cicero Avenue. Killed a boy in a car. I begin

making dinner—mac and cheese, the universal kid food. The boys have a music recital, and since this is Thursday I have aftercare at Chapman. I wasn't about to suggest to Edie that I not go, so the plan is for her eighteen-year-old niece, Sarah—Janice's daughter—to take the boys over to the concert, then watch them until I get back.

Sarah arrives, slim and beautiful, with big brown eyes. She utters a few teenage syllables as she slides onto a kitchen stool and begins digging into the leftover noodles. I wish everybody luck all round, take my leave, and jump into the car. A full-blown blizzard now. Traffic is stopped on Shermer. It budges forward, then stops again, for a full minute at a time, the wipers on the van sluicing the snow off the windshield. It has never been like this in the five years we've lived here. It takes me fifteen minutes to get to Waukegan Road, a mile away, and after a few more minutes, when I finally can make the turn, I see why. A car down the road is engulfed in flames, fire jetting out of the windows. Thick brown smoke rolling off the wreck, making the sky all around brown-yellow. It must have just happened—there's nobody around, just this empty burning car. I roll down my window to look, through the swirl of fast-falling snow—the fire sounds like a blowtorch, the jammed car horn, a long, continuous cry.

I'm not going to make it to aftercare. Not in this mess. Most likely nobody will even be there. It's silly to try. Wouldn't it be ironic to be killed in an accident on the way to therapy? The car ahead of me inches forward and I impulsively pull to the left and put the car into a U-turn. Traffic the other way is fine. I slip into the tiny parking lot in front of Otis & Lee Liquors. No debate, no reflection, as if that were where I was going all along. Inside, brightly lit rows of bottles, the clear vodkas, the brown bourbons. I don't need to choose. I barely need to even look. A pair of scruffy-looking men are in front of the counter, arguing about something. "I bought you dinner," one is saying, as I slide around them and make my purchase, my mind kept a determined blank. In the parking lot, I'm just opening the van door when a snowball barely misses me, splattering against the driver's window. Kids, red-cheeked and laughing, materialize out of nowhere. I open my mouth to say something, but think better. For one second, I look at them, and am struck by the possibility that they are angels, sent to stop me. But I shake off that notion, hop inside the Honda, place the brown bag on the passenger seat, and gingerly back out of Otis & Lee's narrow parking lot.

At home, Sarah and Ross are still picking at dinner. The concert was cancelled by the storm. I tuck the bottle on a shelf in the playroom, among the boys' games. My mother-in-law and sister-in-law, who were going to go to the concert, come over instead, and we all share hot cocoa and cookies and conversation. This storm! And too bad about the concert. We talk of this and that. Finally they leave. Ross puts on his coat and goes out into the snowstorm to say good-bye to them. I tuck the bottle under my arm, slip a shot glass in my pocket, and head up to my office.

I can see the lights of their car, pulling out of the driveway. Ross stays in the front yard, playing by himself in the falling snow. The car lights turn, hesitate, then continue down the road. I set the shot glass on the mahogany computer table and strip the brown bag off of the bottle of Jack. I hold the square bottle in my hand and gaze raptly at its black label.

"Daddy's back," I say, lifting it to my lips and giving it a fervent kiss. I crack the top, pour a shot glass to the brim, the very brim, noticing how the lovely amber fluid glows in the blue light from the computer screen. I don't touch the glass—it's filled so high, I'm almost afraid to, worry about sloshing the bourbon. I go over to the window and look down to check on Ross. He is in the front yard, alone, making angels in the bluish night snow. I lift the glass to my lips, very carefully, take a tentative sip, then pour it down.

I could pretend to be conflicted, torn, agonized. But I'm not. I'm glad. I haven't had a drink in over two months—since Sam's house—and it's about time. The first tastes so good, in fact, that I immediately have another.

Ross comes in, Kent returns from Max's house. I charge up my cocoa—mustn't let them see me drinking!—and the evening rolls merrily along. I sit in the office playing chess with Ross and beat him. *Well, isn't this nice?* I tell myself, taking a covert sip of chocolaty Jack goodness.

Bedtime. I make sure they brush their teeth, splash their faces, and we all pile in my bed to read *Tom Sawyer*: Chapter 11, "Conscience Racks Tom." Ironic, a wink from God—only this time a big friendly wink from a big, friendly God, on my side for once. Conscience racks Tom, but it doesn't rack me. I am happy, returned to my old self, the spheres set right in the world.

The boys want to sleep in our bed. Why not? It's party time. Of course you can. Fun Dad's in charge now. I'll let them drop off, then walk them groggily to their own beds later, just like when they were young. The past is returned. They are delighted, and run and get their animals and blankets and special pillows and arrange them just so.

Mug in hand, I stand before the boys, cozy in bed, and sing "Rock-a-bye." I sing "My Bonnie." I sing "Amazing Grace." Ross asks for "Old Man River"—the *Show Boat* song I used to sing to him when he was very small, dropping my voice low, doing my best Paul Robeson imitation. He remembers! Lovely boy.

"Old man river, that old man river, he must know sometin', but don't say nuttin,'" I begin. "He just keeps rollin', he keeps on rollin' along."

The boys are delighted. The song reaches its climax.

"*Tote* that barge! *Lift* that bale!" I sing, punching the air, then spreading my arms wide and plunging my voice as low as it will go: "You gets a little drunk an' yeh lannnnnnds in jaaaiiiiiiillll!!!" I start to laugh—no kidding. You betcha! Ross' eyes meet mine; he understands immediately, and starts to laugh too. Kent is a little uncertain as to what is going on, but he joins in good-naturedly. Soon we are all laughing, the perfect end to a perfect evening.

———

The next morning I wake up in Kent's room, feeling exhausted and unwell, among the stuffed animals and blankets. A moment of confusion, then: Right, Edie's in California.

Back to our room. The boys are in our bed, asleep. That's good. Pad into the office. Almost half the bottle gone. Geez, I think, even while admiring the amber bounty that remains. I certainly will drink less than that tonight, so it should be enough to get through Saturday. The prudent man will stop on Sunday, to give the alcohol twenty-four hours to leave his system. So Edie will never know. She comes back Monday.

With the boys off to school, I take the train downtown. Sunday's column is written, then I have an errand to run—a pair of little baseball posters that need to be framed, to give to the boys at Hanukkah. So I take a cab to Flax, a frame store on Wabash Avenue, around the corner from the Berghoff. It's about four p.m.

There's a young couple at the front of the store, conferring over an art print spread out on the counter—to decorate their love nest, no doubt. They ponder over which frame most com-

snarl, "Get it done, dammit!" But I wait the five minutes, like a
runner set in the blocks. Finally the clerk gets to me, I conduct
my business, and bolt out of there, hurrying around the corner
to the Berghoff.

The bar is nearly empty. But my pal Dario, the bartender, is
there—a small, neat Hispanic man, thin mustache, dark eyes.
He greets me, perhaps with a trace of wary surprise. I order a
beer, then a beer and a shot.

"Any Christmas plans, Dario?" I ask heartily, making conversation, a foot on the brass rail. The holiday approaches.

"I have Christmas at my brother-in-law's," he says.

"There you go!" I say. "All the benefit and none of the work.
Is it fun?"

"It is," he says. "My wife gets mad at me if I drink too
much."

"Tell me about it," I say, commiserating, draining my shot. I
order another draft beer and a shot of the good Berghoff bourbon, and set to work on a bowl of pretzels. I really should get to
the station—I have to pick up the boys; they're staying with
friends after school and I need to retrieve them. But I felt so
crappy this morning and I feel so good now.

———

Then it's Saturday morning. Another evening melted away, dissolved by the warm ministrations of booze. The boys and I
watched a movie. The Jack's gone. Didn't make it past Friday
night. I didn't save myself a swallow—just a pathetic drop that
trickles out of the bottle as I hold it over my eager baby sparrow
tongue.

My state of mind is simple: I need a drink. Everything else is
a distant second. First I have to get money. My pocket cash was
wiped out at the Berghoff—each shot and a beer sets you back

about ten dollars, with tip. The checking account is not just low, it's empty. Try as I may to ascribe this to something deliberate on Edie's part—a plot to keep me on the straight and narrow by denying me cash—I just can't. She's not that calculating. I can't use the charge card because then Edie would know eventually. So I grab a yellow coffee can filled with coins.

The boys are already awake, playing video games—that's good. "I gotta go outside for a minute," I mutter, rushing out the door, shielding the can with my body. They don't look up.

Rushing into the bank building, carrying the weight of the coins with both hands in front of me, I bump into Sally, the director from Chapman. She's all smiles—what a surprise. How am I doing? Fine, fine, I say, neglecting to mention that I'm dashing to get booze money. The can yields thirty-five dollars and seventeen cents.

The liquor store isn't open yet, so I go to Sunset Foods. I'm a little worried, since a guy from the civic center AA meeting works in the liquor department there. But not that worried. A six-pack of Sam Adams and a bottle of red wine ought to do it. The boys are right where I left them when I return, glued to PlayStation 2.

Drinking beer at nine a.m. does not feel wrong. It feels lovely. There is nothing else I'd rather be doing. I'm never drunk—just staving off the need to drink. My sons feed their addiction in the TV room while I feed mine in the kitchen. I get Kent to his basketball practice, but forget that it's picture day. Just as well. How many sports pictures do you need? Then wine the rest of the afternoon. One bottle goes quick, so I slip out and buy another.

Sunday comes, the day that the prudent man would put on the brakes. I feel even crappier and more tired than the morning before, if that is possible. I have one last gulp of Sam Adams, an open bottle tucked in the refrigerator door. One ounce left, a farewell swallow. Cold comfort, literally. The boys have Sunday school. I drop them off and head to the AA meeting at the civic building across the street.

I can't tell if Hal knows—he is eyeing me suspiciously, but he always does that. Hal asks me how I'm doing and I tell him I'm just hanging on. Today is this meeting's annual Christmas brunch—hot dishes of Swedish meatballs and a tray of cold cuts, donated by Sunset Foods, wait in the next room. I can't face it. Food nauseates me. When they begin their party, I slip out the door.

After Sunday school I get a phone call from Sandi, a friend from the synagogue with two boys of his own. It's a perfect day for sledding! For him, maybe. For me, a perfect day for curling on the couch and facing the wall. But I won't give in to that. I won't. So I toss the old Flexible Flyer sled, with its honey wood slats and red metal runners, in the back of the van and meet them at the big hill. Sandi and I make some kind of small talk— I have no idea what. "Look at the boys sled" or "What a storm we had the other night!" It's like trying to chat with your hand in a vise, tightening unseen. Standing there, in the cold, it grips me. The claw, crushing me. A hurt, a hollowness, a panic. An impetus—*go, now! Now's your chance!*

"Watch the boys for a few minutes, will you?" I ask Sandi. "I'll be right back. I gotta go do something." I briskly walk away to the car, and drive to R & R Liquor at the corner of Willow and Shermer, an even shadier, more marginal place than Otis & Lee, the shelves dusty and half stocked, jutting from pegboard. I spend my last few dollars on a half pint of Seagram's 7 because I don't have the money for Jack. I rip the cap off in the car in the parking lot and take a long draw—ahhhhhh, that's better—then return to sledding, the bottle snugly tucked inside the pocket of my green Eddie Bauer jacket.

The half pint goes quickly. I'm home with Ross—Kent is at a birthday party. I'm out of cash again, so I collect eight dollars in singles, allowance money, from the boys' sock drawers and though I know Kent is being taken home, I pretend I have to go pick him up. Ross is playing video games. I return to R & R and buy a full pint of Canadian Club in a plastic bottle. I don't even like Canadian Club, but that doesn't matter now.

———

Monday morning. Edie is coming home in a few hours. At first I think I can make it, until I realize that I drank twenty-four ounces of whiskey yesterday afternoon—a half pint plus a pint, $8 + 16 = 24$. It's a big jump, from that to nothing. Too big. With the boys off at school, I clean the house for an hour. I put the empty beer, wine, and whiskey bottles in a white plastic garbage bag and walk over to the civic center and toss them with a clink into the Dumpster. Ditching the evidence.

I feel dismal and exhausted on the 9:33 downtown. It's been two weeks exactly since the happy Monday I returned to work. I can't eat. I can't go to the Billy Goat—Phyllis will find out I'm off the wagon and I don't want Phyllis to know. Because she'll think less of me.

So I go to Monk's Pub, over on Lake Street, one of those places where they give you peanuts and you throw the shells on the floor. Fashionable in the 1970s. Not that the setting matters—this is alcoholism at its core, shorn of romance or pretense, where drinking becomes a glamorless necessity, like going to the bathroom. Something you do because you have to, trying not to think about it. I have two vodka tonics for breakfast— slowly sipping, trying not to gulp them, gazing at images on the silent TVs. None of the waitresses setting up for lunch even glance at this puffy guy drinking by himself at ten thirty in the morning, the only customer in the bar.

Back at the office, I sit at my desk, tersely answering e-mails and trying to clear away the clutter of paper, while the vodka tonics wear off. I'm scattered and distracted, worried about Edie coming home. I don't feel right until lunch at the Shamrock Club, the workingman's bar I last went to when I came downtown with Sam. The slat wooden floor, the clatter and commotion, Mary behind the bar, the noon TV news. A big cheeseburger and three more vodka tonics. I'm in control again. Hope flares. This is doable. I can manage this. Back at the office I slide by Cathleen Falsani's desk.

"Cathleen," I say jovially, spreading my arms, radiating confidence. "How do I look to you?"

She looks up, first with indifference, then alarm.

"Like you had a drink," she says, and jots down Frank's number on a yellow Post-it note—she knows him too, knows he's my sponsor. I call him, and he tells me to find a meeting right now and go to it. Go to two meetings, he says. I tell him I will, but even as I say it I know that I won't. In truth, I never consider it—drinking has me in its grip and nothing else matters. Instead I head home—Edie will be there by now. I sip a meager Absolut and lime on the train to prepare myself. Why not? There'll be no hiding it now.

"I just couldn't stop," I tell Edie. I am truly baffled at how it happened; she is outraged. Nor can I stop now. Pretending to duck out for an eight p.m. meeting, I instead go straight to the Three Brothers Tavern. A few men are at one corner of the big rectangular bar, happily drinking their Bud Lights. Normal guys. I linger in a corner by myself, play a few old songs on the jukebox, thinking sadly of my high school girlfriend. Two Sam Adams and two shots of Jack and my hour is up. On some level, I understand that this isn't even fun, but dreary and lugubrious. When I return home, Edie isn't fooled. She knows where I've been immediately, and is even more incensed than she had been earlier in the day—smoldering, unable to tolerate the sight of me. I know the feeling.

Chapter Seventeen

So it's back into the guest room, where I'm up at two a.m., thirsty and squirming, alone and aghast. At four I poke my head into Edie's room. Into *our* room. No, into her room.

"Please," I say. "Let me sleep in here. Put your hand on my heart. I'm begging you." She sends me away. I've got those blue pills—the Zyprexa—somewhere, and I dig through the medicine cabinets, looking. Any port in a storm. But I can't find them.

In the morning Edie is civil until the boys are off to school, until they disappear down the walk.

"Why did you have to drink?" she yells. "Why couldn't you keep it together?"

It's Tuesday—a column due. I get one started, but it's an ordeal, like trying to scrape spit out of a dusty mouth. I get on the phone to Dr. Frisch—he'll see me at eleven a.m. I get there fifteen minutes early. He gives me the chilled water bottle always at the ready. I take it with trembling hands, sit carefully on the chair, and try to tell him how shocking it was. After all this, it's a surprise.

"I just couldn't stop," I say, stunned, not quite able to believe it myself.

"This was probably inevitable," Frisch says. "The question is, what are we going to do about it now?"

The answer, of course, is AA meetings—the lone offering on the menu. "I think I'll have the . . . ahh . . . AA *meetings*, please." Plus really working with a sponsor—laid-back Frank obviously isn't doing the job.

Back home, it's as if I've already died and my restless soul is moving about the house unseen while Edie and the boys get on without me. The bachelor ghost, living in a home with a family.

Edie comes into the office.

"I'm cold," I say, standing up, putting my hands on her shoulders.

"It's not cold in here," she says, embracing me lightly, as if my clothes were dirty. I go to kiss her, but she turns away.

"I was hoping you would rise to the occasion," she says. "The house spotless and a big 'Welcome Home, Mom' banner."

"I cleaned the toilets."

"You did not."

"One of the toilets. I scrubbed it. It was filthy."

"Well, clean up your end table too—it's becoming a junk pile." She turns to walk out of the room. Suddenly, rising to the occasion becomes a lost dream—it never occurred to me, but if only it had. "Rise to the occasion." I never considered it. The phrase itself might have kept me sober. "Rise to the occasion." It would have been so much more satisfying than drinking.

"I'm sorry," I call after her. "I should have risen to the occasion." She goes downstairs in silence.

————

The family is on vacation at the seashore in France. A lovely pale blue room, the sun bright yellow through billowing white lace curtains. The boys and I, tanned and happy, toweling off from the ocean—thick, soft towels . . .

Morning. I clutch at the dream, but it melts away, and I'm in the guest room, the blinds drawn. The boys have never been to France. They have never seen the ocean. A better sleep—less shaking. That's good. I go into the room with Edie and get into bed, and she doesn't seem to mind, which is also good.

"How do you feel?"

"Hurting, humiliated, agonized, remorseful, angry, disappointed, with a burning desire to drink," I say. "Other than that, fine." We both laugh.

She suggests we go out to lunch, to Fujiyama, a small sushi restaurant not far away. First I work on the column, interviewing participants in what I consider a wonder—a community snowblower, owned and operated by a number of families on a city block. While working, the dread abates, until I look up and realize it is gone, when of course it comes back, a cold sea sloshing into a hole scooped out on a wintry beach.

We go to lunch, with lots of hot tea and ice water and a big bowl of hot udon noodle soup. That helps. Stacked in the little hallway on the way to the restrooms are boxes of sake, and I consider, in a desultory fashion, dragging one into the bathroom with me and gnawing it open. But that would be a bad idea.

The first meeting I get to is Techny, my usual Wednesday night. Christopher is running it and he rambles, in an elderly way—he asks twice if there are any announcements. I notice Henry kindly nudging him forward, suggesting we read five pages of the *Big Book* instead of ten. I'm grateful—I'm jumping out of my skin for them to get to me, so I can tell my story and see how they react. Timmy slowly and methodically explains how he feels blessed for each and every day of his sobriety.

Christopher, placid as a Buddha, in his orange sweater, talks about living in train yards, of how he didn't have a drink for three years and then figured, "Heck, I haven't had a drink in three years," so he takes one, and goes on a thirty-eight-day bender.

"I just couldn't stop drinking," he says, words that I had heard before, but that never really resonated with me until now. "That was thirty years ago. I know that if I had a drink now it would come back as strong, and as damaging to my happiness, to my health, as it was then."

Finally time for my story. I outline my relapse. Thursday night I took my first drink in two months. I don't know what I was thinking—I wasn't really thinking anything, just following a route that seemed almost preordained, something I *had* to do. I obviously thought I could pull the reins back when the time came. But I couldn't. That was a surprise. I drank, by my estimate, two bottles of bourbon, two bottles of wine, and nine beers over a three-day period. And it still wasn't enough.

Nobody seems critical, or even particularly surprised.

"You did the next right thing, coming here," says Henry, smiling and chewing, putting his hand on my shoulder. After the meeting, people linger, come over to me, to pat me on the back, say a few kind words. They've been there; they know. Even Christopher, who never talks to me—too new, hardly worth the effort, he seems to think—says something supportive as we go our separate ways. I thought they'd laugh at me, or be envious—I got to drink while they didn't. Instead they felt sorry for me.

Outside, into the night, into the big parking lot outside of Techny, with its sweeping views south and west, the large landfill hill, the planes stacked up over O'Hare, and for the first time in a week I feel nearly myself again. As if the claw that was squeezing my guts simply let go. Maybe it was the meeting.

Meetings help, for some reason. I can't explain why. You go in feeling anxious, conflicted, bad, and you come out feeling less so. Maybe it's the chance to vent, to express what's going on inside your head to a sympathetic audience. Maybe it's the other people, and their stories, so like your own. Maybe it's the familiar readings and catechisms—you may not agree with every line of them, but they do become routine and comforting in their own way. Heck, maybe God smiles down and blesses you and cuts you a break because you went to an AA meeting. I have no idea, but they do help sometimes. They do tend to make you feel better, so I go, and try to find one downtown, near the newspaper. I figure that'll be easier to get to, during the day, than going out at night.

The booklet says there is a meeting at the Chicago Mercantile Exchange, at 30 South Wacker, at noon on Tuesdays, Thursdays, and Fridays, and at a quarter till I head over there—the weather a chilly, fuzzy gray.

There is a metal detector at the CME—I try to hand my money clip to the guard—it always sets these goddamn things off.

"Who are you here for?" the guard asks. I actually hesitate. It's a little late in the day to start getting embarrassed. But still . . .

"The AA meeting," I say.

"Take those elevators to the eighth floor, turn left, and go all the way to room Z."

Waiting at the elevator, thinking: *If I look up at the guard, he'll be looking at me.* I do. He is, and quickly averts his eyes.

In room Z—you can't make that up, can you?—about twenty people are gathered around a big square table, eating take-out lunches and talking. Along the wall, a heavy black curtain hides a window that looks out over the Globex trading floor, and through it comes faint muffled cries of buy and sell. I find an empty chair. There are men in good suits, their neckties sharply knotted at fresh collars, and men in T-shirts. The average age is thirty-five or so, which makes the room about half the age of the guys I am usually hanging out with in Northbrook. *A better crowd.*

The speaker is Randy, and he talks of being a cocaine addict, relapsing three times. "I just couldn't stop," he says. "It got so that I couldn't sleep at night because I would wake up with the drugs out of my system."

His mistakes make my leaving Ross in the children's section of the Northbrook Public Library seem prudent. He invites a homeless man back to his house to smoke cocaine. He gives investment advice while high on drugs—that draws a big laugh from the room, as if they had all been there. Randy talks about acceptance—he reads a passage from page 417 of the *Big Book* from a digital device the size of a pack of playing cards:

And acceptance is the answer to *all* my problems today. When I am disturbed it is because I find some person, place, thing, or situation—some fact of my life—unacceptable to me, and I can find no serenity until I accept that person, place, thing, or situation as being exactly the way it is supposed to be at this moment. Nothing, absolutely nothing, happens in God's world by mistake. Until I could accept my alcoholism, I could not stay sober. . . .

If everything that happens is God's will, then it would be his will if I—oh for instance—stand up right now, leave the meeting, take God by the pinkie, and let him guide me to the Berghoff.

But still "Until I could accept my alcoholism, I could not

stay sober" makes more sense than my approach of "I hate this I hate this I hate this."

While he is talking, I remember Edie's brother, Don, and his esophageal cancer. He, like me, can say again and again how he hates this latest development in his life. He, like me, can cry out, "But I didn't have this three years ago!" And the cosmos' reverberating, echoing answer to the both of us would be: "Yeah, buddy, but you sure got it now."

I sneak out just before one p.m. I'm supposed to meet Sam for lunch, and hurry to the Merchandise Mart food court, where there is a sushi stall, Tokyo Box. Sam is waiting for me, sharp in his suit and tie. We shake hands.

"So how are things?" Sam asks, in line.

"Good, good," I say, paying for my plastic box of sushi and a can of iced green tea. "And you?"

"Good." He seems a little preoccupied. We find a table.

"So how . . . ," he says, ". . . are things?"

"About the same as they were ten seconds ago." We sit. I don't plan on telling Sam about the relapse, worrying he'll be a conduit to the parents. That approach lasts exactly two bites.

"I relapsed over the weekend."

"I know," Sam says. "I could tell over the phone when I talked to you yesterday."

We talked? Oh right. That would explain our lunch date.

"Don't tell Mom and Dad."

He makes an "are you kidding me" face.

———————

Thursday night is aftercare. So I take the train home early, reading the paper, having a hard time focusing on the news. I'm worried about going to Chapman. I hope Linda isn't working, preferring Leah's teddy bear sympathy or Bob's gee-whiz enthusiasm. But it is Linda, and under "Recovery-related activities" on the form she hands out to assess ourselves that night, I write one word—"Relapsed"—and hand it in. *Here we go.*

I tell my story: the snowstorm, the burning car in the middle of the road, the bottle of Jack Daniel's, the sodden weekend that followed. To my relief, nobody reacts strongly. No big surprise; they'd seen it in me for weeks. Linda never flashes the little told-ya-so smile I expect. Just the opposite. She seems genuinely sorry, and the group gives me credit for going right back to meetings. George reminds me that when he relapsed after his first stint at Chapman, he drank for four years.

Chapter Eighteen

Prissy is a small, silent editorial assistant with curly hair, black turning to gray, who has been doggedly going about her business, filing paperwork and answering telephones for decades, since the era of the old Chicago *Daily News*. For the first time in the twenty years I've known her, she stops to make conversation with me.

"So your boyfriend's back," she says, raising an eyebrow. She reads the confused expression on my face. "You better stay away from that Peter Baker. He'll lead you back to your bad habits."

"What do you mean?"

"Haven't you heard? Baker's coming back to the paper."

See what you miss if you spend a day at home, drying out?

"I'd hug you, but it might be taken wrong," I say, rushing off. Information is a commodity, and when you find out something reveals your place on the pecking order. As glad as I am about the news, I'm also hurt to be the last to know. If Baker were such a good friend of mine, I wouldn't be finding out about his return from Prissy.

"I would have told you myself a few days ago were I not threatened with great bodily harm," says Cathleen Falsani airily, savoring the moment. There's nothing to do but shoot him an e-mail and see what's up, but I don't get three steps into my office when a voice beckons me through the wall.

"Neil!" calls Mary Cameron Frey, the society columnist in the office next door. She is a grande dame, wealthy, in her sixties.

"Yes, Mary?" I answer, stripping off my coat and tossing it on a chair.

"I need to have a serious talk with you."

"I'll come over seriously," I say, bustling around the corner.

"Sit down," she orders. I quickly sit, regarding the colorful stack of large gardening books on her desk.

"Peter Baker is coming back."

"I know. I'm excited."

"He's a drunk."

"I'm a drunk."

"He is what they call in the Catholic Church 'an occasion for sin' and he is going to lead you astray."

Mary is wearing her standard office uniform, which I think of as "Hyannis Port Casual"—khaki pants and a light blue Polo man's shirt, her steel-gray hair made up as if for a cotillion, every strand sprayed into place, so she can slip away after work, throw on a dragonfly green ball gown, and be all set for the Women's Auxiliary Board of Northwestern Memorial Hospital's Annual Glitter Gala and Silent Auction.

"I can sin on my own," I say, thinking about my recent relapse. "Look, Peter is the only boss I've ever worked for in my whole career who cared for me and helped me."

She makes a sour face.

"I've cared for you," she says, which is true. For years, I thought of Mary as the Queen in *Alice in Wonderland,* for her habit of ordering about photographers at charity events and brusquely banishing nonentities from pictures as if not being famous and rich were embarrassing personal flaws. But Mary showered me with e-mails while I was at rehab. At first I suspected she was fishing for dirt. But after a while—reading the genuine concern, the way she signed them "love"—it dawned on me that she might actually be sincere, and that while Mary may have imperiously treated me as the help before, my fall has touched some chord within her and she truly cares.

"You're not my boss."

"That's true, but I'm watching out for you, and Baker is no good. I don't know why we're bringing him in here. I've been at black tie dinners where he shows up in an open-necked orange shirt."

I should have laughed at that, but one doesn't laugh at Mary Cameron Frey. She's as imposing as an alp.

"His father was a coal miner," I say.

"My father was a simple man and I'm sure yours was too," she says. "That's no excuse."

"My father was a nuclear physicist," I mutter.

She says she has a dear friend who never stopped thinking of alcohol, never. He goes to two meetings a day.

"That'll pass," I say.

"It's been thirty years."

"I'm lucky then, because it's not an issue for me," I say, mustering bravado. "We'll play racquetball."

"He's coming here to play racquetball?"

"He brings a vibrancy to the paper. Ten marines get killed and we put it back on page 42. The *Tribune* had it as their line. Baker won't make that kind of mistake."

"Well, we'll see what he does here. But you"—and she aims a lacquered fingernail at me—"watch yourself."

"I will," I promise, backing out.

"You know I love you and I don't want anything to go wrong," she calls after me.

Rick Telander fills the doorway of my office at the paper. He's our star sports columnist, lanky, tall, a hero's tousled hair, still resembling the football player he once was. He asks me how I'm doing.

"I'm hanging in there," I say.

"You still want to do lunch?" We had talked of getting together for a drinking lunch not long before my life took its unplanned detour.

"Sure," I say, perhaps a bit too eagerly. "Why not?"

"You drinking?"

"No."

He considers this for a moment.

"You mind if I do?"

"No, of course not," I say. We look at each other, as if each waiting for the other to say, "What would be the point then?"

"We'll have fun!" I finally bluster, and we set a date. He gets his book out and we settle on December 22, though I doubt it will actually happen.

Sunday morning I wake up thinking about it. Eyes open. First thing. Thinking about it.

You must be quite the alcoholic if you have to think about this every waking minute of your life, I tell myself, trying to chide myself out of it. But every door of thought I open, every chamber of mind I rush into, there it is, waiting. Hi, dija miss me?

The bedrock truth of the situation again strikes me: If you have to have a drink, then you shouldn't, because you are an alcoholic. And if you don't have to have it, then why bother, given the obvious downsides? Like having the obsession prey upon your brain.

Edie is going over insurance—we have to change plans, since I moved from management to the newspaper union when

I was booted off the editorial board. That means new forms, new doctors, and devolving to a shoddier form of insurance unless we pay a big premium.

"You have to ask for a raise," she says.

"I just got a raise over the summer!" I say. It came through while I was in rehab.

"Well, ask for another one—we can't afford this insurance." The best costs more. The wheels of our discussion come off very quickly.

"This affects all of us, you know," she says.

No kidding, I think. *Thanks for the bulletin.*

I say something reflecting that, and we really get into it.

"I don't love you," she says.

"I don't love you either," I say. "I don't even like you."

"I view you as a damaged person."

"Well, who damaged me?"

"You damaged yourself."

———

Our video camera breaks and, operating under the antique notion that broken things should be fixed, I take it to a small video repair shop, a tiny warren of scattered parts upstairs at one of the jewelers' buildings on Wabash Avenue. A few blocks from the Berghoff, which draws me in after I drop off the camera. Because it's close by and because I have time and because I want something that isn't dismal in my life, if only for a little while. It's Tuesday—a week and a day since Edie has been home from California. No big rush to get home. I need to make the 5:25 train, I tell myself. And no bourbon. I order a beer, put my foot on the rail, pull out my column, and give it a look, dipping pretzels in brown mustard. Halfway through the second beer I look at my watch—time to head for the station. I take a long draw, then set the beer on the bar. A third of it is left. Wiping my lips on a napkin, I leave the bar, not caring at all about that remaining beer. Or so I tell myself, immensely proud. *So much for powerlessness.*

————————

That's the second half of December; one foot in the drinking world, one foot in the world of recovery. A beer at the Berghoff, a meeting at Techny. A new meeting at the Holiday Inn, a rum and Coke, ordered on the sly at the bar at the bowling alley, while Edie is right there, fussing with the boys and their scores. Takes the edge off.

Sometimes I have one and I'm fine; other times it's all I can do to get home in semipresentable shape. Telander and I actually have our lunch—I get to the empty restaurant at the NBC Tower a few minutes early, so I order a vodka tonic while waiting at the bar. Over a few glasses of wine we talk about my travails—he's full of rumpled sympathy, can't imagine giving it up. "Yeah, it's hard," I say, taking a long sip. He heads to his afternoon work, I go to Rossi's for a shot and a beer.

I parse the situation Thursday nights at Chapman, making the case for drinking so strongly that Bob, the red-haired Louisiana therapist, at one point actually blurts out, "You've got me convinced that maybe you *should* be drinking!" George relapses too, explaining to the group he suspects that my lapses somehow gave him permission.

There's no beer at our Hanukkah party of course—a nod to my theoretical sobriety. I get home from work to find the house filled with my wife's family and friends. Laughter and conversation and clamor that seem to go on whether I am there or not. I feel removed, like I don't belong. The phone rings—Jonathan, heading for a meeting. Do I want to come? You bet.

I put on my coat. "Where are you going?" asks Lise, Sandi's wife.

"I have a meeting to go to."

She looks confused.

"Zoning board meeting?"

"No," I say. "Alcoholics Anonymous."

When I return, after an hour and a half, she apologizes—she feels dense. I tell her it's okay. She isn't used to this, but I am. This is my life now.

New Year's Eve approaches—the time of clean slates. I've given up on December, given up on 2005, and in general given up. We'll try harder in 2006. If Edie notices that I'm drinking, she doesn't say anything, and I'm not about to confess. Unlike when she was in California, my drinking is more measured—I don't want to say controlled. Rather, I get by with as few drinks as possible and get home in decent shape.

First thing December 31, Edie, the boys, and I go to watch the sun rise over the lake, a family tradition for the morning of New Year's Eve. We scramble in the predawn darkness for hats and coats, then pile into the car for a race through the lightening skies to Glencoe. We get there, as we always do, just in time to see the sun crest the deep blue horizon. We talk about the coming year, about our hopes and our fears, then head to Toast, a trendy breakfast place in Lincoln Park.

I park the car around the corner, right in front of an Irish bar. The family gets settled in Toast. "I have to feed the meter," I say, and go back to the car. Can't help but try the door to the bar. It's closed, but a Hispanic guy inside is sweeping up. I tap the glass and gesture hopefully to the doorknob. He shakes his head. But there is a 7-Eleven up the street, and they sell me a half pint of Skyy vodka.

I sip that—and two other half pints I pick up later—throughout the day, as we go about our business, having fun with instruments at the Old Town School of Folk Music, shopping and bopping around the city. I drink them slowly, on the sly, a swallow here, a swallow there, taking the last one at my desk at home at 11:50 before heading down to cheer in the new year with the family. The alcohol is a comfort and a balm.

I'm left with two central thoughts. First, I drank my fill, yet nobody was hurt, nobody was hit, we watched old movies and ate hot dogs wrapped in dough and clinked our cups of nonalcoholic punch at midnight, blowing horns and shouting "Happy New Year!" and "Happy 2006!" So where's the problem? That's the first thought.

The second is: I drank twenty-four ounces of booze in one day and nobody noticed. Edie didn't even seem suspicious. I drank that much, popping into restrooms and ducking into doorways. Drank that much, and wasn't even drunk. Drank that much, just to feel normal. And why would you do that if you didn't have to? Or, as Ross says, "And people do that *because?*"

———

Linda calls me at work; Dr. Manozzi wants to see me. With Edie. To talk about my relapses—first when Edie was in California, and then later in the month.

That isn't going to happen. Edie doesn't know about the most recent relapses.

"I feel like my confidence is being betrayed," I say, scrambling. "I told you about the relapse, I was honest, just like you want me to be, and now you're going to rat me out to my wife as punishment. Is that fair?"

Linda says she'll get back to me. Panicky, I call Sam, even call my father. This isn't right. What should I do? Linda phones me later in the day—okay, she says, I can meet with Dr. Manozzi alone. We make an appointment for the following week.

Sobriety seems to be holding in the New Year, but then it usually does. The boys are on vacation and Ross goes to work downtown with me. Having your ten-year-old son with you at the office should not be a cue to drink, but it is for me. For all the times we stopped by the Billy Goat on the way to the train and he sat at a table and enjoyed his kiddie cocktail while I conferred with Phyllis at the bar and slurped Jack. For all the times we lounged in a booth in the front of Petterino's, when the tuxedoed waiter would set down my Manhattan and I'd sigh with happiness—the booze, the boy, the fancy restaurant, all the spheres of life humming in harmony.

I've still got the son—sprawled on the floor of my office, playing with knights. That's the important part, isn't it? I'll have to do without the rest. Lunchtime approaches. We walk to Harry Caray's and on the way the booze begins to sing its siren song, drawing me toward the rocks. It seems to come out of nowhere—from the gray January chill.

Pushing back, I analyze it—a pressure in my head, a tug at my guts. Nothing extreme. Not a tractor beam, but a motivation. A persistent idea: *Just order it.* A slew of ideas and images, one after another, as if drink were fiddling around with the padlock of my resolve, trying to pick it open. Get set up with Ross in the dining room, excuse myself to go to the bathroom, slip over to the bar—a long room, with its high tin ceiling—and get a Jack on the rocks. It'll feel so good going down

And then what? I mount my defense, slap its fingers away. A flushed lunch with Ross—he won't notice. Maybe a top-off before we leave, to fortify myself. Then we'll have to stop by the Goat after work. It'll be another quick trip down the slide.

Knowing that, I straight-arm the desire, alone—no God, no AA—based on my past experience. It's no fun if you have to. I remind myself that I do not want to order the drink in front of Ross. He either will tell or it'll be a guilty secret and either way that is bad for him. Nor do I want to leave him sitting in the restaurant alone while I pretend to go to the bathroom and instead hurry to the bar. That would be classy.

And even if I do give in, what then? Catch another drink on the way home, and another on the train. Another and another and another. And one on the way to Chapman—it's Thursday. Arrive with a glow, something I've never done. Sit there and talk about sobriety while the liquor fizzles away through my bloodstream? You can't drink your way through this.

Ride it out—you haven't had lunch. Eat lunch. Hold it off. Wait.

We eat quietly—initially I wish I could latch on to something to say, something to talk about, but then realize it's okay for us to just sit and eat. You don't have to talk all the time. The urge passes, or at least cranks down several notches, a lesson that is so obvious but which nevertheless seems a revelation. Every time. The urge can pass without satisfying it—why do I always forget that? An hour can work as well as a shot.

The urge is replaced by a dull bleakness that, believe it or not, is an improvement.

That night at Chapman, I'm almost giddy—upbeat, positive, glad to be here. Melanie reveals her lapse over Christmas—poor girl! I don't talk about my New Year's, since it didn't happen, not officially. I'm already called on the carpet for early December, when Edie went to California, and for the Berghoff; now doesn't seem the time to add to the litany.

When a friend of Kent's is coming over, Kent will often sit by the window, looking out and waiting. I try to tell him not to do that—people sense that eagerness in you and draw away.

"Watching for him doesn't make him come any faster" is all I can think to say.

I have the same waiting-at-the-window feeling at work Monday morning. Baker is back, in the building somewhere. I don't think he'll hurry to my office—though that would be nice. I imagine he'll stop by eventually, and keep looking up, expectant.

I finally see Baker the next day—I walk past the morning editorial board meeting; he notices me through the window and rushes out.

"Sorry I haven't come by . . ." he says. "Busy filling out forms."

"No rush," I say. We shake hands. He asks if I want to play racquetball tomorrow.

"Can't," I say. "I have a doctor's appointment."

"Are you all right?"

"Psychiatrist—for relapses," I say. "Aftercare wants to make sure I'm back on the reservation."

I imagine Dr. Manozzi will chew me out. Maybe she'll prescribe another pill.

Chapter Nineteen

At Highland Park Hospital the next morning, Dr. Manozzi keeps me waiting for a long time. Annoyed, I cast aside the magazines and pace, studying the walls. A poster: "Our name is a promise . . . a promise to C.A.R.E." The "care" is surrounded by a heart, then explained, "Considerate, Attentive, Responsive, Empathetic."

Yeah right. After a half hour, I'm ready to just leave. But then I'd have to come back another day, Finally, the secretary tells me that I can walk down the hall into Dr. Manozzi's office.

"We're dropping you from the program," she says, by way of hello.

I'm stunned.

"But it's helping me!" I blurt out.

"We can't have you drinking; it isn't fair to the others."

"I thought I was supposed to tell you when I have relapses."

"You are. But you can't keep having them again and again."

"I've had two!" Two that she knows about.

"I'm sorry—you signed a contract."

We look at each other. No little speech. No handshake. Don't let the door hit you in the ass on your way out.

I try to think of something pithy, an exit line.

"Not with a bang, but a whimper," I mutter, leaving.

You think I'd be glad—no Chapman, no twenty-four weeks of aftercare. But what I feel is vertigo. My supports kicked away. No guardrail now between me and the cliff. The Chapman Center spat me out. Too much of a drunk for rehab.

Edie is folding laundry in the living room when I get home, setting out neat piles of shirts and underwear on the green sofa. I hesitate before telling her. I'm out, honey. They threw me out.

She is surprised but sympathetic at first, and then angry—at them, thank God, instead of me. How can they do that? Just because of two lapses? Am I sure?

"I haven't had a drink this year," I tell her, honestly, skating past the fact that it is January 11.

At Techny that night, I tell the group about being tossed, and roll out my wisdom, of being sober eleven days.

"It's good not to have to drink all the time," I begin. "I feel like I've lost an obnoxious, insistent companion." Memory of the twenty-four ounces of vodka on New Year's Eve is still on my mind. All that, and not even drunk. Just to feel normal.

"Why would you do that if you didn't have to?" I ask. "Twenty-four ounces a day, or the program. The fact that it sometimes seems a choice I have to think about shows how much I need to be here."

———

The next day, Edie calls me at work. She's had time to brood, and has decided that I'm drinking—now, this week. Why else would I be thrown out of the program? She can't believe they would toss me out in mid-January for drinks I had in early December. She has called Linda, she informs me, to check if that is really the case. Even Linda telling her that it is, telling her I am being cashiered for the two lapses late last year doesn't seem to help. She's still mad, certain I must be lying.

For some reason this does not disturb me. I find it liberating. Edie thinks I'm drinking? Fine, mustn't disappoint her. After work I slide by the Billy Goat. Phyllis isn't there—Gail is. Good. Gail wouldn't care if I drank lye.

The first vodka and lime feels wonderful after nearly a two-week gap. I smoke one of Gail's cigarettes. A foot on the rail, cigarette in one hand, drink in the other, listening to the barflies chatter. Happy. I stay forty-five minutes, then walk into the night, feeling so calm, so peaceful. Three drinks, three cigarettes, and the world is set right. No program. No need to worry about Edie finding out because she already knows—or thinks she knows. No need to worry about her getting mad because she's mad at me already.

"You're playing games with me," Edie says, bustling around the house, getting ready to take Ross to his Saturday-morning chess lesson. "You're trying to fool me, to see how much you can drink without me noticing."

I follow her around the house, trying to smooth things out, missing her already. She is apparently not talking about last night, but generally, so I'm both guilty and relieved at the same time. She brushes my denials aside.

"You're lying to me," she says. "I'm going to get a job so you can move out."

Then she's gone. Kent is mesmerized by the TV, and I head directly to Otis & Lee for some vodka—a half pint of Smirnoff, and a little airline bottle of Jack. I never wonder why I buy so little, but it's obviously some unconscious stab at rationing myself.

Back home, I mix the vodka with lemonade and sit on the couch with Kent, eating peanut-butter-filled pretzels and watching TV. Calm and content.

For a while. But the half pint vanishes. The Jack too. Suddenly it's afternoon and I feel the claw. I tell Kent I have to go to the dry cleaners and walk over to the Landmark Inn, where I have two big vodkas on ice, drinking them briskly and methodically, trying to look at the newspaper and not think about Kent sitting at home by himself. Just get the stuff inside.

The next morning I drink the vanilla.

Up craving booze, twisting around in bed by myself, nothing in the house, nowhere to go—it's early Sunday morning. I can't stand it, so I go into the kitchen and take a pull off the little brown bottle in the tea cabinet. Not the whole thing—half, so there's still some left for later. So much for ridiculing Linda's concern about vanilla as an example of the outrageous zeal of rehab.

It barely helps anyway. Five minutes' peace; then the need comes raging back and it's all I feel. Later in the day we go to visit my friend Kier and his family in Naperville. I'm locked in a desire to drink. At lunch, on our way to Naperville, I gaze through the restaurant windows at a supermarket next door, frantically trying to invent a pretext to go over there by myself. At Kier's house, I idly flip open cabinets in the kitchen, glancing inside, hoping for anything, until Kier notices me doing it and I stop. After dinner we go walk along the riverwalk, watch our boys rolling down the green hillside, and it feels better to get outside, get moving, do something.

And so it goes. Monday I leave the newspaper and head for the noon meeting at the Mercantile Exchange, but know in my heart that I'll be going to the bar later, and can't bear the thought of sitting at the meeting, looking at the clock. So I veer away, skip the meeting altogether, and go straight to the Goat. I phone Sam to join me.

He drinks water. "I have a lot of meetings this afternoon," he says. I'm disappointed. Does he not want to drink with his brother? This is his chance. No. He suggests I leave with him. I do, go as far as City Hall, then peel off, telling him I'm heading to the paper, but instead I go to Cardozo's, a cheesy basement bar on Washington Street.

That evening I show up at Frisch's drunk, or drunkish. He makes the best of it. Some patients, he says, won't even admit they have a problem. That sure isn't me. I see I've got a problem, Doc. Big-time. But what to do about it? Besides not drinking, I mean.

Edie certainly notices now. I want to grin and shrug and say, "Turns out you were right, honey!" But she isn't so concerned with the drinking as the lying. "I can't trust you," she says. "I want the truth. Were you drinking Saturday? Sunday?" I tell her that I was. She says she wants the truth, yet the truth does not make her happy.

I want to pull out, but I can't. I can't stop. Which is terrifying. To keep from going directly to the Goat from the morning train I make three phone calls on my cell phone. I talk to Brent. I talk to Paul, a friendly guy from the Mercantile Exchange meeting. Just to get me the ten minutes' walk to the paper, where I call Frank. I'm just like I was in September, desperate to talk to anyone. Frank tells me to go to two meetings today. Instead I go to the Shamrock for a sloppy joe and vodka. I go because I have to.

The whole week is like that. Some mornings frantic, some in control, but the days all end the same. At the Shamrock, or the opening of a "cigarette boutique" in Wicker Park, where I sit and chain-smoke and drink wine and chat with a friendly waitress, Kelly, who has a bad foot. Four glasses of wine at lunch and the solution strikes me—the wine cure! Simple, dignified, none of this swilling vodka. Wine, it's healthful! Good for the heart.

"I'm just going to drink red wine," I inform Phyllis that evening at the Goat, attempting the stuff they have decomposing in a big green jug behind the counter. She nods. That's a plan. I can tell she's reluctant to serve me, but heck, it's only wine.

The next morning I actually pray to God. "Please," I say. "Take this thing from me. Lift this from me." Because I am desperate and can't do it myself.

By force of will I don't drink on the way into work, but as I walk into the office, all I can think of is that fifteen-year-old Barbancourt rum still sitting on the bookshelf. I want to save it to drink with Baker on some epic occasion, but maybe I should drink it right now. I could snatch a white Styrofoam cup by the coffeemaker, slump low in my chair, scan the empty sports department, then pour a big comforting snootful, the bottle held behind my desk so no one will see.

I don't do that. Somehow I know that if I crack that bottle of rum at nine a.m. in my office I'm a goner. Instead I hold out until lunch, watching the minute hand until it gets to eleven thirty, then flee to the Shamrock—I'm becoming a regular. No pretense of wine this time. Back to the vodka. I return to the office just long enough to get my column in, then head to the Goat. It's crowded; Friday night.

The woman on the stool next to me is drinking margaritas.

"I was in the program for twelve years," she says, quaffing her light green slush. "Very helpful. You have to work the steps."

She wants to talk more, but I've done what I came to the Goat for. I make my farewells to Phyllis, buy the customary half pint of Jack for later, and head out the door.

At home I find Edie in bed, ill. I make dinner for the boys, dropping half-moon-shaped frozen pierogi into boiling water. Afterward, Ross has to weigh in his Pinewood Derby car at Cub Scouts. We trudge over to the school gym. All the other cars seem so finely crafted next to the blue lump I finished the day before, half drunk, getting glue on the wheel shafts so now they don't turn properly. Other dads file down the axles, polish them, dust them with graphite. I get glue on mine.

With the boys in bed and Edie upstairs, sick and asleep, I curl up on the green couch in the living room with the half pint of Jack from the Goat. Eight ounces. Such a bounty, when you start in on it. Then you are half done, and the gong of worry sounds. I nurse the last four ounces for an hour, push the bottle deep in the trash, and go to sleep on the sofa. No use bothering Edie when she isn't feeling well.

Awake at four thirty, under a thin fleece blanket. I know better than to go up to the bedroom and wake a sick Edie by climbing into bed. It's dark. I try to find a comfortable spot, try counting backward, try anything to take my mind off my predicament. Get up, stumble into the downstairs bathroom and look at my face in the mirror. A startling mahogany color high in my cheeks, but very white around the eyes. The face of an ill man.

It snowed in the night, and as soon as it gets light, about seven a.m., I go outside to shovel, because there is nothing else to do. The snow is heavy on the evergreen branches, piled thick, white on green, and heaped tall on the front porch rails. I shovel and shovel—we have a long driveway—pausing to admire the crisp white beauty, the clear blue sky between the trees. Maybe the snow was sent by God, I think, pausing to catch my breath. Sent so I could shovel it, so I could work this out of my system by shoveling. The sweat is cold on my face. My pulse throbs in my ears. Shoveling takes ninety minutes. Inside, Edie is still in bed, and I feel so tired and awful that I dig the half pint out of the trash and hold it over my eager tongue until a few drops dribble out. Then I hold the bottle to my nose and deeply inhale the vapors.

That morning is the Pinewood Derby. I thought Ross didn't care, that he joined Scouts just to sell popcorn—he loves selling popcorn, loves badgering passersby with creative pitches, and is very good at it. But his car comes in dead last—my mangled car comes in dead last—and I discover that he does care. Very much. He doesn't say anything, but I can see it in his face. When I was a Cub Scout, my father helped make—oh heck, made himself, most fathers do—a beautiful little racing car, smooth and enameled and perfect. Like a blue jelly bean. Mine is a lump that came in dead last. At least I stay with Ross, perched miserably on the bench next to him, watching the better fathers and their better cars win. I so want to ditch Ross, to hurry off and get something to drink at Sunset Foods. It feels like holding my breath not to. I am poised to, on the brink of, about to, again and again. But I don't do it. I can't do it to him, can't abandon him at his moment of disappointment.

Somehow, I make it through the day. We take the boys to Hyde Park, to a friend's house. Cate and I sit in the kitchen while our kids play, and I tell her a little bit of what's happened. When she opens the refrigerator, I see Ron's beers lined up in the door and wonder if I should pocket a can and drink it in the bathroom. But I hold back. Not here. We take the kids ice skating in the middle of the Midway Plaisance, with the gothic buildings of the University of Chicago on either side of us. At four thirty, while we sit helping our boys and their girls off with skates, I feel it dial down—the panic, the hunger, the gnawing.

"It passed," I tell Edie with a smile. She doesn't respond. But sitting on the bench, with the skates and the boots and the coats and the kids, the thirst fades, and it feels like a blessing. So I make it through that day. And the next.

————————

I go to meetings, even though I don't feel like I need what they're peddling. My higher power is, once I start, I can't stop. Period, end of story. Meetings are a way to fill an hour at lunch that isn't spent at the Shamrock. A big bluff young man with a red face says this is his first meeting ever, and Russell suggests we have a first-step meeting for his benefit. When they get to me, I say I have been sober for four days and tell the newcomer that he shouldn't be deceived if things go well for a while—even then, do not let his guard slip. It feels good to tell the group the truth.

The challenge is not so much not drinking at the moment, as not to think about drinking. Not going back over it again and again, morning, noon, and night, my mind fixating, grieving, analyzing, despairing. A swooping anxiety. "Your life is over," Baker says in the locker room after racquetball, and I hang my head in silence. He's right. This thing has crippled me.

On Wednesday night I drive myself to Techny Towers, listening to Sarah McLachlan's "Fallen." The song helps, and has become a kind of anthem for me, despite her yodeling voice and Lilith Fair chops. She sings about what a mess she has made of her life, how low and debased, yet she's aware of it now—"Better I should know" is how she says it.

Those last four words comfort and armor me against wishing that I were back drinking, that I never slapped Edie, that I wasn't aware of this. Because bad as it is, I can't deny the truth of the situation. I play the song over and over on my drive to Techny. Better I should know.

————————

One week sober becomes two. I begin to feel better, which is always risky. Maybe this isn't such a problem. Baker, referring to some work situation, says, "We'll have to have a drink and talk about that," then catches himself. "Oh, wait, I guess we can't."

"No," I say, oozing practicality. "We can. We can go to Gene's, have exactly two glasses of wine." Feeling for a crack in the wall.

"No, mate, you're radioactive," Baker says. "I won't be having lunch with you for years. What if you go to that place of yours after, then go home . . ."

". . . and beat my wife, and then you'd be responsible, as a manager?"

"Exactly."

"Thanks, Peter."

The Super Bowl arrives. I was never much of a big sports fan. But the boys insist—we always go to Uncle Sam's to watch the game. It's the first time I've been to his house since I was living in the basement, and being there sparks memories, not so much of September, but of previous Super Bowls, particularly the year we walked our cigars and big snifters of cognac around the neighborhood at halftime. Suburban lords. Not this year. We bring over sparkling pear juice. I close my eyes and pretend it's champagne. Doing that actually helps.

————————

The hat people call—making my flight arrangements for New York next month. My most recent book is, believe it or not, a study of the decline of the men's hat industry, set against the career of John F. Kennedy. Their business organization is having its annual dinner at the Tavern on the Green, and I am the entertainment. When we set the speech up, a full year earlier, I eagerly made the trip as long as possible: a few days in New York, renew my contacts, do some work for the *Daily News*, live *la dolce vita*.

Now I cut back the trip to one day—fly in, give the speech,

spend the night, and fly out. Maybe I can do it. For the first time, I wonder if I can possibly go to New York and not drink. People must do it, right? I mean, it is possible. Physically possible. Isn't it?

Valentine's Day. Tough in a good year. What do you give a practical person? Now is the moment for a grand romantic gesture, but I don't feel romantic at all toward Edie. I feel obligated. I wander miserably through Marshall Field's. In previous years I'd get her an outfit—proud that I can buy her a linen suit that she likes and looks good in. The savvy husband who knows his wife. But I'm not buying her an outfit this year. My confidence is gutted, and I lack the necessary energy to pick something out. We aren't going anyplace special. And I don't know her anymore. Don't know her, don't like her. Just a pair of cats fighting in a barrel as it goes over the falls.

In the end I edge into a busy downtown florist and buy a single long-stem rose from a clerk who can hardly be bothered to perform so minimal a transaction—ten dollars for a rose the evening before Valentine's Day. At home I sneak it inside, tucking it in the old refrigerator in the basement. I'll spring it on her in the morning. Just having a little surprise under my belt makes me feel better about her and me and the whole shebang.

The surprise works—she's happy. A *rose!* Though even her pleased exclamation—"Where did you stash *this?*"—makes me cringe. As if, even in a moment of happiness, she's still sniffing out my hiding places.

Chapter Twenty

The Berghoff is closing in a couple of days after more than a century as Chicago's most beloved German restaurant. Ben Goldberger, assistant to one of the paper's three gossip columnists, tells me that he's going to stop by for a final lunch. Wanna come?

Can you do it? I ask myself. Can you go into the Berghoff and not drink? The Berghoff, its famous stand-up bar the epicenter of Chicago imbibing for one hundred years. Now about to close forever, in the wave of change that hit Chicago about the time my life flipped off its tracks. As if giving up drinking—or at least trying to—weren't change enough, Marshall Field's and the Berghoff have to both go out of business in quick succession. It feels like anything is possible, in the worst sense of the term.

The Berghoff. I love the Berghoff. No greater culinary pleasure than to savor a Thuringer and a cold draft beer, foot on the rail, belly to the bar. Can I really go in there and order a root beer?

Yes, I decide. Yes, I can. I'm that strong.

Ben and I play racquetball, then take a cab over to Adams Street. The place is packed—it usually is at lunch, even without the clock of doom publicly counting down. We get in the sandwich line, buy our lunches—the last Thuringer, sliced in half and set on fresh rye bread, the mound of sauerkraut tossed lightly into the air by a chef with a mustache and a tall white toque, neatly caught in a metal spoon and plopped on the sandwich, warm and moist. The grace note of a pickle. We find a place at the end of the bar. The perfect spot opens up, as if welcoming us, with a view of the long room. A guy just leaving offers us his seat—they put some stools in, a few years back, for the ladies. "No, thanks," I say. "You can sit anyplace."

A bartender pauses in front of us. I let Ben go first—he orders a dark beer. My turn.

"I'll have a root beer," I say. Victory.

"Oh right," Ben says, flustered, realizing he's with the city's official alcoholic. "I probably shouldn't . . . I guess I should . . . I'll get a root beer too. . . ."

"No, no," I say, resolve crumbling at a touch, perhaps because manners overwhelm my self-interest, perhaps instinctively seizing my chance. "I can have a beer with you."

The Berghoff lager is good and cold, harmonizing with the Thuringer, rye bread, mustard, and sauerkraut. Ben and I talk. Young guy, early twenties, bright. Going places and knows it. Back to New York no doubt, where someday I'll be a colorful old coot he knew once—the crusty columnist who befriended him in his Chicago newspaper days. Dead now. So I try to fit the part, doling out my threadbare advice, questioning his youthful assumptions. I look at all the happy faces, the clatter and commotion, note, once again, how the light fixtures hanging from the ceiling are the exact same fixtures in the big framed photo of the bar on the day Prohibition ended. That I have just washed a month's sobriety down the drain never occurs to me. I know I am never going to be here again, that the Berghoff is closing in a few days. Yet somehow I do not feel sad; I feel good. I am having a beer at the Berghoff. I am here now, and I've been coming here for twenty-five years. Everyone who comes after me will have missed it. For a few moments, I don't even think about the beer in the glass.

We have another. "Two's the limit," says Ben, and I agree. This is not a lapse, but a special Berghoff farewell moment. We hunch over the bar, talk, finish our beers. Ben needs to use the men's room, and leaves me standing before the bar alone. I immediately consider ordering a quick shot—seize the opportunity—but can't catch the busy bartender's eye.

That night I meet Edie for dinner downtown. I greet her with a hug, and she steps back and examines me, a long and appraising look. As if she *knows*. I can't believe that a pair of draft beers would show in my face after five hours. Maybe it's just guilt on my part. If she suspects, she doesn't say anything.

So I get away with it. I'm back. I can control it. Saturday she is at a big chess tournament with Ross. I take Kent to his guitar lesson up in Deerfield, and repair to the nearby Red Star Tavern to pass the thirty minutes with two pints of Sam Adams and *In a Sunburned Country* by Bill Bryson. It feels like vacation to sit in a bar and read a book and sip a pint. This is natural. This is normal. The burden of alcoholism has miraculously lifted. "And I only am escaped to tell thee."

Sunday morning I have a few drinks at a bar on my way to pick the boys up from Sunday school. I don't drink Monday—somehow, I have an easier time skipping Mondays. Tuesday after work I stride into the Billy Goat. "Fuck this alcoholism shit," I tell Phyllis, and she laughs and pours me a drink.

"Are you drinking again?" Edie asks me at home that night.

"No," I lie.

This drinking problem is behind me. I can't tell Edie, but in my heart I feel liberated, back to myself, having the occasional drink or seven. What is twenty-eight days of rehab compared to twenty-eight years of habit? Edie seems to be tolerating it, or at least ignoring it. That lasts a day. I come home unambiguously drunk; she moves into the guest room, livid. I continue for another two days, on momentum, enduring her cold shoulder. But without her I have no one.

Seeing Edie's unhappiness drains the fun out of drinking, as does the unquenchable thirst that flares up. The pair of draft beers at the Berghoff deteriorates into a nonstop desire to drink in about five days. Linda used to say at Chapman that rehab ruins drinking for you; what she means is that after rehab, you *know*. You can fool yourself for a while. But eventually the truth is too obvious to ignore: You just can't live like that. Sometime around three thirty a.m. Saturday, alone in the bedroom, I drain the last swallow of Jack and begin yet another stab at sobriety.

In the days that follow, Edie is cold, naturally—there's no big You're Not Drinking Today Party, much as I would like one. She's waiting and seeing. Though there *is* a party—my college friend Cate is celebrating her first self-produced play at a trendy North Side bar with a quaint four-lane, hand-set bowling alley in the back.

I chat and mingle and drink Diet Cokes. With Edie right there, what else can I do? When I head to the restroom, I pass the bar, thinking dully that I could order a Jack here and now and nobody would see me. But the desire is gone, for the moment—it's the first day, again—and I head to the bathroom, congratulating myself.

"For a guy in recovery, I end up in a lot of bars," I joke when I return.

———

The next day it sets in. Dry heaves. Trembling. I go to the ten a.m. meeting at the civic center, searching for any scant comfort. Jonathan is there. The two of us sit at a table.

"How are you doing?" I ask. Trying to get out of myself, think about others.

"Back from vacation," he says. "Molly's under the weather."

"Oh, that's too bad," I say. "I'm not doing too good either. I had a relapse. Drank all last week."

"Happens," he says. "I did that for years. You're here now." He smiles. That's it.

At home, all I want to do is lay around. I can't even read. Snowing outside, big, wet flakes. The boys want a snowball fight. No, I say. I'm tired. "It's getting dark," I say. "It's almost dark out."

They implore. Please, *please*. No, go out without me. Kent puts his face an inch from mine. "Puhleeeeeeze!" No I say no I won't no. But they will not be deterred. They want me to go outside with them. It's no fun without me. How long will they feel like that? I drag myself off the couch. They suit up. The snow is perfect packing. We fight, we run, we make angels, I bury them in the snow as the sky goes from blue to black. We lay there, on the not-so-cold ground, the three of us, spent, staring up at the darkness.

The next day I stay home, exhausted, remorseful. Edie goes about her business—a job interview.

I'm on the green couch. She is in her gray suit. "Let me take a look at you," I say. "I don't have time. I'm running late," she says—still angry—but must realize how petty that sounds, so she strikes a momentary pose, then snatches up her briefcase and goes down the stairs toward the back door. No kiss, of course. "Good luck," I call down the stairs.

Three hours later, Edie gets back from her interview—she didn't get the job.

"So where are things?" I ask. "With us."

"I'm working on myself," she says. "You need to get yourself together."

"The detachment they teach you in Al-Anon. Did it ever occur to you that this is when I need you most?"

"I've been through this already. I'm tired of it."

"That's what relationships are—repetition. The seasons cycle. You pay the bills each month, I drink and I get the lecture. I'm tired of it, but I take it."

"I'm angry and need to separate a bit."

"And I respect that."

"And I appreciate that."

I have a *Newsweek* in my hands. I show her a photo.

"This is that Jessica Alba you thought looked too thin on the Oscars."

"She doesn't look too thin there."

"She's a pretty girl," I say, looking at her. "But I've seen prettier."

"She's twenty-five years younger than me."

"And when she's your age, she won't look as good as you do now." A corny line, but it works. She smiles, and I lean up to kiss her, a light kiss, but the first kiss in five days.

I ask her if she'll sleep in the bed if I change the sheets.

"Maybe," she says.

————————

The rhythm of work, the train, the e-mails, reading newspapers, making phone calls, writing the column. Baker and I have a rare late-afternoon game—we typically play in the morning. He seems in an unusually happy mood.

"Wine at lunch," he explains. "And better for it. Still, if you don't win today, you'll have to join me back on the drink."

"That's a bet," I say, extending my hand. We shake. He grins. "Now don't lose on purpose. . . ."

"Don't worry," I say. "I'm not going to lose."

We play the hardest game we have ever played, without doubt. I win the first, narrowly, 15–13, but the second goes on and on, tying 15–15 and neither can go ahead to win by two points. Back and forth, 16–15, 18–17. Baker's strong, a hard-ass Manchester Brit and he won't give up. For the first time—for the very first time since this whole thing began—I tell myself urgently, "I don't want to drink!" Swinging hard, playing frantically, because if I lose, I've got to drink with Baker and I don't want to. I've just managed a few days sober.

We both are practically staggering, drenched in sweat.

"This isn't fun," I say, getting ready to serve.

Baker wins the second game, 19–17.

The third game is just as hard, but I win the tiebreaker, so I don't have to go back on the sauce. Completely ridiculous, I know, but that's how I feel. Wonderful. Like I went mano-a-mano against King Alcohol himself, ready to pull me back, and won.

———————

Cathleen Falsani is having a book party at the Pump Room in the Ambassador East Hotel. I'm tired, but I have to go: Friends buy friends' books. I mingle, hold my glass of soda water. I can smell the bourbon on my colleagues' breaths, but am never tempted. I haven't been to many parties, haven't seen a lot of people since I've been back at work, and there is a feeling of return to society. People hug and kiss, say they're glad to see me, and pretend like we're going to have lunch someday.

In the cab to the train station, the night city skyline along

Wacker Drive flashing by, I marvel that I had a good time at the party yet did not drink. This is doable. Eleven days and I have this sobriety thing down.

The next day I fly to New York.

The former Traveling Hat Salesmen's Association, now The Hat Institute, has a yearly dinner where the remnants of the haberdashery trade get together to reassure one another that they're still there. I am so happy for a paid trip to Manhattan—the flight, the hotel—that I never even think to ask for a speaker fee.

Of course, being in recovery makes going more complex. To take a trip, to fly on a plane, to stay in a hotel, to be in New York City, all mean drinking. Long lunches with editors. Bar-crawling with my old pals.

I can do it. Arrange the flight for eight a.m. Even I can avoid drinking on an early-morning flight. I whittle down the stay to the briefest time possible—arrive at lunch, get settled, give the speech, leave the next afternoon. How much trouble could I get in?

Plus, I have nearly two weeks of sobriety under my belt. I'm there.

The hat men are friendly. We go out for lunch—no one else is drinking, which makes it easier. Iced tea and a salad topped with a crab cake. Besides, I have a speech to make that night. I need to be sharp.

Going down to the lobby, I gaze at myself in a beveled mirror in the elevator. *Edie will be so proud,* I think, *so proud that I can go to New York, give a speech, and not drink.*

The hat guys all wear hats, naturally—Stetsons, mostly. They laugh and pile into a limousine. I jam in with them. Off to the Tavern on the Green, a garish, mirrored, stained-glassed tourist trap that might have seemed elegant in 1977. I follow my hosts inside. They make an elaborate fuss, checking their hats, handing them over with care and warnings. "Now, don't stack my hat," one says. I get my name tag. The guys I came with see their friends and scatter. Suddenly alone in a roomful of strangers, I notice the bar and walk over.

"Jack on the rocks," I say. Just like that. The bartender fills a wineglass—an eccentricity of the Tavern on the Green—with ice and Jack. I carry the glass for maybe thirty seconds; I'm in New York, I'm in no rush. At one point I take a long pull.

The night dissolves. More Jacks. Standing in a corner of the room, on the phone to the paper, fiddling with the column, on the phone to Edie. People coming up and saying they like the book. Wine at dinner. The speech isn't until late—well after nine. My talk goes smoothly, as far as I can tell. I'm in the bag, but so are most people, apparently.

The dinner breaks up around ten thirty. I have one last free Jack as the bar is closing up, then walk out into the night.

———————

The phone rings—my college pal Rob. We're supposed to have breakfast. Let's meet downstairs in half an hour, he says. I feel awful. Not just tired, but beat-up, exhausted. Twenty-seven years of friendship, however, gets me up and into the shower. The corpse ambulates, dresses in a jacket and tie. I go downstairs to wait for Rob, miserably, the lobby filled with teenage girls. Some sort of school group. They laugh and sprawl on the floor, twiddling electronic devices, making cell phone calls. None of them are drunks.

Rob shows up. We walk to Moonstruck, a restaurant apparently staffed by fashion models. I order food not thinking I can eat, but when it arrives, I do, without pleasure.

It's midmorning; Rob has to get to work. I walk back to my hotel and go up to my room, where I pour the Jacks from the minibar into a glass. Only then do I feel better. It's like a grating, annoying noise, driving you crazy, going on and on, that all of a sudden, stops. I settle in to watch CNN, the sun bright through the window, time slowing down, the way it did during long spring afternoons in grade school. I have a flight at five p.m. and nothing to do but buy gifts for the boys and meet my agent for lunch. We rendezvous at the Blue Water Grill—she is taken aback when I order wine.

"This is my fifth drink today," I confess.

"I thought you seemed a little . . . happy," she says, cautioning me. "You're going back to Edie this afternoon."

I assure her it's my last drink of the day. But it isn't.

The airport is what stands out in my mind. Having drunk away the afternoon in New York and slept on the plane, I'm now back in Chicago. I have to go home, but first need to stock up my system. Four beers, four frantic beers, between the gate and the cab. Four, one after the other, in four different bars throughout the airport. Edie and the boys are on the couch watching TV when I get home. Nobody gets up. I drop my bags and go upstairs.

Edie takes Ross to chess the next day. She is concerned, of course, but not so concerned that she doesn't take him. Life goes on. I have to pick up the Market Days order—the elementary school raises money by selling prepared frozen food in bulk.

On the way, I slide by the liquor store. A half pint won't do—why fool myself anymore?—so I buy a fifth of Gordon's vodka. Odd that I didn't buy Jack Daniel's, but in my mind I am ramping up from the half pint of Popov. Choosing Gordon's is some kind of sentimental tribute to *The African Queen*—

Katharine Hepburn sets bottles of Gordon's gin afloat in the Yulange River after Bogie goes on his binge in the movie.

The day passes, mixing the vodka with Diet Green River soda, sitting on the couch with Kent. I never feel particularly drunk; indeed I drive him to his guitar lesson, sit in the Red Star Tavern and read the *New Yorker* and drink a couple pints of Sam Adams.

Edie comes home about five p.m., but however she reacts to my condition, I neither notice nor care. I admire Ross' trophy, and go back to the television.

I wake up about one a.m., alone in our bedroom, the bottle of Gordon's tucked conveniently in my night table drawer. There's a generous amount left—about a third of the bottle, the top of the clear liquid at the letter "D" in the word "GORDON'S" embossed in the glass up and down the side. I determinedly sit in bed and drink, reading a magazine in the yellow lamplight and watching the level in the bottle get progressively lower. One part of me wants to save some, knows that I'll need it the morning, that I will wake up craving more. But that voice is drowned out by the joy of having the booze here, now, of keeping the party going for another swallow. I get to the O, the N, the S, and the inch below, and then tip my head back, sitting in bed by myself, drinking warm vodka out of the bottle, tapping out the last stubborn drops. It occurs to me that this is my future.

IV

Row Hard for Home

Chapter Twenty-one

"You're stubborn," says Dr. Frisch, who agrees to meet me the next day, even though he isn't feeling well. "It goes back to my original question: Why are you so reluctant to let this experience change you?"

I've told him the full story—the trip to New York, the bottle of Gordon's vodka.

"Are you right? Am I powerless? Did I *have* to drink at Tavern on the Green? I stopped drinking yesterday, even though I wanted to drink, very much. So I have power, umm, sometimes."

"I've been saving this story to tell you, and I think now is the time," he begins. "In the early nineties, I spent a couple years at a halfway house."

As a resident? I think, with something approaching horror. *My therapist used to be a homeless guy?*

"The people there were mostly guys who had just gotten out of prison. Rapists, murderers, child abusers. My first patient"—(*whew!*)—"was a white supremacist who had killed two people when he was eighteen, and had just gotten out of prison after seventeen years. I was the first person he talked to. He lasted a day on the outside.

"I showed up with a laptop in one hand—Radio Shack, lousy

machine—and a bunch of tests in the other I had spent thousands of dollars learning to administer. The guys would make fun of me, ask why I didn't have a microwave under my arm.

"The tests turned out to be useless—these guys had severe psychological problems. Most of them were borderline illiterate. They couldn't take the tests because they couldn't read. I had to throw them all away."

"The point of the story," I say, breaking in, "is that the tools you brought weren't helpful. You're trying to say this elaborate edifice of Neil Steinberg, this palace of memory and thought that I've built for myself, is no good to me in fighting this."

"It makes you a wonderful writer, but it won't help you in this," he says. "You have to find something outside yourself—a higher power—you have to let go of your will and put yourself in the hands of someone else. Get outside yourself and instead of focusing on Neil, focus on other people."

That seems impossible. To ignore myself and concentrate on lending a helping hand to random strangers. The make-the-coffee-at-meetings cure. Sure, some people—maybe many people—can do that. But I can't. At least I don't think I can. I can imagine not drinking; rehab did that much. I can't imagine being good old Neil, the guy who stays to sweep up after meetings. Is that the only way? To call on God and wash the feet of the poor?

"I have such a hard time with that," I begin. "It's as if you said the solution is to embrace Jesus. There's nothing wrong with Jesus. I see that millions of people embrace Jesus. He makes their lives complete. Good for them. But I can't do it. I'd rather die."

On the other hand, I have to do something. Because this, this obviously isn't working. To fall face forward into alcohol, to spend a progression of worse nights, in progressively worse rooms, alone, grimly working my way down the letters in "GOR-DON'S," that just doesn't seem the path of the hero.

"I have a friend, he was at this twenty years," says Frisch. "He fought AA like you wouldn't believe—he makes you seem like nothing. But his wife died and suddenly it clicked for him. He has a sponsor who . . ."

I have a sponsor, Frank, who is ideal in my view, in that he never asks me to meet, nor places demands of any kind upon me. That isn't exactly how sponsorship is supposed to work, however. They are supposed to shepherd your sobriety, redirect your thinking when you wander off the trail, prod you when you dawdle, make you work the steps.

Frisch phones the guy who pounded his head against the wall for twenty years. I notice Frisch never mentions my name. "I have a friend who is looking for a sponsor, and I wonder if Jules would have the time . . ."

He gets the number and calls Jules, who already has two drunkards under his wing—two "sponsees," as they're called—but, heck, the more the merrier. Jules will be my new sponsor. I'm hopeful and apprehensive. "Jules?" Jesus. But what choice do I have? I take the phone number from Frisch.

The next day I call Jules and catch him on his cell phone. I do most of the talking—six months sober, if you can call it that, with frequent swan dives off the wagon.

He doesn't say much, an occasional laugh, an occasional "that happened to me" and "I still feel like that sometimes." Nothing threatening or demanding. He views AA somewhat the way I do—as a kind of black box. "You go through the steps and something happens," he says. It's a mystery.

We agree to get together on Saturday, at the Winnetka Covent Church, to attend the meeting there and then have lunch. He lives in Winnetka, which is also good. Winnetka is classy.

It feels encouraging, to have an appointment with somebody who knows about this nightmare and is going to help me. Four days away—also good, something to set my sights on without having to actually sit with him right now, knee-to-knee, reading the *Big Book*, or whatever it is he's going to have me do. I know I can make it through the next few days, because help is on the way.

Whenever I begin to feel bad about my dry future—and I do, again and again, every few minutes—I try to bring myself up short, thinking: a night of drinking in New York City Thursday. A day of drinking there Friday. An epic, all-day vodkathon at home on Saturday. Let's not decry the dryness of life just yet. I would say that you're getting in your drinking. Drinking o'plenty. You sucked the last vodka back two a.m. Sunday. You've had lots of drinking in the very recent past and, if history is any judge, you will have plenty of drinking again in your bleak and lonely future, whether you want it there or not. So here's a thought, brainiac: Why not try *not drinking* for a little while and see how that works?

What also helps is a beige business card I find in my wallet. A business card for a bar called "Under the Volcano," on East 36th Street in New York. The card shows a dapper skeleton, in hat and morning coat, smoking a cigar and holding a walking stick. A cartoon, but scary, with empty black eye sockets. *Under the Volcano* of course is Malcolm Lowry's searing autobiographical novel about alcoholism. Hell of a name for a bar. I must have been there—I have the card—but no memory of being there. None whatsoever. Still, I keep it in my wallet as a reminder. A bottle a day and you'll be dead.

————

Edie is surprisingly pleasant, from the get-go. They teach you to detach in Al-Anon, and she neither is angry, nor holds my New

York trip against me. The tacit deal seems to be, *you* don't drink, *I'll* be nice to you.

"Love you," she says, when I leave for work a couple mornings after getting back.

"Love you," I answer.

"See you tonight," she says. "With bells on."

"Okay," I say. We kiss.

"Be strong," she says.

"I will," I say.

Baker and I arrange to play at 10:35 "on the dot." Good functionary that I am, I am waiting at the elevators with my bag a minute early.

"So how was your weekend?" I say. He fixes me with a grim look, which I take for "Don't ask."

"I just finished reading this book on Mencken . . ." I say, trying to fill the silence.

"Don't I get to answer?" he says. "Or is that just empty Midwestern formality?"

"I thought you weren't going to answer."

"I did a Steinberg Friday," he begins. "The old Steinberg. Didn't get home until late. . . . " This did not go over well on the home front.

We are walking into the East Bank Club, next to the newspaper.

"Well, come to my meeting, then," I say. "You can tell her you're going and it'll help get back in her good graces. . . ."

"I am going," he says.

"I know that life seems bleak without drinking, but it really isn't," I say, surprising myself a little. "Look at racquetball—do you remember how we started playing?"

He shakes his head.

"We were having these endless boozy lunches at Smith &

Wollensky. Remember? I thought racquetball was something you and I could do besides drink at lunch, maybe three years ago, when I was trying to cut down."

After the game, we grab a cab to the Mercantile Exchange. I brief him.

"There'll be some initial throat clearing and proforma questions to the room. They'll ask if this is anybody's first meeting, and you can raise your hand, if you like, and say your name."

"Do I have to say anything?"

"Not if you don't want. Just introduce yourself and people will clap."

"Do I have to say my last name?"

"No, people generally don't."

We enter the meeting—a different, smaller room, still on the eighth floor, with four square tables pushed together to make an enormous square in the center, the tabletops an executive hue of rich honey veneered wood. I pull back the heavy black drape to show Baker the commotion of the Globex trading floor.

"I love it," he says. "It's like Las Vegas."

The meeting doesn't get off to a good start—the guy running it is filling in for the usual leader, and reads woodenly. When he asks if anybody is here for his very first Alcoholic Anonymous meeting, Baker doesn't respond. But when he asks if anybody is at this *particular* meeting for the first time, Baker raises a finger and says his first name, without any elaboration.

The daily reading is a passage about "wearing the world like a loose garment," from the *24 Hour Book,* a supplemental AA text, read by Carl, a rugged man with a scar on his chin. He talks about what it means to him and we go around the room, introducing ourselves.

It's Peter's turn. "My name is Peter and I'm *not* an alcoholic," he says. The comment sparks an echo of nervous laughter though he's probably correct—I never thought of him as a drunk, at least not the way I am. He then passes to the next person.

"You have to come back more often," somebody says. Drunks have a tendency to ramble, so brevity is appreciated.

When it is my turn, I say, "I have realized that I have a choice, to drink a fifth of vodka every day of my life or to go to meetings, and it's a sign of the depth of my problem that I sometimes have to ponder which it will be. So I appreciate being here and will keep coming and with that I'll pass."

There are about forty people in the room, and each makes a few comments. The younger men and women talked about issues with mothers and roommates, the older with wives and husbands and children. Many highlight the theme of the day, the notion of wearing the world like a loose garment, which they find profound, and a few riff on it—wearing life like a tight jockstrap, like a spandex dress.

"I've been wearing the world like a sweater that's four times too small," relates a woman in a black dress, stringy brown hair with blond streaks, talking about how she went ballistic when her three-year-old daughter lost her shoe in a store.

"If I get away from the program I can't have a good life whether I drink or not," she says.

Just before one p.m., the last man to speak launches into a spiel about positive energy, and how only .04 percent of the general population has it, but 40 to 50 percent of people at AA meetings do—thanks for the hard statistics, pal. Too much time at AA meetings is taken up by this kind of stuff, by people talking about how great the meetings are.

Then we all stand up, form a circle around the room, join hands, bow our heads, say Psalm 23—"The Lord is my shepherd, I shall not want . . ."—and the meeting ends. Baker shoots out into the hall. I hurry after him, but deliberately keep my mouth shut. I want to hear what he has to say about the meeting.

"Lot of good-looking women in there," he begins, then stops. Silence again.

"I wanted to kill myself after my first meeting," I observe, trying to be helpful, to provide comfort in case he's feeling that way. "I think I went straight to a bar."

We get into the elevator.

"These people are all winners," Baker declares, with surprising sincerity. I expect him to pull it back—gotcha!—but he doesn't. "Traders, brokers. They have things going on."

"That's what I like about it," I say. "You can tell by how they dress, how they carry themselves. That's why I like this place."

"So this helps?" asks Baker. "You won't have a drop today?"

"Somehow it does," I say. "No, I won't. Not today."

———————

Wednesday night, Baker, casual in a black leather jacket, meets me at Techny for the evening meeting. I feel a bit of proprietary concern, with Christopher rambling and Henry snapping his gum. It reminds me of when I was thirteen and Miss Maple, my old fourth grade teacher, came to my bar mitzvah. Suddenly viewing the familiar ritual through the eyes of an outsider, I feel self-conscious, responsible for all this. But Baker merely observes, keeping whatever qualms he has to himself.

On Friday we go out of the revolving door at the club after our game. Baker seems surprised when I veer off toward the left to get a cab instead of heading toward the paper.

"So you're going to your meeting, then?" he says.

"Why not come along?" I say. "What if going a third time suddenly makes it click?"

"Haven't the time," he says.

About four p.m. I wander out of my office for coffee, the final push to the end of the day. I return with my Styrofoam cup, and there's a red light on my phone. A message.

A rush of background noise, then Baker's voice:

"There's the problem, mate," he says. "I mean, you're well out of it. A nice game of squash, or racquetball, and a nice lunch and only *two* glasses of wine, which of course leads to *twenty-two* glasses of wine, and I have to say, it's very late now, you're well out of it, and I have to say I wish I was out of it too, in many ways."

And he hangs up.

I listen to the message again. Several times. He sounds so . . . very unlike himself. I think of calling back immediately—no, he'd rake me over the coals, reflexively, out of habit. That's why he was hurrying away after racquetball. Of course—one p.m. on a Friday, time to meet the guys at Gene's. Time to drink. I know that feeling very well.

I stand, gather my papers. I really should call him. And then what? It strikes me, for the first time: Everybody is so concerned about Baker pulling me down. Wouldn't it be extraordinary if I pulled him up?

My new sponsor, Jules, is standing outside the Winnetka Covenant Church Saturday morning, waiting to meet me. Tall, trim, maybe fifty, in Top-Siders and a red sweater. We greet each other, go inside, sit together. The meeting unfolds, but it seems out of kilter, wrong. Honesty is one thing, but they seem unusually focused on what we are, a twist of the knob too much: "I have asked an alcoholic to read the minutes," the leader says. "If I can have an alcoholic volunteer to start off the reading. . . ."

Jules suggests we have lunch afterward—to my surprise—at

Little Ricky's, a nearby Winnetka bar. We huddle together at a back table. The room is dim and mostly empty—a great setting, I think ruefully, to drink away an afternoon. Before our salads arrive, he teaches me the set-aside prayer—asking God to let me ignore everything I believe so I can better absorb this stuff. I say the words. There is a Norman Rockwell painting of a family praying in a diner, while the grizzled blue-collar types glance over, and I think of that image as Jules and I pray and talk and read together at a table in a corner of the bar.

By way of homework, he wants me to read the first 164 pages of the *Big Book*—twice. This leaves me with a sinking feeling. Once I can understand, but twice? It smacks of indoctrination.

Oh, and phone him every day. Just to check in.

Every day? I want to give this a chance—people who fail invariably say they didn't have a sponsor and didn't work the steps. So if I'm going to have a sponsor, and work the steps, I have to actually do it—I can't dismiss it out of hand, at the start, having never even tried. Maybe reading those 164 pages, twice, and phoning him every day will beat that old alcoholism right down into its hole. I agree to do it, and to meet him next week.

———————

"You're invited to Gene & Georgetti Friday," says Baker. "We talked about it and decided that it was time to bring you back in. The publisher will be there."

My first thought is: Of course I can go and have an iced tea. It might be hard to see the big glasses of red wine, but that will be okay. Other people do it—Wallace Waters, a powerful lawyer at the table, always has his Diet Coke. Everybody still likes him.

I'm confident, until I remember the Berghoff. I was confident then, too, up until the moment I wasn't. The sober thing would be not to go to Gene's—it's too early. A couple weeks since New York. Too early to be in a slippery place, as they say at Chapman. I will go and slip and the whole damn thing begins again. Or go and not slip and give myself a false feeling of confidence that crumbles at the second temptation.

But I have to go. I can't stay sober, I tell myself again, just because I don't know where the booze is. You're asked to go to lunch with the publisher, you go. I have to go and not drink. Show Baker it can be done.

We get out of the club about 12:35—just enough time to go back to the office, turn around, and go to Gene's for my big debut. Or we could go straight to Gene's . . .

"Let's go have a drink," I say, as we leave the club. Baker looks quizzically at me.

"I don't want to be the one responsible for your drinking," he says gravely.

"You'll be having a drink," I say. "I'll . . ."

"Oho!" he says, brightening. "You'll be having an *iced tea*, some poofy nancy drink." He shifts into a high, girlish voice: " 'I'll have an iced tea, thank you.' " Then his regular voice. "Not for me, mate. None of that for *me*. I'll be having a man's drink."

I can only smile. We change our course to the restaurant, three blocks away.

We push through the door and into the dark wood dimness of Gene's. The prodigal is welcomed home. I shake hands with the owner, Tony. "Good to have you back," he says. We pass the barnacles at the bar. They're here every single day, rich men who have decided to drink away the rest of their lives. Their BMWs and Mercedes—even a Bentley—are parked prominently out front. Past the tables filled with stolid individuals who all look like they run construction firms, thickset, potato-nosed men who shoot you a quick, appraising glance, as if they're trying to decide whether to let you pass or drag you out into the alley and work you over with a pipe.

Upstairs, we're the first ones there. The room is entirely empty. We take our seats at a big table and a waiter hurries over. I gesture grandly to Baker; he gestures back to me with an equal flourish. I hold my ground, wait—I don't want my order affecting his.

"I'll have a glass of red wine," he says.

"I'll have an iced tea," I say. "With lemon."

"Make that a Coke," Baker says. *Oh gee,* I think.

". . . and rum," he continues. "Just a bit of rum." He holds up his thumb and forefinger close together, then spreads them as wide apart as they'll go.

The boys arrive. A few prominent attorneys, a few elected officials. I get a hearty "Look who's here!" and a blustery "Welcome back from the dead." The wine is ordered. Nobody mentions anything directly about my drinking. Guys don't do that. Not directly. Instead the subject is discussed generally. A fixer tells a story about driving for Phil Rock, a once-powerful state senator, both of them soused, to a dinner where he had to sit next to the famously teetotaling and uptight governor, Jim Edgar. Bottles come and go. At one point the guy to my left pours and plants a wine bottle directly under my nose. I pass it to the right.

I'm not tempted—not licking my lips and wishing I could drink, though there is a moment when I conjure up the warm, round, slightly salty pull of a good glass of red wine. I just don't want to begin the slide, not today anyway. Around the fourth bottle, the guys soften a bit, as if they all shift out of focus. But the conversation always remains interesting—the intricate dance of city and county politics.

Toward three p.m. the mood lags. I stand up and begin to

make my good-byes. One of the big benefits of not drinking is that you know when it's time to go.

"Where are you going?" Baker demands.

"I haven't filed my column yet."

"You're not leaving without me."

"I couldn't. Then whatever happens afterward would be all my fault," I say, grinning. "I would be *responsible*."

"You're damn right."

We walk out together, into the bright sunshine of a crisp March afternoon.

"That was fun," I say. "Thanks. I like Tom O'Neill—a good guy."

"Incredibly rich," Baker says. "And you were good." He smiles, as if embarrassed to catch himself saying something positive. "Though I like you better drinking."

"How come?" I ask, half indignant, half curious. "How come you like me better drinking? I held up my end of the conversation, didn't I? I passed the wine. I wasn't sitting staring glumly at people. I was talking. You like me better in what way?"

Baker ponders this as we turn down Orleans and approach the newspaper.

"Maybe a little better," he says.

Back at the office, I reflect with satisfaction upon lunch. I had fun and didn't drink. Nor do I wish I had—who looks back on any event in the past and wishes he had drunk *more*? Nobody. I'm proud that I could pull it off. It seems to bode well for the future, and brings to mind Edie's words, spoken at the beginning of all this: proud every day.

Epilogue

After that night spent working my way down the letters on the side of the Gordon's bottle, I don't drink for a year. Something clicks—perhaps the pure seediness of the moment, with its grim indication of things to come—and a year passes without a single alcoholic beverage.

A year and counting.

There are two ways to view a year of sobriety. It can be seen as little more than a good start. I've gone to too many meetings where somebody, telling the story of their current low state, recounts how they didn't drink for a year or three or ten, and then suddenly they're back "out there" and it all goes to hell and quickly too.

Or a year can be seen as a triumph. I never thought I could make it a year. Three hundred and sixty-five days where I wanted to drink but didn't. Inconceivable, back when I was just trying to make it through the next hour, the next minute. I can scarcely believe it now.

I've come to view the struggle of alcoholism as a fight, not so much not to drink—which I have discovered I can do successfully, at least for a year—but to not constantly think about drinking. That's a dicier proposition. Some days I hardly think about drinking, but other days I hardly think about anything else. Here time helps, and work, and family. The problem comes to mind less frequently, a few times a day instead of dozens. And when it does, it isn't a sharp pang, but a softer, gentler, regret.

I know the problem hasn't gone away because I can feel it down there, like a beast in the basement, throwing its weight against the cellar door. Yet sometimes it ebbs to such a degree I find myself hoping it has gone away for good.

"You ever seen anybody get better?" I ask Phyllis, when I am finally able to go back to the Goat, drink a nonalcoholic beer, and leave. "Does it ever go away?"

She shakes her head. "It doesn't get better," she says. "It gets worse." Her words, unwelcome though they are, stick with me, because Phyllis *knows*.

———————

For our sixteenth wedding anniversary, Edie and I drive up to a little bistro, Cafe Central, in Highland Park, of all places, not far from the hospital. I feel wistful, walking in, seeing the bottles on the tables, and thinking of the days when we might have shared one. But we sit at the copper bar, and I have a St. Pauli N.A., which really isn't that bad, and the wistfulness passes. We enjoy a nice dinner. We talk, as we've been doing for twenty-five years now. She looks beautiful, has smart things to say.

After a year, we've clicked back into our old selves, for the most part, talking in bed in the morning about the day ahead. Eventually, it begins to dawn on me that perhaps I have found the higher power that the program keeps saying I must have—Edie. It is she who has always stuck by me, even when I lost myself. It is she who gives me the strength to resist drinking, so as not to let her and myself down. It is she who is proud of me, every day. Maybe my higher power was Edie all along. As much as I love to drink—as much as I *loved* to drink—the bedrock truth is I love her more.

Acknowledgments

This book would not exist without my extraordinary agent and dear friend, Susan Raihofer at the David Black Literary Agency, whose enthusiasm for the project began immediately and never wavered. Many thanks to her, and to Trena Keating at Dutton, who championed this memoir from the start, and to my editor, Lily Kosner, who gave the book a thorough and intelligent reading. Gratitude as well to Jaime Wolf, for his sensitive legal vetting.

I want to express my regard and my gratitude to the professionals at Highland Park Hospital's Chapman Center. Thanks as well to Dr. Steve Frisch, and to all the men and women I have met through Alcoholics Anonymous—a fine program that has helped millions attain sobriety and is in no way responsible for the words and actions of this particular participant.

Thanks as well to all those I met in recovery and to those who stepped forward to offer their assistance, to all my wonderful neighbors on Center Avenue, whom I obviously will not name, but whose efforts are greatly appreciated.

My bosses at the *Sun-Times* have been kind to me during this process, and I thank John Cruickshank, John Barron, Don Hayner, and Michael Cooke.

Thanks as well to my colleagues at the paper, Leslie Baldacci, Esther Cepeda, Roger Ebert, Robert Feder, Scott Fornek, Mary Cameron Frey, Janet Rausa Fuller, Ben Goldberger, Dan Haar, Rich Harris, Jack Higgins, Mark Konkol, Tom McNamee, Carol Marin, Nancy Moffett, Maureen O'Donnell, Abdon Pallasch, Cheryl Reed, Richard Roeper, John H. White, and Bill Zwecker.

Thanks as well to my friends on the Chicago scene—Rich Melman, for his lovely book parties, Dick Babcock, Lee Bey, Phil Corboy, Robert A. Davis, Grant DePorter, Jay Doherty, Dick Durbin, Lee Flaherty, Gale Gand, Harry Heftman, Jim Houlihan, Tim Joyce, Rick Kogan, Ed McElroy, Ken Price, Phyllis Smith, Wayne Waylan, Bill Zehme, and Eric Zorn.

Special thanks to Cate Plys, for suggesting that I take notes.

I'm grateful that my old friends are always there—Jim and Laura Sayler, Robert Leighton and Val Green, Kier Strejcek and Cathleen Cregier, Larry and Ilene Lubell.

My sister-in-law, Janice Sackett, was particularly kind to me and I want to express my love and appreciation to her.

This book is dedicated to my brother, Sam, in recognition of his lifetime of wise support and loving friendship. This experience was obviously hard on my family, and the publication of this book will also be difficult. So thanking them in advance for bearing with me, love and appreciation to Robert and June Steinberg, my sister, Debbie, plus Dorothy Goldberg and the entire Goldberg clan: Alan, Don, Jay, Cookie, and all the girls, Julia, Rachel, Esther, Sarah, and Beth. Thanks to Yuri Steinberg, as well as to Rina and Ryan Steinberg. To my cousin Harry and his wife, Yi—congratulations and good luck.

To my boys, Ross and Kent—I'm sorry for putting you through this, and would have left you out of the retelling, but you are too important a part of my life. I needed your sunshine to balance the darkness. All children bear the burden of their parents, sooner or later, and I hope mine rests lightly on you, and that you do not come to judge me too harshly for my flaws and weaknesses. I love you.

To my wife, Edie, a private person who has endured too much in public already, a private word, borrowing from Dante who, as always, said it best: *"Tu m'hai di servo tratto a libertate. Per tute quelle vie, per tutti modi. Che di cio fare avei la potestate."*

And since, as you so levelheadedly point out, most people don't speak Italian: "You have led me from my bondage and set me free, by all those roads, by all those means that were in your power and charity." You are my world.